Beautiful Cosmos

Beautiful Cosmos

Performance and Belonging in the
Caribbean Diaspora

TINA K. RAMNARINE

First published 2007 by Pluto Press
345 Archway Road, London N6 5AA
and 839 Greene Street, Ann Arbor, MI 48106

www.plutobooks.com

Copyright © Tina K. Ramnarine 2007

The right of Tina K. Ramnarine to be identified as the author of this work has been asserted by her in accordance with the Copyright, Designs and Patents Act 1988.

British Library Cataloguing in Publication Data
A catalogue record for this book is available from the British Library

Hardback
ISBN-13   978 0 7453 1767 0
ISBN-10   0 7453 1767 7

Paperback
ISBN-13   978 0 7453 1766 3
ISBN-10   0 7453 1766 9

Library of Congress Cataloging in Publication Data applied for

This book is printed on paper suitable for recycling and made from fully managed and sustained forest sources.

10   9   8   7   6   5   4   3   2   1

Designed and produced for Pluto Press by
Chase Publishing Services Ltd, Fortescue, Sidmouth, EX10 9QG, England
Typeset from disk by Stanford DTP Services, Northampton

For Kumar,
who first taught me to look at the stars

CONTENTS

List of Tables and Figures viii
Acknowledgements ix

Memories 1

1. Home in the Diaspora 18
2. Performing 'Britishness'? 42
3. Towards Beautiful Cosmos 76
4. Dancing Diaspora 109
5. Riddim in Lyrics 129
6. 'I'm a Stranger' 161
7. Reaching for the Trickster Gateway 183

Appendix 207
Notes 210
Bibliography and Discography 219
Index 234

LIST OF TABLES AND FIGURES

Tables

A.1 Members of the Trinidad All Steel Percussion Orchestra — 207
A.2 Steelbands in Britain listed by the British Association of Steelbands, 2001 — 208

Figures

1.1 Models of the relations between 'home' and 'diaspora' — 21
2.1 Handwritten (a and b) and printed (c) scores of 'They Came Upon the Windrush' — 58–60
2.2 Alexander D. Great — 62
2.3 First Historical Café and Bar in Tobago — 65
2.4 Notices about Tobago's folk music on the walls of the First Historical Café and Bar in Tobago — 66
2.5 Carnival at the Victoria and Albert Museum (2002) — 72
3.1 Ebony performing in Leicester Square, London — 78
3.2 Salah and Family Steelpan Academy performing in Toronto, 2001 — 79
3.3 Skiffle Bunch and Dynamic Tassa Group in performance at the October Gallery, London (2004) — 98
5.1 Alexander D. Great (right) and Sheldon Blackman teaching at a music workshop — 131
6.1 The panyard of Phase II Pan Groove — 169
6.2 A steelband class for tourists — 170
6.3 Preparations for Panorama — 171
6.4 Rikki Jai performing on the chutney stage, Brian Lara Promenade — 174
6.5 The stage of the Kendra Phagwa Festival (2001) — 175
7.1 Louis Saldenah (right) at his mas camp — 199

ACKNOWLEDGEMENTS

My thanks are extended to everyone who contributed to this project, providing information and answering questions. Special thanks are due to Wayne Marshall (ethnomusicologist and hip-hop artist), Alexander D. Great (British calypsonian), and W. A. Henry (sociologist and British dancehall DJ) for contributing to my ethnographic experiment in chatting (Chapter 5). The scope of this project emerged in dialogues with Alexander D. Great, who first approached me in the late 1990s to ask if I would be interested in writing about British calypso, and with my publisher, who encouraged me to consider other examples of musical practice in the Caribbean Diaspora. I am indebted to them for encouraging me to pursue this wide-ranging research when I was formulating my ideas at an early stage of the research process.

I gratefully acknowledge the various grants that have enabled me to pursue this project. The British Academy funded fieldwork on Carnivals in Trinidad and Tobago (2001). The Arts and Humanities Research Board funded my exploration of Carnivals in Toronto and New York (2001, 2002). Funding awarded by the Department of Music, Royal Holloway University of London, enabled me to present some of my research materials in earlier stages of preparation at the Society of Ethnomusicology conference in Miami (2004) and at the British Forum for Ethnomusicology conference in Aberdeen (2005). The Department of Music, RHUL, the Music and Letters Trust and the British Academy co-funded my participation in the conference on 'Caribbean Soundscapes' at the University of West Indies in Barbados and field research on CropOver (2005). I have also benefited from invitations to present extracts from this work in research seminars at Cardiff University, Goldsmiths University of London, Roehampton (University of Surrey), Sheffield University and Sussex University. Chapter 2 is partly based on an article I published in the journal *World of Music* (volume 46/1: 7–82). As I was in the final stages of writing this book, Shubha Chaudhuri invited me to present some thoughts on music and diaspora at the 'Remembered Rhythms' Seminar and Festival in Delhi (2005), funded by the Archives and Research Centre for Ethnomusicology, American Institute of Indian Studies. Mark Slobin invited me to present my work at the International Council for Traditional Music colloquium on the theme of 'Emerging Musical Identities' (2006). These were opportunities that allowed me to participate in deeply inspiring discussions on this topic and which provided the final impetus for completing this script.

Special thanks to Mark Slobin for also kindly commenting on an earlier draft and helping me to find a way of polishing the text. Every effort has been made to obtain permission to reproduce song lyrics and due acknowledgement has been given where appropriate. Please contact the publisher if any omissions are noted. Thanks also to the British Calypsonians who have allowed me to quote their song lyrics extensively.

MEMORIES

Crimson in the sky. The sunset ricochets in the meandering waters of the River Thames as two men from St Lucia joke with me about their arrival in Britain. Another man, from Trinidad, joins the conversation, telling us about a steelband performance given in 1951 at the Festival of Britain. We are on the deck of a boat, moored to the banks of the river opposite the Royal Festival Hall, in which that performance had been given. We can see St Paul's Cathedral if we look down the river and, looking in the other direction, the Houses of Parliament. Just out of sight, docked in a river bend by the once decrepit warehouses that are now newly polished dwellings, is a clipper ship. It floats in museum-like preservation as a reminder of past exploration, trade and imprisonment, of the making of empire, of traffic in people, of exchanges in textiles, tea and spices. But this evening we are thinking of a different ship, a later one, and we are, along with everyone else, in a festive mood. There is food. Speeches are being given. This is an invited gathering in celebration of the 'Windrush Years' hosted by the Greater London Authority.

The two men from St Lucia did not arrive in Britain on the SS *Empire Windrush*, the ship that has become a symbol of post-Second World War Caribbean migration to the motherland, but I am at the celebration with my microphone and recording equipment, exploring the musical expressions of the Caribbean Diaspora, and they wish to contribute their tales of migration during the 1950s. They joke about their first impressions of London: the contrasts of landscapes, tropical sun, damp fog, settling in. Just as the conversation begins to take a serious turn, with the two men's reminiscences of their early experiences of London life, the official entertainment begins in the interior of the boat and we are all once again laughing with the performances of a poet, 'Because I come from the West Indies, some people think I am an expert on palm trees' (John Agard); a calypsonian, 'They came upon the Windrush in 1948' (Alexander D. Great), and a comedienne, 'Oh, memories!' (Angie Le Mar).

The comedienne's sketch unfolds to enthusiastic applause. We become increasingly aware of the different ways in which 'home' and the moments that mark migration (arriving at harbours, at train stations, at doors looking for rooms to rent) are experienced through the generations. We are laughing, but there is seriousness in this comedy. Angie Le Mar tells us about the shock of seeing her mother return to Jamaica after 25 years. She had not really paid attention to her mother saying, 'I going home one day. One day, Angie, I going home. I going home.' When that day arrived, Angie cried. Troubled by her mother's absence, it was not long before she travelled across the Atlantic to see her:

'She left in June; I was in Jamaica July. With my three children, asking, "Who's going to raise these children?"'

The invitation to perform at the Windrush celebrations was worth reporting, and in excitement Angie telephoned her parents in Jamaica:

'I'm going to be doing the Windrush celebrations.'

'Oh that's fantastic, let me tell your dad.'

Her mother left Angie hanging on the telephone for half an hour. On resuming the conversation with her daughter she sighed,

'Yes. Oh, memories!'

'No, mum I can't hear your memories now because it's too expensive; write to me.'

Memories are prominent threads woven into, shaping and giving expression to the movement of populations that have come to be known as diasporic. Connecting people to the past, memories contribute important dimensions to thinking about belonging, homelands and diaspora. For Angie's parents, memories are viewed through the changing political landscapes of colonial and postcolonial experiences. Yet memories are only a part of feeling that one lives in a diaspora. The claims of the past cannot overshadow people's current struggles. Contemporary political activisms and creative expressions – the ways in which homes are made – are also aspects of the struggles over diaspora. Perspectives through the generations highlight the dynamics between diaspora, history and politics, so vividly captured by glimpsing the memories of Angie Le Mar's mother, of migration to Britain, the motherland of her childhood, a place in which she would dream of returning to her Caribbean island home. Britain – a place that her children and grandchildren would learn to call 'home'.

Where is home in the diaspora? Why is it necessary to pose such a question? What kinds of politics come into focus in responding? While nations, identities and borders attract renewed scrutiny in view of contemporary migrations, global processes and geopolitical shifts, people still feel the need, intently, to belong to specific places. In contrast to the transformations of home through generations that we see in Angie's case (and which provide some responses to the questions posed here), diaspora discourses are often preoccupied with the themes of exile, migration and dislocation. It might appear incongruent to ask about home in the diaspora. Traditionally, diaspora has been seen as a space of non-belonging, of being away from a place called 'home'. As Cohen notes, the classical notion of diaspora has been one that 'highlights the catastrophic origin, the forcible dispersal and the estrangement of diasporic peoples in their places of settlement' (1997: 177).

While recent analyses of diasporas have been more diverse (Cohen 1997 suggests 'victim', 'labour and imperial', 'trade' and 'cultural', for example), echoes from the past, assertions of the historical specificities that shape people's everyday experiences, and an insistence on remembering remain central to diasporic sensibilities. Questions about origins continue to inform debates about diaspora, and they interweave with considerations of imbalanced relations of power between people. Such questions have led to new ways of reading history (between the lines of colonial documents and through oral testimonies, for example) so that diverse perspectives on the past can be layered to produce fuller accounts of what has happened. In many diasporic contexts there is something more at stake than simply being 'at home' or 'away from home'. The national, the diasporic and the postcolonial are configured together in the politics of – and claims to – place, and in the reclamations of cultural heritages.

Diaspora is inflected, moreover, by increasing possibilities for travel between diasporic site and homeland, and by the movements between these two places that may become a 'mode of dwelling' (Minh-ha 1994: 15). In this mode of dwelling, both places are transformed. Minh-ha writes about a loss of home and of becoming a stranger in a strange land, of home for the exile and the migrant being hardly more than 'a transitional or circumstantial place, since the "original" home cannot be recaptured, nor can its presence/absence be entirely banished in the "re-made" home' (1994: 14–15). We can think in very different terms, however, about such a mode of dwelling. Instead of loss and subjective uncertainties about the places which one inhabits, we might focus on diaspora as being about the relations between people as well as between places. The mode of dwelling between two places, then, is an expansion in which multiple homes are established through a transnational community of kin relations, as in the cases of St Kitts-Nevis (Olwig 1993) and Trinidad and Tobago (Ramnarine 1996). Goulbourne and Chamberlain similarly observe the importance of transnational kinship relations in thinking of a 'unified Atlantic world', noting that return migration plays a role in maintaining these links (2001: 8).

In drawing attention to historical processes, place, dwelling and kinship ties, we have moved some way towards a response to my initial question: where is home in the diaspora? Between uneasy transformations of place and transnational communities of relatedness we find that diaspora is something more than a concern with migrations, movements over territories, displacements. The circumstances that have led to the formation and recognition of various diasporas – the African, the Indian, the Jewish, the Armenian, the Caribbean, for example – have been diverse. People's experiences of migration, therefore, are not uniform, even if they sometimes seem to share a sense of longing for a place called home, which is somewhere else. People have been compelled or forced to move. They have moved voluntarily. They have moved through the routes of empire, trade, slavery, indentureship, labour and persecution. While the modern world has witnessed large-scale human movements around the globe, migration is nothing new. How can we account, then, for the rise in the discursive modes of self-awareness described as diaspora consciousness?

The reference to 'consciousness' reveals that diaspora can be understood as a political concept through which people claim their rights to belong, not just to 'homelands' left but also to 'homelands' inhabited. In the context of civil rights and independence movements, these politics have been forcefully articulated through the reggae song texts (often described as 'conscious lyrics') of Bob Marley, for example. Reaching out from Caribbean island to global spaces, these song texts, rooted in a longer history of musical narrative performance, refer to resisting Babylon, weeping by its rivers, the Exodus, and thus draw on the tropes of, and find resonance with, the Jewish dispersion to which 'diaspora' originally referred.

'Consciousness' also brings to mind Du Bois's notion of 'double consciousness' as the 'peculiar sensation' of 'always looking at one's self through the eyes of others', of feeling 'two-ness' (1999 [1903]), a formulation that carries contemporary resonance in considering how identifying 'diasporas' continues to both mark cultural and ethnic boundaries (with their attending potential for exclusion) and enable people to hold on to the past. In the opening passages to his influential book, *The Souls of Black Folk*, Du Bois refers to Moses (a 'stranger in a strange land') to pose the question that forms the 'bitter cry' of his classmates: 'Why did God make me an outcast and a stranger in mine own house?' (1999 [1903]: 10). Each chapter of that work is introduced with musical notations of African-American spirituals that draw us into the world of performance and attune us to the expressive dimensions of diasporic experiences. A contemporary variation on 'double consciousness' might be 'multiple subjectivity', a concept that emphasises process, practice and experience. Diaspora can be understood, therefore, as a practice in which multiple subjectivities are rehearsed and experienced. Rather than understanding these in terms of dispossession, disconnection, fragmentation or fracture, the experiences and articulations of a plural, changing consciousness that shape diasporic subjectivities might lead to different ways of thinking about belonging altogether. In the diaspora, people often feel a sense of connection to places in which they both do and do not live. They belong to more than one geographic location, even if they never travel to their ancestral 'homeland'. These multiple subjectivities emerge from the interplay of diaspora, nation and generation, crosscutting the frames of time and place and providing important perspectives on questions about identity formation and belonging. The recurrent tropes of multiplicity and plurality throw static formulations of identity and the polarities of either inclusion or exclusion into relief.

As the tenacity of the past, as a political concept, as a practice, diaspora alerts us to the limitations of thinking about diaspora as being concerned with 'at' and 'away from' home. While Caribbean populations have emphasised political and historical factors in explaining their movements across places, thereby nurturing diasporic consciousness, the study of diaspora has been promoted within academic discourses recently. One of the most influential journals in the field of diaspora studies, *Diaspora: A Journal of Transnational Studies*, was launched in 1991. Over the past decade, it has highlighted a number of thematic trends in analysing diaspora, including nationalism, transnationalism, globalisation, identity, citizenship and 'race'. Slobin edited a special issue of the journal on music and diaspora in 1994. (Also see Slobin 2003 for an account of the use of the term 'diaspora' in ethnomusicology.) The ethnographic literature on diaspora in Caribbean contexts predates this recent analytical focus, extending back to the mid twentieth century and therefore providing further resources for this study. Research projects on diasporic performance, kinship structures, rituals and village life in the Caribbean, focusing on issues surrounding the preservation and transmission of cultural knowledge, cultural retentions and cultural creativities, have resulted in a substantial ethnographic literature (for example, Herskovitz and Herskovitz 1947, Klass 1961, Myers 1998, Henry 2003) which, together with sound recordings (such as the collections of Alan Lomax from the 1960s and Emory Cook, 1956–62), and historical research (Dabydeen and Samaroo 1987, de Verteuil 1989), have inspired me to consider similar questions about diasporic cultural production in relation to the Caribbean Diaspora.

Academic discourses have played their role in legitimising, identifying and constructing 'diasporas'. Emerging from an increasing preoccupation with 'identity' (despite the intangibility and resistance of this concept to neat categorisation), these discourses intersect with expressions of diasporic consciousness at 'grass-roots' levels in interesting ways: at times in resonance; at times providing dissonant counterpoints; at times pointing to the complexities of the topic. Particularly illuminating in these debates have been the contributions of writers who have reflected on their own experiences of migration. Edward Said's memoir *Out of Place* (1999) discusses, for example, the disjunctures of growing up in one place and moving to another, of thinking in two languages at once, of an early uneasiness with a name that did not signify a clear identity ('a foolishly English name yoked forcibly to the unmistakably Arabic family name', 1999: 3). Yet, towards the end of his life, struggling and learning to prefer feeling out of place, he observed:

> I occasionally experience myself as a cluster of flowing currents. I prefer this to the idea of a solid self, the identity to which so many attach so much significance. These currents, like the themes of one's life, flow along during the waking hours, and at their best, they require no reconciling, no harmonizing. They are 'off' and may be out of place, but at least they are always in motion, in time, in place. (Said 1999: 295)

While diaspora as a displacement from a homeland is a prominent feature of different kinds of diaspora discourse, many writers and cultural commentators who were part of the 1950s and 1960s wave of Caribbean migration to Britain note the in-between states of arrival. Among them is Stuart Hall who talks about a diasporic experience that has left him with a sense of not feeling 'at home', either in Jamaica or in England:

> This Jamaica [of the 1970s] was not where I had grown up. For one thing, it had become, culturally, a black society, a post-slave, postcolonial society,

whereas I had lived there at the end of the colonial era. So I could negotiate it as a 'familiar stranger'.

Paradoxically, I had exactly the same relationship to England. Having been prepared by the colonial education, I knew England from the inside. But I'm not and never will be 'English'. I know both places intimately, but I am not wholly of either place. And that's exactly the diasporic experience, far away enough to experience the sense of exile and loss, close enough to understand the enigma of an always-postponed 'arrival'. (Interview with Stuart Hall in Chen 1996: 490)

Hall's acute sense of both distance and proximity in thinking about feeling 'at home' has particular relevance for subsequent generations who do not experience the move that can be described as a geographically determined 'exile'. Caryl Phillips also turns to a personal narrative in an essay on 'The High Anxiety of Belonging'. He writes:

I grew up in Leeds in the sixties and seventies, in a world in which everybody, from teachers to policemen, felt it appropriate to ask me – some more forcefully than others – for an explanation of where I was from. The answer 'Leeds' or 'Yorkshire', was never going to satisfy me either. I soon recognized that no sooner had the words 'Leeds' or 'Yorkshire' fallen from my lips than a corollary question would be asked. My interrogator would paste a smile of benign patronage to his face. 'No lad, where are you *really* from?' ...

Today there is a tacit understanding that Britain has changed. It has been a few years now since a Briton had the temerity to ask me 'where are you from?' I take this as a sign of progress. Sadly, however, I am coming to understand that despite these welcome changes, the constant questioning of those early years and concomitant undermining of my sense of belonging, has inevitably affected my ability to embrace Britain as 'home' with the degree of vigour that I might wish. (Phillips 2001: 8–9)

The personal accounts of Hall and Phillips emphasise the point that the notions of diaspora, homeland and home raise problematic questions about the borders of belonging. Both writers grapple with identifying 'home' in ways that allow us to glimpse the discomforts of feeling excluded. While Avtar Brah notes that a diasporic sensibility does not mean a desire 'to return to a place of "origin"' (1996: 192–3), Rosemary George asks whether we should look for ways to move beyond the notion of 'home' altogether (1996: 199). We do not have to think about home and diaspora in polarised terms. Both 'diaspora' and 'home' place subjects in locations to which they seemingly do or do not belong. This is a suggestion that results in disorientation, registering our own complicities and investments in (non-) belonging. The contradiction of diaspora is that it opens a way to move beyond a circumscribed notion of home because it exposes the boundaries of (non-) belonging. If first generation migrants may never feel the sense of 'arrival', for their descendants the diaspora may have to be the space of belonging, or at least – and perhaps more importantly – a place to which they lay claim. Another view of 'home' is needed. While Stuart Hall is the 'familiar stranger', not wholly of Jamaica or England, Caryl Phillips deals with the anxiety of belonging by actively cultivating 'a plural notion of home' (2001: 9).

Ultimately, the sense of multiplicity that is provoked by the experience of diaspora, what I earlier called 'multi-local belonging' (Ramnarine 1996), emphasises the permeability of boundaries and identities and draws attention to the connections between people across geographic and temporal distances, such that the currents that make up life experiences are always 'in time, in place'. In posing a question about home in the diaspora, this book, which can be viewed as a recitation of that mantra 'in time, in place', attempts to shift academic diaspora discourses away from the boundaries of marginal/minority spaces, away from the emphasis on certain kinds of migration as reducible to a movement away from home, and away from descriptions of some diasporic populations (some but not all) living in a 'host land' irrespective of settlement through generations. Away from, in short, always feeling 'out of place', a 'stranger in one's home'. Focusing on diaspora as politics, as history and as subjective practice in relation to the Caribbean Diaspora (and all studies of diaspora are necessarily historically and politically specific), I will suggest that rather than focus on diaspora as a dislocation we start from an alternative premise: that diaspora can be the space in which people establish 'home'. This is an alternative premise in relation to predominant academic discourses. But it is the premise with which I began writing this book; one that at first seemed almost too banal to be presented as an argument, a perspective that has revealed itself as being rather a radical assertion in view of contemporary academic orthodoxies only as I read more and more of the academic literature on diaspora. It is a premise that invites us to reconsider the insuperabilities of difference ingrained in everyday encounter and ethnographic modes of thinking, to imagine the possibilities of different kinds of politics, and to struggle against the traumas of human separations.

The suggestion that 'home' can be in the 'diaspora' provides a way into rethinking both concepts. To understand diaspora as a space of belonging challenges knowledge about identities, cultures, hybridities and, above all, diaspora as only being about displacement – compelling us, in exploring performance, to question long-cherished ideas about the bounded nature of cultural transmission, to invite new paradigms through which to investigate memory and creativity, and to focus on the relationships between place and generation. With its multiple diasporas forged out of the mass movements of populations in the making of the modern world and connecting people across the globe, the Caribbean Diaspora provides an appropriate way into such critical enquiry, confronting us with the brutalities of island histories and the fixations of difference that continue to plague the region, whilst heartening us, nevertheless, with abundant evidence of the human capacity for creative expression. The Caribbean, populated by diasporised people from different parts of the globe and generating its own multiply situated Diaspora, constantly prompts us to avoid the absurd simplicities that reinforce the dichotomies of 'Us' and 'Other' or produce analytical models of communities living in 'host lands' harbouring a nostalgia for a home elsewhere that they (or their parents, or grandparents, or ever-distant ancestors) may never have seen.

Promptings

Caribbean popular music is now heard all over the world. Its global impact has been given added impetus through the Caribbean Diaspora, which spreads across the Atlantic, from Miami to Manchester to Montreal. This book is concerned with the role of some of the most widespread Caribbean musical expressions in diaspora politics. In Britain, Caribbeans came mostly from Jamaica, Barbados, Trinidad and Tobago, and Guyana, their numbers standing at 304,070 in 1971. It is more difficult to reach a figure that includes British-born children, though Owen, noting the ways in which census categories hide this population, suggests 633,425 on the basis of the 1991 census (Owen 2001: 65). In the Netherlands, Caribbean population figures stood at 308,000 in 1988 and most of the migrants were from Suriname. In France, the Caribbean population migrating largely through government sponsorship stood at 180,448 in 1982. These are patterns of migration that point to the connections established through empires. Most migration from Cuba, Puerto Rico and Haiti has been to the United States of America (these figures are from Peach 1991, cited in Chamberlain 2001: 35–40). Music and musicians travel through overlapping networks between diasporic contexts and Caribbean island spaces, and between Caribbean communities in diasporic settings. Arriving at Tilbury Docks in 1948 on board the *SS Empire Windrush*, the Trinidadian calypsonian, Lord Kitchener was greeted by news reporters requesting an impromptu performance. He sang 'London is the Place for Me'. The performance was captured on Pathé newsreel and has provided one of the most enduring images of mid-twentieth-century migrations from the English-speaking Caribbean to the mother country. The zouk band, Kassav, the leading voice of the French Caribbean, launched their international career in Paris in 1979. New York, with a Caribbean population of over 2 million by the 1980s, saw the development of salsa. Other mediums for the wide dissemination of Caribbean popular music have been commercial recordings since the early twentieth century, from biguines recorded in Paris in the 1920s and popular calypsos recorded in Britain during the 1950s, to reggae of the 1970s and contemporary dancehall expressions. The UK and USA popular music charts have featured several Caribbean and Caribbean Diaspora artists, including Jimmy Cliff, Eddy Grant, Gloria Estefan, Ricky Martin, Shaggy, Desmond Dekker and Harry Belafonte. Tourism has contributed to a transnational music market and to the spread of Caribbean musical sounds. Political movements in various contexts have turned to models of musico-political articulation from Caribbean repertoires. Contemporary bands as diverse as the Brazilian Afroblocos, the Serbian Eyesburn, and the Australian Aboriginal Yothu Yindi attest to the legacy of the Jamaican reggae singer, Bob Marley.

The music considered in this book includes calypso, reggae, salsa and steelband. This is not a comprehensive survey of music in the Caribbean Diaspora. Given the breadth of the topic, one study cannot hope to be exhaustive. There are simply too many musical examples and Caribbean diasporic contexts to be considered. The examples are not arbitrary choices. They have been the sounds (together with chutney, discussed elsewhere: Ramnarine 1996, 2001, 2007) of the Caribbean Diaspora in Britain that have reverberated through the urban landscapes that I inhabit. Through selected ethnographic examples, I address questions such as: how do musicians reveal the dynamics between diasporic and national sensibilities? What do musical performances and sounds tell us about the movements of music and people? How is 'home' experienced, and belonging asserted, through musical practice?

Why music? Music is a way of telling stories about connections and particularities. Music provides an apt medium for thinking about diaspora: holding a crucial place in the diasporic imagination, having the capacity to interrogate social theory, and raising complex questions about boundaries, identities and politics. Through the aesthetic, expressive and performance medium of music, diaspora is practised and enjoyed; experienced emotionally, somatically and temporally. In listening to people preserve the sounds of a home somewhere else and create new sounds inspired by their new environments, we become aware of overlapping domains, of complex geographies and temporalities of belonging. Between musical preservation and musical creativity we find music held in the moment but linking people to the past. In its representational ambiguity, music lends itself to multiple interpretations, performed, for instance, in the rituals of lifecycles over generations or on the stages of contemporary political life. The portability of music means that it is often retained and practised in the diaspora. People carry their musical voices, musical instruments and musical memories with them.[1] People are also influenced by the sounds they hear circulating through transnational spaces, increasingly transmitted through a variety of media – live performances, recordings, films and virtual technology. Cultural theorists such as Gilroy (1993a, 1993b) and Sharma, Hutnyk and Sharma (1996), as well as ethnomusicologists such as McDaniel (1998), Monson (2003), Myers (1998), Ramnarine (2001), Slobin (2000) and Sugarman (2004) have emphasised the significance of musical practice in diasporic contexts. The capacity of music to travel around the world, to cross boundaries but still evoke places, to provide sonic windows into the past but exist in contemporary soundscapes, gives it a special role in maintaining diasporic sensibilities, creating new homes, and revealing complex histories of creative interactions.

Music is in the everyday, providing sonic border crossings. Goulbourne writes that 'it is hardly necessary to detail the obvious cultural presence of Caribbean people in Britain, but it is important to note that this presence continues to have a significant impact in various areas of British national life' (2001: 16). The 'visibility' and 'audibility' of musical performance (to use Goulbourne's descriptors of DJs and loud music in clubs) also take us beyond the subjectivities of diasporic experience into the realms of political struggle and activism, interacting with the political work of diasporic assertion. This is one reason why Du Bois's *The Souls of Black Folk* includes musical notations of African-American spirituals, revealing the extent to which he drew on Herder's ideas of the folk as tradition bearers connected to the past, which were to become so implicated in nationalist projects. If the politics of diaspora, like the politics of nationhood, sometimes reinforce the boundaries of identity ('we are these people, they are those people'), looking at musical practice in diasporic contexts may help us, nevertheless, to respond to the political philosophies of difference, to dislodge their essentialisms and intolerances. In thinking through time and through place, we find histories and politics entwined. While my emphasis lies in considering musical practice as a way of dislodging the essentialisms that shape how people think about themselves, diaspora discourses nevertheless offer ideological contradictions between essentialist and more fluid conceptions of identity. Theorisations of identity constructions and the politics of cultural practices in terms of the 'in-between', the 'hybrid' (for example, Bhabha 1994) or the 'intercultural' (Bharucha 2001, for instance) offer ways of negotiating these contradictions, but might not entirely escape them.

The main centres of diasporic Caribbean communities include Paris, New York, Toronto and Miami, and musical scenes in some of these metropolitan centres will be considered here. Although the focus in this book is Britain (London in particular, which is the area that has the greatest concentration of British-Caribbean populations: see Owen 2001: 71–3), I carried out multi-sited field research to situate my research findings within the wider frameworks of the Caribbean Diaspora.[2] Following the methodological approaches of the ethnographic-based disciplines of ethnomusicology and anthropology from which this study emerges, I wanted to hear people's stories, observe and participate in performance events, ground my understanding in having been present. This involved short visits to many field contexts in which people's wide-ranging perspectives on music and diaspora could emerge. Multi-sited field research has been one of the new methodologies developed within ethnographic-based disciplines in trying to understand processes that take us beyond clearly demarcated field sites. Multi-sited empirical methods have become essential to reach understandings of how people and places are connected and they are increasingly applied in researching migration, globalisation and mass media processes. Between 2001 and 2005 I was present at performances in Trinidad and Tobago, Barbados, Toronto, New York, Miami and London with the specific intention of 'doing fieldwork'. I interviewed musicians, their students and members of their audiences and attended meetings in which cultural policy matters were debated. I participated in music education projects both as a teacher and as a student and examined the websites of Caribbean musicians. The multi-sited field experience proved to be invaluable in highlighting the circulation of musicians and repertoires, in following performance trends in various Caribbean Diaspora locations and in exploring the networks between Caribbean island and its diasporic communities at various levels (the links woven between performers, audiences, policy-makers and performance organisers). In all of the field sites, specifically local concerns came to the forefront. In Canada, practitioners spoke about 'Caribbean heritage' and 'Canadian Carnival' while in London, calypsonians spoke about calypso as 'British folk music'. In Barbados, the winning soca song of 2005 began with the line 'If you're proud to be a Bajan, put all your flags out', and several calypsos of this season commented on the debates about whether the island should become a republic. While Carnival and calypso are thus global forms, helping people to forge a sense of multi-local belonging, they also show us how music in global spaces takes on multiple significances, featuring in local debates on politics and aesthetics and interweaving between national and transnational spaces. Carrying out multi-sited fieldwork means that I have been able to look at performances in a variety of contexts that share a politics devoted to exploring displacement and placement and reveal contestations over national spaces. These performances are the musical spaces between diaspora and nation that map onto the political spaces of colonialism, postcolonialism and nationalism. Ultimately, they are the musical spaces of 'home'. Yet the relation between the national and the transnational is complex. While multi-sited field research revealed the habitual foregrounding of the 'local' (expressed in terms of the national), the transnational circulation of musical ideas, recordings, performers and audiences that connects the Caribbean and its multiply situated diasporas provides the context within which Caribbean diasporic musical production must be understood.

The insights generated by multi-sited field research are significant. To supplement the short-term fieldwork, other fruitful methodological approaches included performance participation, consulting historical sources, and considering 'oral histories' or 'biographies' as a way of looking at how the experiences of diaspora are revealed through the stories of individuals. Ethnographic work has provided a way of listening closely to what people say about diasporic performances and describing musical events and practices, but each ethnographic context included here merits further attention. For this project, the contextual details demanded by ethnographic writing are placed ultimately in the service of a grand narrative gesture that is concerned with a politics of possibility – thinking of home in the diaspora. Grounded in ethnographic approaches, this book critically engages with key concepts such as 'culture', 'hybridity', 'multiculturalism' and 'others', shifting emphasis away from the idea of 'difference' and turning to the details of musical practices to unravel processes of musical memory, innovation and cultural production in diasporic politics.[3]

Outline of the Book

The following chapters present kaleidoscopic perspectives on connections and collaborations that might move us towards thinking about home in the diaspora. Chapter 1 introduces the main themes of this book and outlines the theoretical frameworks that have shaped my analysis of music in the Caribbean Diaspora. Chapter 2 focuses on the connected musical spaces between diaspora and nation, emphasising the limits of musical canons defined by their geographies. How does performance create new spatialities and what do these tell us about the relationship between diasporic, national and postcolonial sensibilities? Drawing on the testimony of one of its most active practitioners, the aim is to show how calypsonians in Britain are involved in the performance of 'Britishness' even as they maintain links with a Caribbean island home and adhere to Caribbean calypso models. Examining some of the challenges presented by theoretical ideas enjoying a current vogue that attempt to account for the creative expressions that emerge from encounters between 'musical cultures', Chapter 3 looks at musical fusions and multiculturalisms through steelband pedagogy, one of the beneficiaries in trends to foster a multicultural music education. Challenging some of the assumptions that underlie models of people living in discrete cultural groups and examining the moral dimensions of culture theory that inform fusions, hybridities and multiculturalisms, begin to move us towards 'beautiful cosmos'. Chapter 4 further explores the theoretical possibilities of 'hybridity' discourses and rethinks inscriptions of belonging on the body such that appearance might tell us where people are 'really from'. Chapter 5 turns to lyrics that imagine the possibilities of global political action for connections, assessing the legacy of a Caribbean musical superstar (Bob Marley) and presenting an ethnographic experiment in 'chatting': a way of presenting collaborations with performers and implicating the researched in self-reflexive accounts that contribute to this research project. Through chatting, the explicit spiritual politics of lyrics are highlighted. The last two chapters are interrelated, tracing Carnival performances in both the Caribbean and its Diaspora to discuss the parallel discourses on the development of Carnival tourism and contestations over performance histories.

Through the details of musical practices, *Beautiful Cosmos* presents an argument for a politics that takes issue with strategies of exclusion and recognises that the boundaries that seem to separate are, and have been, crossed over and over again. Music and diaspora act as figurative and literal metaphors of these crossings. This is not, then, an argument for easy visions of global utopia, but for a politics of rethinking difference. This argument suggests a way of thinking about political possibilities through everyday processes of creativity. The traumas, losses and exiles of diaspora, the memories and consequences of which are sustained through generations and through centuries, alert us to the struggle involved to reach any utopian sense of connection that might be described as 'belonging'. Music of the Caribbean Diaspora is manifold. This study charts my ongoing journey through this musical terrain, marking my encounters with musical sounds, musicians, dancers and audiences, and presenting some reflections on belonging and its expressions.

1
HOME IN THE DIASPORA

Diaspora has become fashionable. It has been highlighted in attempts to analyse contemporary global processes, raising questions about home and belonging. It is worth beginning with an obvious question. What is diaspora? A response is provided by the Trinidadian calypsonian, Chris Tambu Herbert, who sings: 'The journey don't stop. Never look back look ahead... I say travel on, travel on...' (Tambu n.d.). Journey metaphors signal the political dimensions of migrations to the New World as well as the subsequent journeys to which they have given rise. Tambu's song text provides a route to exploring the articulation of (dis)placement, resonating with Avtar Brah's observation that 'at the heart of the notion of diaspora is the image of a journey' that involves leaving one place and arriving and settling in another (1996: 182). Brah discusses diaspora as composite formations, as a pan-ic concept, and as a conceptual category rather than as a description of different migrations that 'delineates a field of identifications where "imagined communities" are forged within and out of a confluence of narratives from annals of collective memory and re-memory' (1996: 196). Brubaker similarly focuses on the conceptual, writing that where boundaries and identities are emphasised, diaspora can represent 'a non-territorial form of essentialized belonging', the problems with which might be overcome by thinking of diaspora 'not in substantialist terms as a bounded entity, but rather as an idiom, a stance, a claim' (2005: 12).

Memory and stance (history and politics) are central to my exploration of diaspora. In focusing on issues about belonging in the diaspora, this study adheres to a classical concern with 'homeland', although my argument is not about homelands elsewhere but about homes established in diasporic contexts, and about networks of homes (real and imagined) that might stretch our views to thinking about home in global terms. In thinking globally I have not been persuaded by the wide application of diaspora, embracing such diverse categories as digital, trading, liberal, fundamentalist, and so on, in which semantic significance seems to be lost. An adherence to the diaspora-home continuum reveals that I share Tölölyan's (1996) view that some 'stringency in definition' of the term 'diaspora' is required. As Brubaker notes, 'If everyone is diasporic, then no one is distinctively so. The term loses its discriminating power – its ability to pick out phenomena, to make distinctions. The universalization of diaspora, paradoxically, means the disappearance of diaspora' (2005: 3). In a radical political project towards global belonging, the removal of descriptors attached to some populations, such as 'new', 'refugee', 'migrant', 'exile', 'outsider', might be no loss. But that political project is not on the horizon and what the wide application of the descriptor 'diaspora' does is to obliterate the politics of diaspora relating to migrations and labour, often forced; the histories of exploitations and inequalities, and the secondary diasporas (as in the Caribbean example) that are the fallouts of empires.

The Study of Music and the Study of Diaspora

How might the study of music offer a route to revising views of 'home'? Can we turn to music to respond to the question, where is home in the diaspora? I explored a plural notion of home in an earlier study on an Indian-Caribbean popular music in which I stressed that music in the diasporic imagination is never only about displacement. It is also about establishing a space of belonging perceived in multi-local terms. To elaborate briefly, music can refer to a heritage beyond the Caribbean (say, in India or in Africa), but can also be used in the expression of different senses of cultural placement because of the ways in which the music itself is put together. Musical sounds, timbres, melodic and rhythmic characteristics: all of these simultaneously reference a heritage elsewhere and people's sense of belonging in the Caribbean (Ramnarine 1996, 2001, 2004). This sonic referencing remains ambiguous, making music a medium equally appropriate for holding onto the past or for re-imagining places, histories and traditions. Music circulates between diasporas and homelands, nourishing multi-local sensibilities. Mediated through cassette, CD and video technologies, and mediating, as Sugarman observes, between the tensions resulting from poles of experience relating to distant homelands and lived realities that represent 'different visions of self and community', music presents possibilities for 'new forms of subjectivity' (2004: 21).

It is the presentation of possibility and, for that matter, an ambitious one writ large, that I wish to pursue. Diaspora does not transcend any of the categories through which people conceptually and politically divide human spaces: nation, region, ethnicity, religion or community for example. Neither, for that matter, does music: often one of the creative forms to which people turn in articulating specific identities, in marking the boundaries that separate, in feeling diasporised. But through looking further at music as practice, as experiential and as a way of engaging the creative imagination, I want to elaborate the potential offered by diasporic cultural production for expressing the sense of multi-local belonging that begins to move us closer towards Kuper's insistence on similarity rather than difference in human experience (Kuper 1999) and Gilroy's vision of a planetary humanism (Gilroy 2000). This elaboration brings into play another trope that is often linked with diaspora – that of globalisation. In thinking globally, we are removed from the model of diaspora as exile (as being away from home) via multiple homes and the transformation of home and diaspora (see Figure 1.1). My approach to globalisation departs from analysis of music in global, commercial processes and hegemonies to thinking about musical performance, situated in the dialectics of diaspora and home, as an agent in the development of a global political action committed to the vision of a shared 'One World'. There are two layers to be considered here. The first concerns the role of musical performance in and as political action. The second concerns the role of musical analyses and ethnographic descriptions of musical practices in contributing to the political project of thinking through human connections. While some studies of diaspora have overlooked performances as being 'only fun', 'depoliticised', demanding 'nothing except enjoyment and consumption' (Werbner 2002: 12, 252), ethnomusicologists have reiterated the view presented in Gilroy's (1993b) seminal work on *The Black Atlantic* that the expressive

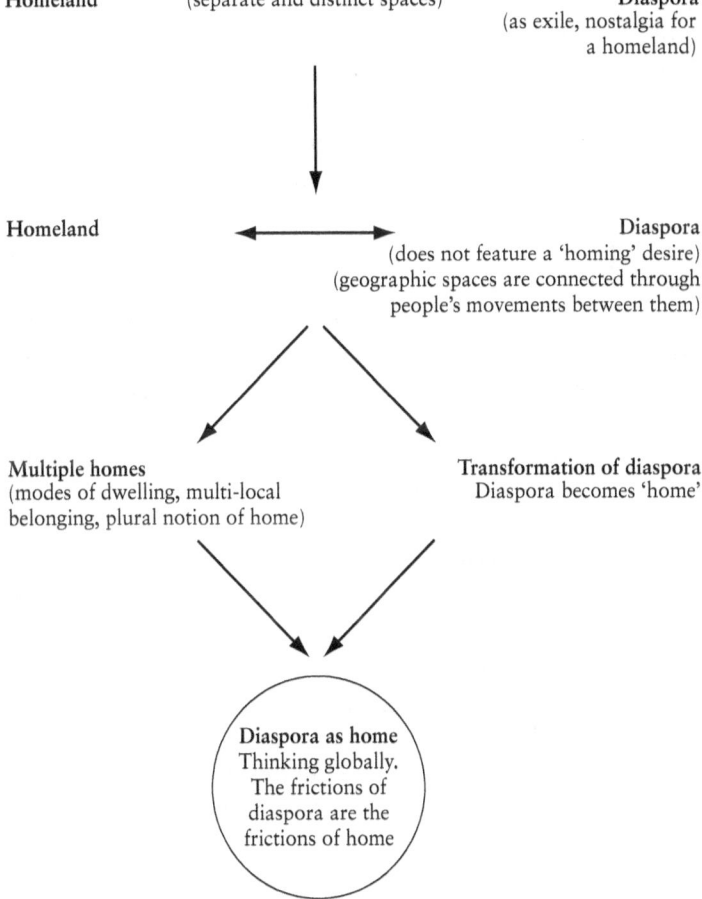

Figure 1.1 Models of the relations between 'home' and 'diaspora'

and performative arts are profoundly political and central to the theorisation of diaspora. In fact, musical practices always make us look at theory again, to reconsider, revise and even reject existing theoretical models. Analysis of what is going on in music, of the ways in which sounds are put together in the processes of creation and performance may also prompt some revisions to theoretical understandings and to social analyses of diaspora in terms of the marginal, minority and problematic.

Multi-local belonging experienced through music encourages us to think about home in the global space: to feel connected with people and places elsewhere. It is worth making explicit the fact that this statement highlights the implication of musical analysis (talking about timbres, melodies, rhythms, for example) with political activism (advocating a move towards global political action). This link between analysis and activism demands further comment given that the cursory treatment of performance as only fun (mentioned above) finds some response in musicological angst about the discipline's social relevance. As Cook and Everist ask: 'Where does musicology come on anybody's list of global priorities?' (1999: vii). The range of approaches to music confirms Samson's observation that in analysing 'we construct the object of our analysis according to certain presuppositions' (1999: 44), which alerts us to considering not only methods but also motivations in undertaking studies of music. There is a social and political agenda for the kind of study of music with which I engage here. This agenda points to the social relevance of musical analysis and critical thinking about musical performance, as well as of performance itself. This is a project which could be described as contributing to an 'ethnomusicology of engagement' (see Ramnarine, forthcoming), drawing attention to the ways in which musical understanding finds a place in the political world and offers alternative possibilities. In this sense, it confirms that musicology is indeed a political act, as Bohlman suggested in a landmark essay, and that the field has moved some way from insisting on its apolitical status to come not only 'face-to-face with its own political acts' (1993: 419), but also to actively engaging with the politics of scholarship and with the wider political world within which music scholars are located. This project points to some fruitful intersections between cultural studies (seeing the cultural as the political) and ethnomusicology (based on ethnographic production of musical practices as socio-cultural phenomena that gives us a close-up view of what is going on in any context under study, so that we can study the details of performing and political practices).

The journey towards music in the realms of human connectedness is not easy for the processes whereby musical sounds are combined into the textures and forms explored here lead us into questions about the politics of musical creativity that pull us into opposite directions. How do we analyse the combined timbres of sitar and steelpan? How do we interpret reggae in Australia with a prominent use of the didgeridu? As postcolonial musical experiments? In relation to resistance politics? As the blurring of discrete 'musical cultures'? On one hand, music as a cultural product, a commodity from which some profit and others lose, sensitises us to the borrowing or plundering of musical resources as being yet another aspect of power and its inequities. As Perry Hall suggests in exploring the dynamics of appropriation and innovation in African-American music, separating music from people

> not only 'exploits' Black cultural forms, commercially and otherwise, but also nullifies the cultural meaning those forms provide for African-Americans. The appropriated forms become ineffective as expressions and affirmations of the unique cultural experiences from which they arise. (1997: 32)

On the other hand, the realm of the musical imagination may attune us towards the possibility of thinking through alternative paradigms, of developing a much-needed 'theory of global political action' (Pieterse 1995: 59) capable of addressing those very inequities. For 'difference' can dissolve in musical practice. When steelpan players collaborate with sitarists, when didgeridu musicians experiment with reggae, they may be more concerned with timbres, textures and structures, with music as an aesthetic and performing, rather than political, practice. They may simply be tuning into the sounds that they encounter in their everyday sonic environments. In tuning in, they show us resonance between people's experiences. Such sonic manifestations of tuning in may contrast, nevertheless, with discursive and political formulations of musical practices in relation to cultural appropriations and products. The musical examples to be explored in the following chapters navigate us across the precarious tightropes that stretch between these two divergent trajectories.

If a theory of global political action to address inequity is needed, thinking globally is becoming easier. Perhaps the fashion for considering diasporic experiences has arisen because, as Stuart Hall observes, movements away from homelands have become such an important feature of modern geopolitical landscapes. Hall argues that, 'since migration has turned out to be *the* world-historical event of late modernity, the classic postmodern experience turns out to be the diasporic experience' and the diasporic experience can therefore be understood as being central to the articulation of the postmodern and the postcolonial (interview with Stuart Hall in Chen 1996: 490). The Caribbean Diaspora as a postwar example is paradigmatic for looking at the experiences of people undertaking more recent economic and political migrations to Britain from other places (Hall 2001). Despite the proliferation of writings on this topic, establishing diaspora as a space of belonging and not just one of separation or rupture from a place of origin in the ever-more distant past remains an urgent project. Dealing with the imagery of exile while disrupting the links posited between territory and origin, diaspora necessitates revisions to notions of national belonging (cf. Gilroy 1987). Focusing on the Caribbean Diaspora further disrupts notions of a homeland elsewhere. For where is the homeland? Is it in the Caribbean? Or should we look back further in history to Africa, India, China, Ireland, England or somewhere else? This point lies at the centre of an understanding of diaspora that does not look to one homeland elsewhere. As a secondary diaspora, the 'Caribbean Diaspora' is similarly encompassing. The 'Caribbean Diaspora' is a term that indicates a level of inclusiveness not always found beyond its own diasporic spaces. As George Lamming observes in his novel, *The Pleasures of Exile* (1992 [1960]: 214),

> No Barbadian, no Trinidadian, no St Lucian, no islander from the West Indies sees himself as a West Indian until he encounters another islander in foreign territory. It was only when the Barbadian childhood corresponded with the Grenadian or the Guianese childhood in important details of folk-lore, that the wider identification was arrived at. In this sense most West Indians of my generation were born in England.

Kasinitz likewise writes about a New York-based pan-West Indian identity (2004: 276).

How can we forge ways of thinking of 'belonging' in a world in which we might nevertheless, like Stuart Hall, never feel quite 'at home'? How might moving towards a view of diasporic spaces as spaces of belonging turn out to be vital if people are ever to feel 'at home' in the world? In a world of agitation and frictions, musical performances can be used to cultivate an easy vision of global utopia. Musical performances can sometimes, as Gilroy suggests, provide 'a space in which the competing claims of ethnic particularity and universal humanity can be temporarily settled' (1987: 154). But, more often, they reveal levels of difference within communities. Music for Puerto Ricans in New York, for example, does not just serve to unify an 'ethnic' community. Audience reception within the New York Puerto Rican community is complex and the music provokes diverse responses from its listeners (Glasser 1998). These kinds of mediations are central, I believe, to experiencing diaspora as home for they reveal a struggle to belong that goes beyond the simple polarities of insider and arrived outsider. As George suggests, the notion of 'home' is itself an organising principle for 'a pattern of select inclusions and exclusions' (1996: 2). Both diaspora and home can be places of unease, of not quite fitting in, of difference.

History and the Musical Narratives of Belonging

European imperial expansion, slavery, indentureship, postwar labour shortages; postcolonial movements; the convergence of several diasporas such as the African, the Chinese, the Indian, the Jewish; the histories of sugar, tea, and transport systems: these all render the Caribbean Diaspora multifaceted, in which memories, old allegiances and new belongings are juxtaposed. Probing diaspora invariably invokes historical narratives. As these historical narratives deal with the consciousness of having come from some other place they seem to offer a reminder of displacement; and diaspora, as has been noted, is habitually analysed in these terms. Nevertheless, as I have already suggested, diaspora discourses with their attendant historical narratives are as much about placement as they are about displacement. This is the ambiguity of (dis)placement to which the Trinidadian novelist V. S. Naipaul refers in his 'Prologue to an Autobiography'.

Naipaul writes that he grew up with 'two ideas of history'. The first idea of history that he tells us about is 'history with dates'. This was the kind of history that 'affected people and places abroad... ancient Rome.... Nineteenth century England; the nationalist movement in India' (1984: 51). Naipaul says more about his second idea of history, a history that was more personal but less well known to him as a child. He continues:

> Chaguanas, where I was born, in an Indian-style house my grandfather had built, had no dates. If I read in a book that Gandhi had made his first call for civil disobedience in India in 1919, that date seemed recent. But 1919, in Chaguanas, in the life of the Indian community, was almost unimaginable. It was a time beyond recall, mythical. About our family, the migration of our ancestors from India, I knew only what I knew or what I was told. (1984: 51)

Naipaul's grandfather had returned to India, leaving a family in Trinidad. Travelling through India in 1962, the year of Trinidadian independence, a time when histories were becoming increasingly reclaimed and re-imagined in the postcolonial project, the novelist visited his grandfather's village. 'I wasn't prepared for the disturbance I felt,' he writes, 'turning off from the India where I had been a traveller, and driving in a government jeep along a straight, dusty road to another, very private world. Two ideas of history came together during that short drive, two ways of thinking about myself' (1984: 52). For Naipaul, the two ideas of history come together in the juxtaposition of place – real and imagined. While India, for Naipaul, turned out after all to be the remote and imaginary place, he realised in that journey to his ancestral land, that for his grandfather, the Indian village had been the 'real place' and Trinidad 'the interlude, the illusion' (1984: 52). Within two generations, then, the homeland, the 'real place', had shifted from India to the Caribbean. Yet Naipaul shared with his grandfather the experience of diaspora and the confusion over the real and the imagined. Naipaul's text points to the dilemmas of cultural placements and displacements, of known and illusory places, of diaspora as historical narrative and contested terrain.

Musical performances highlight the dilemmas of (dis)placement. What are the musical sounds of the past and where have they come from? What can musical performances tell us about real and imagined places? What are the sounds that people remember, forget, create? While orally transmitted performative expressions are now read as historical sources that give voice, literally, to agents once rendered 'historically inarticulate', these expressions are not fixed but result from processes of transformation. They are the products 'of interaction between the past and present' (Levine 1977: 5). The real and the imagined become even more blurred, then, in the various ways in which people experience musical sounds and events. Diasporic performance practices can be analysed usefully as encoding memory and identity, but divergent notions of the history, narrated about or contained within the performance, bring forward the problems associated with projects aimed at assembling 'fragmented' (cf. Walcott 1992) historical narratives. Consider, for example, the analysis of historical memory, social meaning and compositional process in McDaniel's study of the Big Drum Ritual of Carriacou (1998). The myth of the 'Flying Africans' recited by the Carriacouan performer, Gentle Andrews, provides McDaniel with a framework for an interpretation of this song, dance and drum ritual which is performed at major life events, for tourists and for political celebrations, as host to mental travel that 'inspires the connaissance, the fascination with homeland, the revival of ancestral connectedness' (1998: 124). In the words of Gentle Andrews, the 'Flying Africans' myth is as follows:

> The Africans who were brought here did not like it. They just walked to the sea. They all began to sing as they spread their arms. A few rose to the sky. Only those who did not eat salt left the ground. The Africans flew home. (cited in McDaniel 1998: 2)

McDaniel links musical parameters to the myth of flight, a reading contained in the story itself – the Africans sing as they spread their arms in preparation for flight. For McDaniel, then, the myth deals with a 'flight from enslavement' on one level and, on another, with 'compositional flight'. These two levels can be seen as being ultimately interrelated for the subjective response to ritual performance can do more than merely evoke a sense of merging with a distant homeland. Practitioners claim that one's ancestral identity can be uncovered through becoming aware of the particular rhythms in the performance to which one is drawn. Carriacou drummers identify nine rhythmic patterns, 'nation rhythms' that signify ancestral heritages: Cromanti, Igbo, Manding, Arada, Moko, Kongo, Temne, Banda and Chamba (McDaniel 1998: 86–7). To choose a rhythm is to choose an identity. This story is about that which is not known but can be chosen. It tells us about musical performances as strategies of empowerment. It tells us about the emotional, spiritual and transcending significances that people experience through musical performances. It tells us about music giving expression to diasporic sensibility.

There is another aspect to the Big Drum Ritual of Carriacou, though, that emphasises what might have been forgotten. Hill notes that the Big Drum Ritual is presented as a folk entertainment although its purpose is the propitiation of the ancestors. There are indications, in the trembling of dancers, that possession may once have been part of the ritual even though contemporary practitioners regard it simply as an entertainment, perhaps 'a vestige of a long forgotten ruse foisted upon eighteenth-century estate owners and the Catholic Church' (1998a: 186).

Both music and diaspora are conceptual, expressive and political spaces in which people creatively work and rework expressions of self. The labour of identity formation is of course crucial to analysis of Caribbean diasporic experiences. From sugar plantations to London Transport, music has provided the soundtracks for daily life, offering a shield against harsh work conditions and evoking memories of peoples and places elsewhere. In theorising diaspora, music of the Caribbean and its Diaspora provide especially interesting cases to consider. We will not find any simple polarities here. The musical expressions of the Caribbean look to various diasporas, showing us how one diaspora interacts and overlaps with another diaspora, how diasporas cut across each other, how diasporic identities are shifted and transformed, and how one person can hold several diasporic identities – as African or Indian or Jamaican or Cuban or Caribbean. Music and diasporas spill over the boundaries that people too often insist on marking.

A Question Posed in Theoretical Mode

This 'spilling over' deserves further attention in relation to the ethnographic production of cultural difference, to marketing representations of cultural diversities and to concepts like hybridity that seem to rethink static models of culture by emphasising cultural encounters. Hybridity discourses offer another way of approaching the question of where is home in the diaspora by focusing on intercultural creativities, processes and strategies. Embraced by ethnographic disciplines, like ethnomusicology, as a trope that seems to be able to explain complexities, hybridity is read, too often though, as simply the creative mixes that result from culture contact, thus reinforcing rather than challenging 'cultural difference' and, in fact, misreading the more provocative politics of hybridity in relation to colonial and postcolonial frameworks. Such a misreading results in a convenient, if misleading, adjunct to established ethnographic projects of musical mappings, using the familiar tropes of cultural boundaries to inform hybridity discourses. The ethnomusicologist Bruno Nettl neatly outlines these tropes in observing that musicologists and ethnomusicologists have typically seen the musical world in terms of distinct musical traditions. Nettl explains that a basic assumption has been that:

> a society has a music, or at least a principal music, that consists of a set of rules and principles that govern ideas about music, musical behaviour and musical sound... There is Italian music, Chinese music, Arapaho music, and Ewe music. This congruence of society and music is certainly an oversimplification and readily subject to criticism from several perspectives, but it is a point of departure. (Nettl 1995: 87)

I do not aim to add a further critique to this model here. Rather I wish to ask a question, 'What does the musical world look like if we do not take this model as our point of departure?' This is a question that is inevitably posed in thinking about music in contexts of migration. Recent trends in ethnomusicology have been moving away from the simple model that maps music onto a society as ethnomusicologists have become increasingly preoccupied with considering what happens when musicians from different societies encounter each other. A substantial vocabulary has been applied to the description of such encounters. Terms such as acculturation, fusion, multiculturalism, creolisation and hybridity have become common in analyses of global process, social change and musical creativity. While theoretical models of creolisation, acculturation, fusion and hybridity have been important in challenging assumptions about cultural boundaries and in trying to make sense of contemporary global processes, they rest, too often, on the theoretical orientation that begins with the idea of 'a society with a music'. Looking at processes of music-making, I hope to indicate ways in which we might avoid the pitfalls inherent in the analytical models of 'a society with a music' and of musical 'cultures' encountering each other. What analytic possibilities emerge from moving away from the idea of diasporic creativity configured in relation to cultural mixes? Through examination of calypso and steelband practices in particular, I will suggest that a paradigm shift is necessary; that thinking about 'a society with a music' does not provide an appropriate starting point. Its restrictions lead us to making conceptual moves in the wrong direction – resulting in ideas about cultures meeting and mixing in ways that reproduce tropes of cultural difference and projects of mapping music onto people and places.

Once viewed as a negative trope entailing the loss of 'pure' cultures, hybridity has become celebrated as a way of dealing with mixtures, fusions, crossovers, indeed all kinds of processes that cut across categories previously held as distinct. 'Hybridity' (like its variations, cultures in contact, acculturation or syncretism, for example) has been identified as a defining characteristic of diasporas (Braziel and Mannur 2003: 9, Turino 2004: 7), drawing attention to the reconfiguration of relations between cultures and accounting for the emergence of new creative expressions based on a variety of models. I am not convinced that it is sufficient to analyse creative processes as the consequences of diasporic movements. Are the new musical expressions that emerge from diasporic contexts simply the result of encounters between musical cultures, the mixing of separate canons? Applying the concerns that have emerged in postcolonial studies (assimilation, mimicry, disruption or destabilisation) it is worth asking what the terms of 'musical mixtures' are and how we read the power relations configured by them.

In posing a question about how we view the musical world if we reject our most cherished presuppositions about music and society, we are led into thinking about how musical hybridity is situated within debates about planetary humanism (or global consciousness) and processes of globalisation. If we accept the view that accelerated contemporary processes of globalisation reveal the hybridities of all cultures such that hybridity is nothing new (Bhabha 1994, Pieterse 1995) then the politics of hybridity in relation to creative processes invite some critical scrutiny. Nettl's comment above provides a starting point. Laying bare the essentialism of conventional readings of hybridity (music in mixes), the model of a society with a music hurls us into the problems of all the tidy conceptual modes that underlie thinking not just about ontologies of musical creativity but also about 'culture', 'nation', 'race' and 'ethnicity'. It is possible to criticise the assumptions of hybridity discourses without departing from the models of society and music on which they rest. In one of the most recent critiques of hybridity, for example, Hutnyk focuses on market processes and on World Music festivals as spectacles to discuss race relations and cultural appropriations. Musical practices are thus read in terms of texts and representations resulting from unequal power structures that allow for the marketing of exotica (Hutnyk 2000). Such perspectives provide valuable insights into production and power in the practice of music. Yet, I would like to suggest a different elaboration on this theme that is informed from within the music itself, from the sounds and testimonies of those involved in the performance and production of music. This entails moving from a product-based analysis to a practice and process-orientated perspective in which the model of a society and its music becomes increasingly blurred in view of what is actually going on between musicians and their audiences, producers, policy-makers and other musical agents. In thinking about musical processes in diasporic contexts I have found it useful to bear in mind Pieterse's observations about the shortcomings, as well as understandings, of models mapped onto experiences:

> the hybridization perspective releases reflection and engagement from the boundaries of nation, community, ethnicity, or class. Fixities have become fragments as the kaleidoscope of collective experience is in motion. It has been in motion all along and the fixities of nation, community, ethnicity and class have been grids superimposed upon experiences more complex and subtle than reflexivity and organization could accommodate. (Pieterse 1995: 64)

In rejecting an understanding of hybridity as the simple result of cultural interaction, I have been guided by Bhabha's view that hybridity is not 'a third term that resolves the tension between two cultures' (1994: 113), but that it presents an interruption to assumptions of difference that mark power stratifications and an intervention in the 'exercise of authority'. This is a reading of Bhabha that is central to my project but that departs from a more habitual emphasis on his notions of the transformative powers of the third space, ambivalence and mimicry. Viewed from the perspective of interrupting difference such that the assumptions on which power is predicated have to be interrogated, hybridity not only offers a theoretical tool in the musical and ethnographic analysis of music in diasporic contexts, but also, more fundamentally, poses a challenge to conventional ethnographic understanding of 'the cultural' and forces us to keep looking at the ways in which the ethnographic enterprises have been implicated in the construction of 'cultural difference'. As Bhabha writes, 'To see the cultural not as the *source* of conflict – *different* cultures – but as the effect of discriminatory practices – the production of cultural *differentiation* as signs of authority – changes its value and its rules of recognition' (1994: 114). Bhabha rescues 'hybridity' from simple understandings of cultures in contact to offer a critique of difference, but in asking about what the musical world looks like if we do not begin with the model of cultural creativities mapped onto societies I will suggest that our musical analyses might rest on alternative foundations altogether.

'People From Here'

Let me shift the discussion towards considering the ways in which ethnomusicologists and cultural theorists have drawn attention to the political dimensions of musical practice. Working with the dominant paradigm of music in and as society, ethnomusicologists have paid much attention to the ways in which people use music to express a sense of identity and place. While exploring the musical practices of people in diasporic contexts offers a challenge to the idea of music *in* place, the conditions under which a 'diaspora' has been formed also invites us to consider how diaspora intersects with issues of contested identity and power. Contemporary studies of music in global, transnational and diasporic forums have thus shifted an emphasis on music 'in context' that once 'allowed ethnomusicological discourse to bracket itself outside the very real world of colonialism, power relations, and the social production of meaning' (Waterman

1991: 179). Caribbean musical performances, however, have never allowed us to ignore issues of power and meaning. These performances are explicitly political, simultaneously addressing national and transnational audiences, and have been extensively analysed and described in the ethnomusicological literature (for example, Averill 1997, Berrian 2000, Cowley 1996, Guilbault 1993, Ramnarine 2001, Steumpfle 1995).

The intensities of alterity, the politics of exclusion and movements across musical spaces are related in complicated ways. Musicians in the Caribbean Diaspora, as in the Caribbean, explore the interstices of diasporised conditions: the ties of island homes to the global ecumene, reformulations of national identities and racism. The dancehall DJ and sociologist W. A. Henry analyses the reggae/dancehall scene in relation to the 'politics of oppression' and focuses on how people actively mark boundaries through music. The dancehall scene emerges as an 'alternative space' in which Black British youth negotiate ways through a hostile racist environment. Taking issue with social theories of the 1970s and 1980s, which talked about the 'problem' of Black youth in Britain, Henry's study is based on individual experience as a dancehall DJ and on extended discussions with a core group of practitioners. It focuses on DJ lyrics. Henry suggests that 'exposure to the lyricism contained in Yard-tapes provide many British born Blacks with an alternative set of knowledges from which to form a more inclusive and positive notion of a blak [sic] self' (2002: 7) and that lyricism provides 'an alternative pedagogy for much of the African Diaspora' (2002: 32). DJ-ing as a space 'to partake in a diasporic system of intellectual exchange' (2002: 89) is explored in relation to the networks for the exchange of lyrics that span the Caribbean (Jamaica in particular), Britain and the USA.

In his book *Cut 'n' Mix* (1987), Dick Hebdige considers reggae and hip-hop in Britain, concluding with observations on music's capacity to herald social change:

> More and more people are growing up feeling, to use Colin MacInnes' phrase, 'english half-english'. There is an army of in-betweens and neither-nors out there who feel that they belong to no given community. They realise that

any community they might belong to in the future will have to be *made by them* or it won't get made at all. In some parts of Britain, West Indian patois has become the public language of inner-city youths, irrespective of their racial origin. When I interviewed a crew of (one white, two black) teenaged B-boys from Walsall in the West Midlands in 1984, they used three separate common languages. They talked to me in the local 'Black Country' dialect. They joked and teased each other in Jamaican patois. And when describing their dance moves, they used the specialised South Bronx jargon of hip hop. Perhaps there is another nation being formed for the future beyond the boundaries of race. If that nation can't yet be visualised then it can perhaps be heard in the rhythms of the airwaves, in the beat that binds together histories, cultures, new identities. (Hebdige 1987: 158)

While Henry suggests that dancehall DJ lyricism provides an example of how musical and social boundaries are built even as Yard-tapes and DJs circulate in transnational, diasporic contexts, Hebdige emphasises the role of musical and linguistic expressions in helping to make us rethink the boundaries of the nation. Both writers are concerned with the interfacing of the national and diasporic. If DJ originality is implicated in the articulation of a 'Blak British' space, not Jamaican (because it uses different thematic materials) or African American (Henry denies the influence of rap suggested by other commentators) this tells us something about the diversity of 'Black' musical expressions and social experiences that distinguish between the national and the transnational. Henry's dancehall DJ-ing in Britain is concerned with struggles to mark out musical spaces of belonging within racist structures, although on closer inspection these turn out to be open rather than closed spaces. No one is precluded from joining them. As such, Henry's DJs turn out not to be so contrary to Hebdige's West Midlands crew in welcoming creative and social interactions that predispose them towards rethinking national belonging. It is never easy, though, to settle into the cushions of musical utopias. What prompts the maintenance of musical and social boundaries? What and who crosses them? The difficulty with the metaphor of the 'rhythm of the airwaves' is that people can become dislocated from the sounds they produce, such that new claims to particular sounds can be asserted. Since the very early days of recording technology the ontologies of music have had to be rethought. Sounds can be separated from the people who produce them. It is no longer necessary to have the performers present. And this is true for the Yard-tapes. While these products of recording technology circulate through diasporic exchange systems they also reach other consumers, who may care little about intellectual discourse or the promotion of positive images of Black identities. In confronting the question about how 'black' music can be situated within 'white' racist cultures, Les Back records this startling exchange:

> Daniel was a fifteen-year-old skinhead from the English Midlands. He was not a follower of Screwdriver but rather a devotee of rave and house music. I tried to use the fact that house music was crucially influenced by black gay DJs in Chicago before it was imported to Britain. Something of an antiracist pantomime ensued in which I insisted, 'Oh yes, it *is* black,' and Daniel replied, 'Oh no, it *isn't*.' I cautioned Daniel that if he threw all black people out of the country, then his music would go with it. A moment of silent reflection ensued, and Daniel cocked his head to one side. He finally replied, 'No, because we will still have the tapes, won't we!' (Back 2000: 146)

People's sense of dislocation is often a response to the ways in which they are perceived in the diasporic context. As DJ Lezlee Lyrix (otherwise known as W. A. Henry) says, you can be born in a place but not feel that you belong there (personal communication). Through the making of 'others' and of marking differences that deny historical, geographic and political interconnectedness, diasporised peoples may be viewed as outsiders to places and spaces that may be the only ones they know and inhabit.[1]

Carnivals in Brooklyn, New York and Notting Hill, London, reveal many of the struggles around racism. Chapters 6 and 7 of this book will focus on these dimensions in relation to the Trinidad, Toronto and Notting Hill Carnivals. As a prelude to that discussion I would like to turn to the Brooklyn example because it raises questions about the unity of the category 'African-Caribbean'. Allen and Wilcken note that New York 'has emerged as a Caribbean crossroads in two important respects: first as a geographic center of interactions among peoples from different island backgrounds; and second, as a gateway between the islands and mainland America' and that it is in the realm of popular music that the 'transnational crossroads phenomenon' of New York is most apparent (1998: 1–2). While pre-Lenten Caribbean music and dance events had been held in Harlem as early as the 1920s, the Brooklyn Carnival became an annual event from 1969 following increased migration from the Caribbean after the 1965 immigration reforms and the revoking of a parade permit in Harlem in 1964. The event is essentially pan-Caribbean although it follows the Trinidad Carnival model.

Such pan-Caribbeanness has proved to be ambiguous, however, and exploring the musical repertoires of Carnival performances shows contestation within as well as beyond New York's Caribbean community. Kasinitz outlines the various musical styles that have featured in the Brooklyn Carnival. Trinidadian-style calypso tents, steelband and costume competitions were dominant in the early 1970s. Reggae and Haitian dance troupes were included in the programme of 1976 and reggae had become more prominent by the early 1980s, to be itself taken over by Jamaican dancehall a decade later. If Trinidadian soca was the music that most mas (costume) bands chose to play during the parade in the 1990s, the sound systems lining the side streets played contemporary reggae and dancehall. Steelband leaders, who were being drowned out by recorded music, called for a performance authenticity to restore the Trinidadian roots of Carnival and started the 3am parade (know as 'J'Ouvert') in the late 1980s (Kasinitz 1998). These contestations over musical repertoires show island-specific affiliations. Kasinitz notes other kinds of struggles around issues of ethnicity including the differentiation of Caribbean communities from the rest of Black New York despite discourses of Black unity and pan-Africanism, and the violent confrontations in 1991 between the Caribbean and Hasidic Jewish communities. Further controversy in 1994 between these communities was resolved peacefully, appealing to the media's 'comfort with ethnic celebration over racial confrontation' and resulting in increased media coverage of Carnival the following year (Kasinitz 1998: 110; and see Kasinitz 2004 for further details).

The emergence in 1990 of organised rara performances in New York, in which people gathered together to sing, dance and socialise, further marks the distinct as well as shared musical spaces created by Caribbean diasporic communities. Rara in Haiti is a yearly festival that follows Carnival – beginning on the eve of Lent and lasting until Easter Week. While rara shares 'characteristics with other Black Atlantic performance traditions like Carnival, Jonkonnu, capoeira [etc.]...', it is 'explicitly religious' (McAlister 2002: 7), and rara bands perform music and rituals for African-Haitian deities. In New York, raras have become performances that speak about the diasporic experience and with the continuous circulation of songs between Haiti and the United States (paralleling similar movements of people and songs by other islanders) they are a feature of transnational life. By 1995, four rara bands were performing in New York in secular contexts. Songs circulate between Haitian social spaces rapidly – 'a song created in Léogêne could be sung in Brooklyn a week later' (McAlister 2002: 185). McAlister points out that these performances show us how important music is at the level of grass-roots transmigration (2002: 186) and that the kinds of musical flows that occur in rara reveal diasporic groups constructing themselves in relation to other Black groups, near and far, as well as with reference to a dominant culture in the nation-state context (2002: 198).

Berrian's (2000) study of French Caribbean popular songs highlights the same kinds of movements, in this case between the Caribbean and Europe. These popular songs explore some of the legacies of colonialism and feelings of exile that are generated when musicians realise that they are considered to be 'others' in the former colonial centre. Yet Berrian suggests a view of exile that emphasises opportunities for critically reflecting on social processes rather than focusing on marginalisation. While migration leads people to question their sense of belonging and identity in a new place, it also prompts looking again at oneself and one's 'home' country from alternative perspectives. Thus ideas about neo-African unity (explored by Aimé Césaire from

Martinique, Léon Damas from French Guyana and Léopold Senghor from Senegal in the movement called négritude) were developed in Paris in the 1930s. Aimé Césaire's daughter, Ina, wrote lyrics with her cousin, Mano, for the on-and-off soloist of the band Malavoi as he prepared for his first solo album, *Exil*. While her father wrote about the disfranchisement of the Black man in Martinique, Ina has written about the island's landscape providing a sense of security and belonging. For Ina, brought up in France, living there meant always feeling like a foreigner, an emigrant (cited in Berrian 2000: 22). Berrian suggests that music provides a 'safe space' for critical reflection on the experience of migration and on society. It is a space for creative expression that allows bands like Malavoi to confront dislocation, speak openly without fear of censorship and promote values and memories of Martinican social life (2000: 25). Despite Ina's ambivalent views towards France (she returned to Martinique after more than 20 years), the lyrics she co-wrote for the song '*Exil*' reveal that sense of 'feeling at home in the world' that I have suggested above.

It is worth reminding ourselves of the different kinds of musical spaces that have been discussed thus far, from the musical journeys across geographic spaces to the spaces of musical memory, from alternative and confrontational spaces to safe spaces, from temporary spaces in which the competing claims of particularity and universality are settled to the shifting, ambiguous theoretical spaces between 'a society with a music' and musical hybridity. Pieterse (1995) calls for a theory of global political action addressing inequities. Veit Erlmann suggests a space for musical performance within such a theory, seeing the arts as a way of recognising 'interdependency' and 'complicity' in a globalised world. For him, the tension between music in identity politics and music in global politics offers an unrealised political vision of a fully globalised world:

> while we may well have to take seriously the sort of strategic essentialism implied in musical constructions of modern black political cultures as pure and unified, the more pressing question to me seems to be this: how fictions of black identity, and, for that matter, any diasporic identity may

invigorate a different kind of hyperpolitics, a future politics and cultural practice that is perhaps better understood as the art of the impossible. (Erlmann 2004: 91)

It would be a mistake to read such questions as arising from misguided visions for a global utopia that do not address the abundant inequalities, poverties, aggressions evident all around us, just as it would be unfair to interpret the theoretical paradigms of human *similarity* through the inflections of creative, political and social *sameness*. A vision of global connectedness does not have to rest either on new corporate and cultural dominances (the terms in which processes of globalisation are often analysed) or on the erasure of difference that relates to different histories and experiences. In this respect, the paradigm of human similarity allows for an acknowledgement of different stories whilst striving for a revision of human relations that might lead to the promises and potentials of equitable global political action. An impossible politics? Perhaps so, but that does not silence the chorus. What more potent political voice is there than the one that asserts the realisation that we are all here, speaking our languages of identity, nationalism, diaspora, community, but connected in myriad ways, even ones of which we may be unaware?

If focusing on diasporic Caribbean musical practices in relation to the politics of belonging means having to consider uncomfortable questions about racism, marginality and the construction of otherness, I hope that, ultimately, this book will end on an optimistic note. Not just in celebration of the richness of the musical expressions considered here, but also in aiming to develop theorisation on diasporic musical practices and on the significance of music in cultural politics and identity formation in ways going beyond 'otherness' and performance in the margins. I aim to contribute to the critique of those worn-out concepts of 'race', ethnicity and culture (see Gilroy 1987, Kuper 1999, Trouillot 2003). The distinctiveness that emerges within Caribbean diasporic communities, thereby pointing to the complexities of 'Caribbeanness', in Kasinitz's exploration of the Brooklyn Carnival, McAlister's analysis of music circulating in diasporic contexts showing the kinds of relationships that are developed between people at grass-roots levels, and Berrian's view of music as a safe space for looking at boundaries all provide important insights into how we might move beyond 'otherness'. But a passage from Ina and Mano Césaire's lyrics for the song '*Exil*' best captures an expression of diaspora that I will try to develop in this book. An old song says: 'We are not people from elsewhere. We are people from here.'[2]

2

PERFORMING 'BRITISHNESS'?
The Performance Politics of British Calypsonians

Calypso is a prominent Caribbean song genre associated with Trinidad and Tobago. Calypso is a British folk music. Calypso is a commercially recorded, globally marketed genre. How do these statements about calypso relate to each other? What do they tell us about musical canons and about sources of musical authority in canon formation? What are the connections between calypso performances in national and transnational contexts and what do they tell us about the musical spaces between 'diaspora' and 'nation'?

Calypso is characterised by the social and topical commentary of its song texts. During Carnival in Trinidad and Tobago, calypso is sung in performance spaces known as calypso tents. In the streets of Port-of-Spain, Carnival mas bands (costume bands) often use calypsos as their musical accompaniment for the parades. Spectacular costumes and dancing unfold one after the other and alongside there are trucks with sound systems playing the mas bands' soundtracks. This is a rich acoustic environment; one mas band moves into the distance and another comes into focus, playing songs that overlap and replace each other over and over again. The most popular song of the season is known as the 'Road March' and it represents the audience vote for the best Carnival song.

The song text plays an important role in calypso aesthetics and in the performers' displays of calypso virtuosity. In the most virtuosic displays, calypso texts are often satirical, critical, humorous, and they are set to memorable melodies. The ability to extemporise is a feature of the calypso virtuoso and calypsonians engage in picong duels in which they demonstrate verbal dexterity through the exchange of insults. The texts are multi-referential, drawing on literary sources, other calypso texts and topical commentaries. In a picong (from the French *piquant* – to hurl jokes or insults) duel between Mighty Sparrow and Lord Melody recorded in 1957, for example, Sparrow invites a response, singing 'Well Melody, come close to me, I will tell you plain and candidly, Don't stop in the back and smile, because you have a face like a crocodile'. One of Melody's responses is 'You know that I'll be proud and glad, if Samson and Delilah come back to Trinidad, But when they come I wouldn't go in the theatre, because look, the jawbone of the ass right here' (recorded by Emory Cook 1957, LP 1185). Audiences as well as calypsonians enjoy the demonstration of verbal mastery and performers are often able to express sentiments in song that might be unacceptable in ordinary discourse. Texts were subject to colonial censorship during the 1930s in particular, but during this period the calypso became a national form of musical expression and calypsonians became important figures in promoting nationalist causes against the censure of colonial authorities.

Calypso has been recorded across the twentieth century through commercial interests in the USA and Britain (for example, the Victor Talking Machine Company recorded calypsonians in Trinidad and New York from 1912 onwards and British Parlophone recorded calypsonians in England in the 1950s). Researchers such as Andrew Pearse (1950s) and Alan Lomax (1962) also made recordings of calypso. The live recordings of the sound engineer Emory Cook, made during the 1950s, capture some key moments in calypso performance history, including Mighty Sparrow's 1956 competition-winning performance of 'Jean and Dinah', using the latest technological developments in sound recording of the era. The widespread availability of calypso recordings means that not only was calypso one of the first global popular genres, but also that there is a large body of recorded materials for research into calypso performance. In Britain, calypso received much attention with the arrival of famous calypsonians during the 'Windrush Years'. British recordings of Caribbean music during the 1950s focused on Trinidadian styles, particularly calypso. The themes that singers dealt with included the problems of migration, politics, racism and personal relations. Other Caribbean music recordings included examples of biguine from Martinique, folk songs from Jamaica, and Cuban dance music like rumba. While calypso is a Caribbean island song genre, which has found audiences in global spaces, this chapter considers how the genre has come to be described as being 'British' by the late twentieth century. What does 'British calypso' signify?

In the 1950s, Young Tiger composed the 'Coronation Calypso': (Verse 7) 'Troops from Dominion and Colonies, Australia, New Zealand and West Indies, India, Gibraltar, Newfoundland and Canada. (Chorus) They were there at the Coronation. I was there at the Coronation'. Commenting on Britain's imperial spread around the globe, the 'Coronation Calypso' resonates with the observation of the nineteenth-century historian J. R. Seeley that 'the history of England is not in England but in America and Asia' (cited in C. Hall 2000: 2). Seeley emphasised the importance of thinking about empire when thinking about England, for the English (rather than the British) had made other parts of the globe 'English throughout'. After empire, though, what does the nation look like? How is a sense of national identity now being constructed? The performance politics of British calypsonians alert us to a post-Seeley disjuncture between Englishness and Britishness, highlighted by Catherine Hall who asks 'if Englishness is no longer a hegemonic identity, defining the national characteristics of all those who claim belonging in Britain, then what does it mean to be British?' (C. Hall 2000: 2). Young Tiger's 'Coronation Calypso' offers routes through the intersecting traffic of nation, empire and diaspora to exploring the suggestion that 'diaspora forces us to rethink the rubrics of nation and nationalism, while refiguring the relations of citizens and nation-states' (Braziel and Mannur 2003: 7). As a widespread, commercially recorded, transnational genre, calypso points to the complexities of national projects for it features in different kinds of nationalist politics in different geographic spaces. Nevertheless, calypsonians in Britain, as we shall see, are concerned with the performance of 'Britishness'. They challenge the idea of ethnic absolutes in defining the nation and tell us something about the importance of imperial and historical legacies.

The composition of the 'Coronation Calypso' may have been prompted, as Stuart Hall (2002) suggests, by a royal visit to the London club, the Orchid Room. Young Tiger (George Brown's stage name) was a seaman from Trinidad who, on disembarking in Glasgow in 1942, developed a musical career in Britain, appearing on a television programme, *The Minstrel Show*, and singing in London's clubs. When Prince Philip turned up at the Orchid Room, Young Tiger improvised a calypso text to mark his visit. Composing in response to the constituency of the calypso audience, to the immediate performance context is characteristic of calypso performance. Calypsonians often engage in dialogue with their audiences and with each other, commenting, sometimes competitively, on other calypso texts and highlighting the performance as being both an event and a process. They reflect and influence public moods and audience interpretations of their texts depend on knowledge of local and topical debates. Whilst commenting on social concerns, then, calypsonians entertain, combining social critique with comedy. Calypsonians are attuned to the contents and the contexts of their performances and their abilities to respond to the conditions of their environments indicate the levels of their skills in calypso performance.

Young Tiger was reprimanded for his impromptu commentary on the royal visit by the Orchid Room management. But he was surprised when a royal party arrived the following evening to hear his new composition. Such positive reception reveals ways in which musical performance can nudge social relations in different directions and explains the ongoing affection displayed by British calypsonians for the British monarchy through calypso texts of tribute. It moves us away from Blacking's view that music (although essential for human survival) only 'confirms what is already present in society... [adding] nothing new except patterns of sound' (1976: 54). More recently, phenomenological approaches within ethnomusicology have suggested that performance articulates a way of being-in-the-world and highlights the relational dimensions of human encounters. The relational dimensions of musical performance allow for the possibility of transforming human realities. Thus music can be understood as sonically significant in empowering people and in giving shape to their political expressions. Through music, people remember the past, enacting and contesting cultural memories and they dream of the future, imagining what the world might become and what their place in it might be.

Looking at performance as a way of exploring political possibility, this chapter focuses on diasporic, postcolonial and national sensibilities as articulated through calypso in Britain. It is against the backdrop of the musical spaces between diaspora and nation, as well as calypso's wide dissemination in transatlantic settings through migration, recordings and the circulation of musicians and their repertoires, that this chapter aims to show how contemporary British calypso practices challenge notions about difference in the British context.

Calypso in the Politics of 'Race' and Place

Racism makes 'race' matter. Academic discourses argue against the acceptance of 'race' (see Gilroy 2005 for a recent example) as being a concept that is outdated in its categorisation of people. But 'race' discourses show no signs of disappearing. They have become connected, in fact, with alternative propositions, which originally hoped to evade categorising people according to 'race', such as 'ethnicity'. Racism makes talking about 'race', as if this were a scientific fact, dangerous. As Stuart Hall notes, 'race' is 'a political and social construct' (2000: 222). While one can dismiss the concept of 'race' as an objective category, the effects of racism are pervasive. Two approaches that highlight inclusion and exclusion in national spaces based on ideas about 'race' provide an apt frame for analysing British calypso practice. The performance politics of British calypsonians can be thought of in relation to the politics of 'race' analysed by Gilroy in which concepts of national belonging and homogeneity inform representations of the nation in biological and cultural terms such that some people are always excluded from truly belonging to the nation. Gilroy writes that the central achievement of the new racism in Britain is the precise coincidence of national frontiers with the limits of 'race': 'bounded on all sides by the sea':

> The effect of this ideological operation is visible in the way that the word 'immigrant' became synonymous with the word 'black' during the 1970s. It is still felt today as black settlers and their British-born children are denied authentic national membership on the basis of their 'race' and, at the same time, prevented from aligning themselves with the British 'race' on the grounds that their national allegiance inevitably lies elsewhere. This racist logic has pinpointed obstacles to genuine belonging. (Gilroy 1987: 46)

For Gilroy, music has the power to develop black struggles for recognition within the nation by 'communicating information, organizing consciousness, and testing or deploying the forms of subjectivity which are required by political agency'. He notes the moral dimensions of music, as a medium through which people can articulate alternative social visions and express demands for 'non-racialized justice and rational organization of the productive processes' (cited in Braziel and Mannur 2003: 72–3).

Sensitivities to the politics of music, 'race' and exclusion have been demonstrated too by ethnomusicologists. Radano and Bohlman note that ideas about 'race' have been mapped onto music and that musical repertoires within Europe that are associated with marginalised people (including those from the former colonies, Roma and Jewish communities) are not regarded as belonging to the canon of Western music:

> In a continent where radical political change has a truly global impact, the brutal results of racist histories are everywhere palpable. Whatever else can be said about music in the New Europe, it is impossible not to recognize the proliferation of musics outside the Western canon – indeed, music that gives voice to the peoples politically and ideologically excluded from European history. Music gives voice to this postmodern European otherness; the new musics of the New Europe insist that we confront race and racism. (Radano and Bohlman 2000: 24–5)

As we shall see, British calypso confronts the intersections of music and 'race' to issue the ultimate challenge to the biological and cultural exclusion from the national space explored by Gilroy. Its practice prompts a rethinking of ideas about 'race' in the national imagination. Resonating with Ina Césaire's emphatic formulation, 'we are people from here', British calypso similarly challenges the idea that this genre, so strongly identified with Caribbean island musical practices, stands outside the Western canon. There can be no better example than Lord Kitchener's British debut at Tilbury Docks, when he sang 'London is the place for me ... I am glad to know my mother country'.

During the 'Windrush Years', over 40,000 people from the English-speaking Caribbean migrated to Britain. With this debut performance, Lord Kitchener touched right to the core of ideas about belonging to the imperial homeland. Like many other Caribbeans who undertook this journey, Lord Kitchener believed that he was arriving in the 'motherland'.[1] In the heart of Empire, Kitchener was to come face to face with the dilemma of 'otherness'. Kitchener's initial musical expression of belonging contrasted with a later feeling of being out-of-place, a consciousness of diaspora, and he was to return to Trinidad. The disenchantment expressed in Kitchener's subsequent calypso texts: 'You can never get away from the fact, if you're not White you're considered Black' ('If You're not White you're Black', Lord Kitchener 1953), for example, confronts us with issues of colonial politics at the end of Empire, postcolonial sensibilities, and contemporary constructions of difference in the national imagination. Lord Kitchener's recordings were marketed in the Caribbean, Europe, the USA and West Africa. He was invited to compose a calypso to mark Ghana's Independence, and the popularity of calypso in Ghana and Nigeria during the 1960s and 1970s influenced the West African styles of jùjú and highlife (Waterman 1990: 96, Liverpool 2001: 76–7).

The story of British calypso began before Lord Kitchener and the two other calypsonians, Lord Beginner (Egbert Moore) and Mona Baptiste, who were also on board the *SS Empire Windrush*. Their arrival added impetus to the already existing

Caribbean musical scene. As Cowley notes, London, like New York, has been a centre for musical activity that offered jobs for Caribbean musicians in clubs, theatres, radio broadcasts and even opportunities to record on gramophones throughout the twentieth century (Cowley 1990: 60). While the *SS Empire Windrush* marks the beginning of the 'official' Caribbean migration to Britain, the activities of Caribbean musicians in Britain have been well documented since the early twentieth century.[2] One of the earliest recollections of Caribbean music in London refers to the end of the First World War (1918). The Trinidadian-born bandleader Gerald 'Al' Jennings formed a band during his naval service, which played for Caribbean soldiers and sailors who had fought for the Empire's cause before their return to the Caribbean:

> In World War 1, I was stationed at La Palice, and while there we got together a little band for our own amusement. After the war we gave a few concerts for wounded coloured soldiers in London before their repatriation. A war had just been fought; the West Indies had sent their sons then as they did in this last war [1939–45]. Those concerts were not a success because, as I learnt later, they were for unwanted coloured soldiers – men who were the remnants of thousands who would never see their homes and loved ones again. (Jennings 1946: 5, cited in Cowley 1996: 220)

Two Guyanese bandleaders, Rudolph Dunbar and Ken Johnson dominated Britain's Caribbean musical scene between 1930 and 1945. They employed pan-Caribbean personnel, performed mainly for white audiences and their repertoires were drawn from popular music of the time, including African-American jazz. Musicians who were also active in the USA, like Sam Manning and Lionel Belasco, recorded in and toured Britain during this period. In addition to pan-Caribbean musical performances in London there was also a transatlantic Caribbean music scene. While Caribbean musicians achieved a high profile in club performances during the Second World War, many of them struggled to keep their bands active after the war. Mass migration from the Caribbean beginning in 1948 marked a new era and a renewed impetus to Caribbean musical activities in Britain.

Calling attention to issues of 'race', calypso texts offer perspectives on the various strands that make up British life and testify to the claim that 'there may be no better evidence that music is more intensely present than ever in the European racial imagination than in the New Europe at the end of the twentieth century' (Radano and Bohlman 2000: 27). With their thematic parallels, calypso in Britain can be analysed in relation to the performance poetry of writers such as Linton Kwesi Johnson, John Agard and Benjamin Zephaniah and to the British Caribbean fiction that emerged from the 1950s onwards. This literature became the fastest-growing branch of the so-called 'new literatures in English' that emerged from writers tied by the links of the former Empire.[3] Innes (1995) observes a shift away from feelings of alienation in this literary output that applies to calypso practice too. She notes that a new generation of writers from the 1980s (including female voices)

> have been concerned with re-creating and reflecting upon the experience of those who came from Asia, Africa and the Caribbean, and the experience of their children. Many of these younger writers were born in Britain or came as young children. Almost all of them recognise that they have made their home, or at least one of their homes, there. (Innes 1995:22)

In speaking through calypso texts to a recognition of home in Britain, British calypsonians have challenged ideas about 'race' in the national imagination, contributing calypsos to a CD album titled *Born in Britain* (1999) and locating their musical practices within a postcolonial, national context.

Musical Spaces Between Diaspora and Nation

Kitchener's calypso, 'London is the Place for Me', resonated with the Duke of Iron's (Cecil Anderson) 1930s text about being in the United States of America: 'I am happy just to be, in this sweet land of liberty' (Varsity 1939, cited in Hill 1998b: 76). With the movements of musicians between the Caribbean, London and New York, calypso has circulated in transatlantic spaces. Thus, the practices of British calypsonians can be compared to those of their counterparts in the United States, who have been active in New York from 1912 onwards. The calypsonian Lovey (George Bailey) went to New York with his band in 1912 to make recordings that would be marketed to audiences in Trinidad, not to New York's Caribbean communities. It was not until the mid 1930s that calypsonians began to turn their attention to North American themes. The Roaring Lion (Rafael De Leon) and Atilla the Hun (Raymond Quevedo) sang about the reception they received from influential American musicians like the singer and orchestra leader, Rudy Vallee: 'We were making records for the Decca Company, when we were heard by Rudy Vallee. Well he was so charmed with our rhythmic harmony, he took us in hand immediately' (Decca 1938, cited in Hill 1998b: 77). The introduction of North American themes paralleled changes in calypso performance contexts. While calypso in Trinidad was an integral part of Carnival, in New York this song genre was heard through recordings, radio and club performances. Through these performance contexts, calypso entered a mainstream popular entertainment scene. Calypsonians performed for Caribbean and African-American audiences, but by the late 1930s they were also singing for 'middle-class white listeners' (Hill 1998b: 79). By the 1950s, the stage was ripe for a singer like Harry Belafonte (a New York singer born of Jamaican parents) to establish calypsos and Caribbean folk songs as popular music (and a passing fad) and to achieve greater commercial success than Trinidadian calypsonians. Hill observes that by the late 1940s in New York, 'calypso was, on the one hand, folding into a broadly Caribbean culture in the United States, while on the other it was about to become a popular style of music performed by North Americans as well' (1998b: 89). While calypso in the United States could have turned into a passing fad, it was revitalised following the 1965 Immigration Act with a new wave of Caribbean migration. Calypso is now performed in Carnivals in cities such as New York, Miami and Boston.

In Britain, as in the United States, calypso performance changed trajectory throughout the twentieth century in response to local audience expectations. The calypso in postwar Britain was an important Caribbean genre, boosted by the presence of influential calypsonians like Lord Kitchener, Lord Beginner, The Roaring Lion, The Mighty Terror and Invader. Following Trinidadian Independence in 1962, however, these calypsonians began to return to Trinidad. Calypso practice in Britain faded from prominence during the late 1960s and 1970s. Caribbean audiences in Britain, many of them from Jamaica, were listening to popular music in the shape of The Beatles and to Jamaican ska followed by reggae. There were a few Trinidadian calypsonians still active during the 1970s and 1980s, including Mighty Tiger (who was the first to be awarded the title of Calypso Monarch of Britain in 1971) and Lord Cloak.

In 1991, calypsonians established a formal structure – the Association of British Calypsonians – to promote their song genre. The principal aim of the Association of British Calypsonians (housed as a community group by the Yaa Asantewaa Arts and Community Centre set up by Westminster Council in 1974) is to promote calypso in Britain and more generally in Europe. The methods pursued in doing so include reaching audiences through education programmes and setting up performance rights through appropriate copyright agreements. The Yaa Asantewaa Arts and Community Centre is also home to the only calypso tent in Britain in which calypsonians perform and compete as part of the Notting Hill Carnival celebrations. Since this Association is the only organised forum for British calypsonians, its membership indicates the extent to which calypso remains within a predominantly Trinidadian community and on the fringes of national musical life. A decade after its inauguration, 16 calypsonians and 21 juniors were members of the Association (see Appendix, 'British Calypsonians'). The majority were London-based; only four members were based in other parts of Britain (two were in Birmingham and two in Reading).[4]

These numbers might suggest that the British calypso scene could be described as one of the city's 'micromusics' – the various 'small' musics within bigger systems that intersect and interact with each other, and move among societies' different levels (Slobin 1993). Thinking about British calypso in relation to the concept of micromusics is surprising given that calypso has been a popular music in the global domain since the early twentieth century. But it is worth interrogating further as it focuses attention on contradictory facets of the performance politics of British calypsonians in which 'race' (or ethnicity) as an aspect of authority in musical canons is both embraced and rejected.

Highlighting small-scale performance spaces within larger superstructures, the concept of micromusics works well with recent analyses of political mobilisation and the trends towards marking ever more distinctive spaces within Black communities. Seen as a micromusic, British calypso can be read in relation to the dramatic shifts in the political responses and organisation of Caribbean communities over the last 50 years towards ever increasing ethnic identities marked as distinct from a British mainstream. Early organisations concerned with postcolonial politics, operating from the margins of British politics and maintaining an interest in the Caribbean island political scene during the 1950s, began to be influenced by Black Power movements of the late 1960s and 1970s. By the 1990s, Black political organisations were entering the mainstream of British political debate (Shukra 1998). A contemporary accent on ethnic differences *within* Black communities is observed by Gilroy (1993a). Like Shukra (1998), Gilroy notes the brevity of a political 'Black' movement:

> The precarious political grouping, which for a brief, precious moment during the late 1970s allowed settlers from all the corners of the Empire to find some meaning in an open definition of the term 'black', has been all but destroyed. Today, polite 'anti-racist' orthodoxies demand an alternative formulation – 'black and Asian'. This involves the sacrifice of significant political advantages but is presented as a step forward. (Gilroy 1993a: 93)

Dealing with the 'new ethnicities' in an exposition of this point, Shukra argues that 'the development of politics based upon competing identities institutionalised and reinforced fragmentation among Black groups into more specific ethnicities'. The term 'Black' itself was broken down into various groupings such as 'African', 'Caribbean', 'Indian', 'Bengali'. Black political organisers ceased being primarily concerned with 'creating unity among Asian, African and Caribbean communities in the search for a black consciousness to bring about wider social change'. Instead, a Black alternative view has been 'fragmented into a search for smaller, minority perspectives' and each perspective rejects 'the idea of a universal human history in favour of the notion of different histories and identities' (Shukra 1998: 59). The pursuit of British calypso space (competing for resources and funding on the basis of musical distinctiveness) and calypso's promotion as one of the many genres that deserve space in multicultural programmes can be interpreted within Shukra's frameworks. For Shukra, the new constructions of ethnicity 'have been concerned with making special efforts to include hitherto excluded groups which are able to demonstrate that they are distinctive from the British mainstream. Ethnic identities today are thus seen as a lever to gain a portion of power' (1998: 61).

Promoting musical distinctiveness and thus contributing to the competitiveness of British calypso and helping to establish a market for it is one way of 'levering a portion of power'. British calypsonians have certainly been involved in talking about distinctiveness. In 'Oh Gosh Man', Totally Talibah reinforces the association of calypso with Trinidad and Tobago: 'Oh gosh man, I in kaiso competition, oh gosh man, oh gosh man, but I am a Jamaican' (Totally Talibah 1999). In 'My Kinda Music', Mighty Explorer makes a series of distinctions between repertoires and the audiences for them:

> (Verse 3) Is rock music, is that your kinda music? Is ragga music, is that your kinda music? Is salsa music, is that your kinda music? So-calypso, is my kinda music... So-calypso, my kinda music. Tell me what's your kinda music... (Verse 4) Is jazz music, is that your kinda music? Is pop music, is that your kinda music? Is country music, is that your kinda music? Is reggae music, is that your kinda music? Is highlife music, is that your kinda music?' (Mighty Explorer, 1999)

Yet musical behaviours are not necessarily tidy. Discourses about distinctiveness refer both to the Caribbean island home (Trinidad) and to the British national space. I will return to distinctiveness expressed as an aspect of musical competition in the music industry, but first I want to consider how British calypsonians refute the notion of minority status altogether, how they work against the idea of micromusics and how they make us reconsider national canons. Rather than accept the designation of only musically expressing a minority 'Blackness' or a 'new ethnicity' in Britain, British calypsonians have begun to describe their practice as 'British folk music'. In doing so, they claim the national arena as their musical space and contribute an important perspective on questions about imperial legacies in modern European nationalist politics.

'British Folk Music'? Questioning the Canons of Nation and of Diaspora

'Is music that is good music for one country or one community necessarily good music for another?' wondered the English composer Ralph Vaughan Williams. He suggested that a 'composer cannot expect to have a worldwide message, but he may reasonably expect to have a special message for his own people' (1963 [1934]: 8–9). Like Mighty Explorer's articulation of musical distinctiveness, in the calypso 'My Kinda Music', Vaughan Williams promoted the view that certain sounds captured the national spirit and urged his readers to 'cultivate a sense of music citizenship' (1963 [1934]: 10).

In Trinidad, the calypso became a national form of musical expression during the 1930s and 1940s and calypsonians became important figures by promoting nationalist causes against the censure of colonial authorities. As well as capturing the public imagination through voicing the political sentiments of the era, calypsonians gained prestige because of the attention paid to their art outside of the island context. Recording companies such as the RCA Victor company in the USA and the gramophone company HMV in England and France began to market recordings of calypso and calypsonians sought work opportunities in metropolitan cities such as New York. From early in the twentieth century, then, calypso was an island music that was being established as an important genre within Trinidad but that was also reaching beyond the island space.

Looking at the global movements of music in the late twentieth century, the Trinidadian calypsonian Hollis Liverpool suggests that 'Trinidad-style carnivals throughout the diaspora... have transformed calypso from folk to world music' (2001: 77). Liverpool's view of world music specifically refers to globalisation via diaspora: 'the exportation of the calypso to Africa is an example of Africans from the Old and New worlds influencing one another in the acculturation process, through which, as is the route of African traditions, the music reflects continuity and change' (2001: 77). The 1999 report of the Association of British Calypsonians presents a rather different perspective on how calypso can be categorised in Britain. For Association members, calypso is not only a Trinidadian or an African music. Neither is it, in its dissemination beyond the Caribbean island, 'world' music. Members of the Association of British Calypsonians have argued that calypso in Britain should be recognised as being 'British folk music' (Association of British Calypsonians 1999). Such a categorisation is remarkable, all the more so because it is made despite the insistence of association members on 'performance authenticity' and on looking towards Trinidadian calypso models (discussed further in Chapter 7). In making the claim that British calypso is British folk music, calypsonians suggest alternative readings of the Western music canon and place calypso alongside those repertoires that have shaped a British national imagination. In Europe, myths of origin, culture and territory have linked the folk to the nation and folk musics are regarded as 'belonging' to particular peoples.[5] If folk music has been held up to bear witness to the geographic origins of particular musical practices that express national belonging, those musical practices which have been associated with migrating peoples would seem to lie beyond the national musical spectrum. Nation and diaspora are thus held in musical opposition to each other. Yet the term 'British folk music' speaks to the location of music-making, the where of its happening, diaspora within the nation. Given the strong association of folk musics throughout Europe with specific national spaces and nationalist enterprises, 'British folk music' is a description asserted against the constructs of earlier generations, against Cecil Sharp's exhortation, for example, 'English songs for Englishmen' (1907: 135). Sharp was of course active in promoting the view that 'local' musics should feature more prominently in the national arena through, for example, educational reforms to the music curriculum. But, given the views of his time and of contemporaries such as Vaughan Williams, whether Sharp would have embraced the idea that calypso (even British calypso) belongs to the canon of 'English songs' is doubtful. This brings me to some of my central points about British calypso performance as creating presence and suggesting possibility. Challenging the national imagination, calypso as 'British folk music' is a description of musical practice that insists 'we are here', that reminds us of migrations from former colony to metropolitan centre. Such a description expands Sharp's perspective on 'English songs for Englishmen'. It raises the possibility of rethinking the idea of national belonging by striking against those formulations (like folk music as the musical expression of people who belong to and guard the treasures of the nation) that have contributed to imagining the nation. *It places postcolonial politics in the midst of modern forms of European nationalism.*

Emphasising 'Britishness', British calypso discourses erode an opposition that has been fundamental to conceptualising 'race' in Europe 'between musics that historically participated in the construction of a European canon and those that did not' (Radano and Bohlman 2000: 25). Vaughan Williams, who demonstrated much interest in folk music, provides an example of the rhetoric on musical nationalism, similarity and appreciation in posing the question, 'Should music be national?' He suggested that music 'uses knowledge as a means to the evocation of personal experience in terms which will be intelligible to and command the sympathy of others' (1963 [1934]: 1). Such a formulation could apply to a calypso recorded in 1998 by the British calypsonian Alexander D. Great ('They Came Upon the Windrush', see Figure 2.1 for the musical scores), which provides a potted history of the Caribbean experience in Britain from the 1950s onwards, were it not for his elaboration on the 'others': 'These others must clearly be primarily those who by race, tradition, and cultural

(a)

Figure 2.1 Handwritten (a and b) and printed (c) scores of 'They Came upon the Windrush'

PERFORMING 'BRITISHNESS'? 59

(b)

60 BEAUTIFUL COSMOS

(c)

Figure 2.1   continued

'They Came Upon the Windrush: Multicultural Britain Today'
(Verse 1) In May '48, the Empire Windrush set sail from the Caribbean for Britain.
Five hundred on board coming to seek work,
Most of them ex-RAF service men.
The fare was only twenty eight pounds ten,
but that was a whole heap of money way back then.
On the twenty second of June, the ship dock at Tilbury,
To the discomfort of the government led by Clement Atlee

(Chorus) They came upon the Windrush in '48.
The flame of hope in their hearts whatever fate.
A few who formed the vanguard
Came through although the doors barred,
It's true that most find it hard
But survivors always find a way.

They came a part of the great Diaspora
To claim our right to be part of what we are.
This land so fit for heroes,
must hand the laurels to those,
who stand as history shows
built multicultural Britain today.

(Verse 2) These were not the first, thousands came before
to put in their bid for democracy.
Many of them died, doing their duty
To ensure that Britain would remain free.
On Windrush they thought they were British citizens,
Until they felt the iron fist in velvet mittens.
No longer required citizens soon became immigrants,
Which Mosley and Powell used to fuel ignorance.

(Chorus)

(Verse 3) The living was hard all through the fifties.
Some people even believed we had tails.
Then through the decades, we read about the riots,
The suss laws, school suspensions and jails.
But Linton, Bob and jazzy soul to soul
Could soothe our hearts while we reach for our goals.
With Black presence now in the media and Black MPs,
This next generation is getting there by degrees.

(Chorus)

(Verse 4) Now fifty years passed, many things have changed;
we now leading music, fashion and sport.
But make no mistake, some still find us strange,
Many battles still out there to be fought.
This world we share belongs to all of we,
We must take care to respect multiplicity.
Survivors of Windrush know, that in love and war all is fair.
The Empire has crumbled, only Commonwealth left to share.

(Alexander D. Great 1998)

experience are the nearest to him; in fact those of his own nation, or other kind of homogenous community' (Vaughan Williams 1963 [1934]: 1). On the basis of 'race', at least, many Caribbean migrants would seem to stand outside of the nation as imagined by Vaughan Williams and their musical expressions thus would be less likely to be received with understanding.

Today, the idea that music can be somehow bounded by a static national space such that people can express musical citizenship is outdated, but Vaughan Williams's comments highlight the point that in playing out national politics, British folk music has to be thought of within 'postcolonial' as well as national parameters. Exploring the pre-1948 Caribbean presence, experiences of migration and racism, changes in social status from 'citizen' to 'immigrant', Alexander D. Great's 'Windrush' text nevertheless ends on an optimistic note (Figure 2.2). It notes the end of former political relations of power and the moves towards a 'multicultural' society. In reflecting on the process of song text composition, Alexander D. Great noted that in this example he wanted to 'encapsulate as much as possible in four verses of the general experience of the Caribbean "vanguard" in Britain' (Alexander D. Great, personal interview June 2001). Alexander

Figure 2.2 Alexander D. Great

wanted to highlight Caribbean experiences framed in relation to a general sense of 'difference' during the early 1950s to dealing with institutional racism. The early experiences outlined in the second verse of the song marked 'a type of difference-ism. There weren't enough Black people here for them to be a threat yet... So they were a mixture of being interesting and slightly quirky.' Yet the next verse refers to 'the real struggles of maybe the last ten, fifteen years, of having to deal with the institutionalised racism which shows up in things like the police and school exclusions'. The last verse is perhaps the most interesting in terms of calypso poetics and the use of double entendre.

> The final thought is that eventually all sides will have to recognise that there's nowhere to go; that we're stuck with one another. 'Survivors of Windrush know, that in love and war all is fair. The Empire has crumbled, only Commonwealth left to share': now the Empire is a double take. For the Empire is the name of the boat, the *SS Empire Windrush*. So the Empire's crumbled which it has. It has disappeared now. It's a wreck. Also the British Empire has crumbled. 'There's only Commonwealth left to share'. There's only common wealth left to share now, which is everybody's wealth. The whole thing is peppered with double entendres of some sort, and there are levels which people can either see or not see. (Alexander D. Great, personal interview, June 2001)

Why does Alexander D. Great feel compelled to explain this history, to reflect on the ironies of common wealth? His preoccupations with Commonwealth and postcoloniality exist because the moves towards independence and the end of empire are still held in living memory. As Hobsbawm suggests, the end of empire lies in the 'twilight zone between history and memory.' It is 'still a part of us' if not 'within our personal reach' (Hobsbawm 1987: 3–5). What does postcolonial mean to people born and brought up in Britain? Stuart Hall alerts us to the point that the 'post' in postcolonial is not just a reference to temporal frameworks or to 'different' kinds of political organization:

> the term post-colonial is not merely descriptive of 'this' society rather than 'that' or of 'then' and 'now'. It re-reads 'colonisation' as part of an

essentially transnational and transcultural 'global' process – and it produces a decentred, diasporic or 'global' rewriting of earlier, nation-centred imperial grand narratives. (Hall 1996b: 247)

This rewriting of imperial grand narratives shows that postcolonial projects are 'specifically political'. Postcolonial expression is an attempt 'to dismantle the hegemonic boundaries and the determinants that create unequal relations of power based on binary oppositions such as "us and them", "first world and third world", "white and black", "coloniser and colonised"' (Gilbert and Tompkins 1996: 3). In questioning musical canons and rewriting imperial narratives that contrasted 'our' music (focusing on the folk as the preservers of traditions) and 'other' music, British calypso discourses reveal the strands that cut across 'national', 'postcolonial' and 'diasporic'. These discourses offer a reminder of intertwining musical histories and the ways in which Empire has shaped calypso practice. British folk music emphasizes the centrality of the 'Other' in representations of Britishness and of the 'Other' now part of British life in Britain, reminding us that because of Empire talking about Caribbeanness also means talking about Englishness, and vice versa.

This takes me, then, to the Caribbean island of Tobago, which was colonised in 1498, belonged to various European nations, was finally ceded to the British in 1814 and gained Independence, becoming part of the Republic of Trinidad and Tobago, in 1962. Driving along the island's winding roads during a field trip in 2001, I was drawn into a café by the sign at the front: 'First Historical Café and Bar' (see Figure 2.3). Its walls were covered with notices outlining the history of the island's folk music (Figure 2.4). One of the Caribbean's most prominent music anthropologists, J. D. Elder, who began collaborating with Andrew Pearse of the University of the West Indies in 1951, wrote about studying the folk music of Tobago:

> We started at Charlotteville and then went back west to Plymouth, working our way village by village up the North Side Road, finally stopping at Parlatuvier on the sea coast. Returning to Scarborough, we collected folk music and folk tales as far East as Roxborough. (Elder 1994: ii)

Elder classified the island's repertoires into four streams: (i) early post-Emancipation songs with texts that deride the White planters; (ii) the adoption of European recreational music from the late nineteenth century with the most common genres that they collected including reels, polkas, jigs, quadrilles, scottisches, sea-shanties and nursery rhymes; (iii) popular music that developed as a result of musical education programmes organised by missionaries; and (iv) a contemporary stream that demonstrates intensive cross-cultural processes, artists drawing 'upon musical material irrespective of its ethnic or cultural origin' (Elder 1994: 5). By classifying folksong into four streams, Elder notes both that the social history of the island is clearly reflected in the island's musical repertoires and that the strongest colonial influence was that of the British. Marches like 'I'm a Soldier Bound for Glory' (sung to the 'Marseillaise' tune) became popular in the 1930s when British authorities undertook intensive missionary work in Tobago (1994: 95). The Tobago reel dance references African themes, for example, invoking ancestors to dispel illness brought by jumbies or ghosts ('Wind'ard Car'line', Elder 1994: 126–9).

Elder summarizes the 'cultural base' of folk song in Tobago in terms of degrees of Africanness and Britishness. By the early twentieth century the cultural base is 'very British/slightly African'

Figure 2.3   First Historical Café and Bar in Tobago

Figure 2.4 Notices about Tobago's folk music on the walls of the First Historical Café and Bar in Tobago

(Elder 1994: 9). My interest in Elder's summary of cultural base is not in his quantitative assessment of cultural origins but in his attention to the impact of colonial power on musical expressions and in his emphasis on European influence. This study of folk music in Tobago shows us that the same genres have featured in the construction of both 'English' and 'Tobagonian' folk tradition. From this perspective, then, there is nothing remarkable about the British calypsonians' claim that they are creating musical expressions within the frameworks of 'British folk music'.

Situated in a nexus of nationalist impulses in both the Caribbean and Britain, of transatlantic exchanges, of recording industries, of imperial histories and postcolonial politics, calypso articulates people's socio-political concerns, remaining intimately connected to local specificities while criss-crossing global spaces. To what extent does British folk music remind us of overlapping and intertwining histories? To what extent is British folk music a move towards erasing the boundaries of difference, configured in terms of 'race', genre and imperial history, within national spaces in contemporary Britain (in relation to Gilroy's formulation)? To what extent is British folk music a strategic term to secure a place in a national music market? British folk music certainly marks historical processes, engages in erasing boundaries of difference and features in cultural competition, but the descriptor *British* provides the central clue. 'British folk music' signifies the location of musical practices – the 'where' of musical activity. British calypsonians privilege the post-imperial diasporic space as one where their musical practice belongs and from where it emerges. Yet, in describing their practice as 'British' rather than as 'English' or 'Scottish', for example, calypsonians continue to demonstrate sensitivities towards questions about national musical ownership and the politics of exclusion. After all, this is still a Britishness based on imperial legacy. It is a Britishness that insists on remembering Empire and its effects.[6]

The New

If British folk music tells us about the politics of calypso in Britain, it also tells us about the promotion and marketing of a musical genre in a competitive industry. A need for distinction is found in cultural markets: 'to sell oneself and one's products as art in the marketplace, one must, above all, clear a space in which one is distinguished from other producers and products – and one does this by the construction and the marking of differences' (Appiah 1996: 59). The demands of the marketplace mean that innovation is sought. An emphasis on the new also characterises diaspora identities 'which are constantly producing and reproducing themselves anew, through transformation and difference' (Hall 1996a [1990]: 120).

While the term 'British folk music' makes a clear statement about national and musical belonging it is also one that distinguishes a particular repertoire. The mission of the Association of British Calypsonians is to 'promote the culture of calypso originating from calypsonians based in the UK to audiences in the UK, Europe and worldwide'. Yet submissions to the Greater London Authority Review of the Notting Hill Carnival (undertaken in 2001 to develop safety and tourism and resulting in a report: Greater London Authority 2001) revealed internal contradictions regarding the classification of calypso and highlighted both the interplay of Caribbean and British histories and the moves to promoting the genre in a competitive musical marketplace. The following statements, submitted by the Association of British Calypsonians for the review, provide some examples:

1. Calypso is the *traditional and official music of Carnival* and should therefore be recognised and promoted as such.
2. Calypso is the first music of the Caribbean.... Originally it was linked just to the pre-Lenten Carnival in Trinidad and Tobago, a legacy of religious festivals however, as its popularity grew, it became acceptable to be played throughout the year.
3. In the UK, calypso is not linked to the Trinidad and Tobago formula.... It is absolutely *the world music of the people*.
4. ABC's vision is to hear calypso being played on all major UK and European radio stations.... The organisation's dream is to see calypso *recognised as a contemporary Caribbean art form flourishing in the UK*, and eventually in Europe. (Association of British Calypsonians 2001: 4–5, emphases mine[7])

Calypso discourses raise issues about traditional practice – looking to Trinidadian calypso models as a way of shaping Carnival performance in the British context; and calypso as world music (music of the people) but also as a specifically Caribbean form in Britain. The first track on the *Born in Britain* CD, with its references to 'my kinda music' and 'your kinda music', neatly captures the ambiguities of constructing and deconstructing musical boundaries.

Resonating with the aesthetic judgements of Trinidad, the island 'home' of calypso, British-based calypsonians regard the Mighty Sparrow and Lord Kitchener as being outstanding performers who have provided models for the possibilities of working within the calypso genre. For many younger audiences in Britain, however, calypso is often thought of as 'old-time music'. Even in Trinidad recent trends have been to perform soca and 'jump and wave' songs rather than calypso as a social and political commentary. Responding to these trends, with a variation on the term 'British folk music', Alexander D. Great promotes what he calls a 'New British Calypso'. He emphasises musical innovation and complexity:

> The last wave of British calypso was when Kitchener, Beginner and Terror were in Britain in the 1950s. It was really known then, very popular, and the Royal Family loved it. Their liking for it made it more generally popular, particularly Kitchener's stuff. In the same way that there was a first Viennese School (Beethoven, Mozart and Haydn) and a second Viennese School (Schoenberg, Berg and Webern), I like to think of New British Calypso (which has never really died out because it has always been there) – there's an upsurge...
>
> Where I write the songs it has definitely been going in that direction [New British Calypso]. I don't think I've written a song yet which uses three chords, which the majority of modern calypso does. I always look for new ways of structuring the verse–chorus relationship. I try four line verses, six lines, eight lines. I've even tried nine lines, with each set lined in three groups of three. So I'm cutting across all sorts of structural barriers and experimenting in new ways. I have choruses in remote keys from the verse if I can. A trick that Kitchener did, he was very good at putting the verse in a

minor key and the chorus in a major key and vice versa. I've taken that and stretch it all the time when I can. Bringing a sort of classical key relationship, variety to the whole thing. I won't do horn arrangements that don't have harmony. All my horn arrangements are harmonised in as many parts as there are horns. I don't like unisons because it is easy to do unison octaves with a couple of brass and then say that's your line. That's more the sort of jam and wine, three chords, twenty words – I'm not into that. So New British Calypso is as exciting as Motown was to Black music. (Alexander D. Great, personal interview, June 2001)

Kitchener clearly provides some musical models for Alexander D. Great. But like contemporary calypso in the Caribbean, British calypso draws on musical ideas from a wide range of sources. Alexander (who spent over 20 years working as a 'commercial' session musician before turning his attention to calypso in the early 1990s, becoming the BBC's resident calypsonian and offering workshops to schools in London) has experimented with Chaucerian rhyming iambic pentameter couplets and with the textures of baroque cantatas: a top melodic line and a continuo part – 'It's bringing all the things that I've learned to bear on using the calypso genre' (Alexander D. Great, personal interview, June 2001).[8] Such experiments offer further ways of disrupting any sense that calypso may be located outside of the Western canon and point to the coalescence between creative processes, marketing strategies and political representations.

Performance Spaces

The spaces of British calypso performance contribute to current discourses on 'race' issues, the most obvious example being the Notting Hill Carnival. Variously viewed as a noisy spectacle, a site of conflict or a display of Black Power, carnivalists found new performance spaces in 2002 – indications of radical transformation in public perceptions of London's Notting Hill Carnival. British calypsonians performed at the Royal Opera House, Covent Garden. Masquerade featured prominently in Queen Elizabeth II's jubilee celebrations. Alexander D. Great composed a calypso of homage for Queen Elizabeth II. Changes in the organisational structures of Notting Hill Carnival and an increasing emphasis on highlighting the economic benefits of the event as Europe's largest street festival also contributed to shifts in public attitudes. Post-Carnival, the Victoria and Albert Museum ran a two-day event featuring the 2002 carnival costumes as part of Black History Month. In the dimly lit Raphael gallery, steelbands performed in front of an early fifteenth century altarpiece, the retable of St. George attributed to the German artist Marzal de Sas. Mas (costume) bands paraded through the galleries, moving past those holding treasures from India, Korea, China and Europe of the Middle Ages. Visitors to the museum crowded along the sides of the procession route moving with the mas bands towards the open air garden spaces of the museum (Figures 2.5(a) and 2.5(b)). They were also able to participate in procession preparations – face painting for children, costume design and steelband workshops. Junior calypsonians performed their competition songs and seminars on Carnival musics and collecting oral histories were offered. A play about British calypso history that drew on oral history projects that had been undertaken at Kensington and Chelsea College, London, was put on in the India galleries. The play emphasised early hardships and celebrated the musical creativity of calypsonians. Such a spectacle lies at the intersections between cultural production and political action. Set in a museum with cultural treasures from around the world, the event might have been seen as an interrogation of imperial legacy, of past ethnographic displays of 'exotic others'. For some commentators, such activities put on in a month allocated to 'Black History', are only token gestures of inclusiveness. For others, such community initiatives are a way of using artistic expression to enhance public education and move towards a more egalitarian society. One seminar speaker observed that the Victoria and Albert Museum with its display of culture was an appropriate place for a discussion on Carnival musics also 'rich in culture and heritage' (a comment by Roy McEwen, representative of the Caribbean Music Association). In the grand entrance hall, Alexander D. Great set up his microphone and backing system and sang some of his calypsos to launch the event.

Figure 2.5 Carnival at the Victoria and Albert Museum (2002)

'Big Party for Your Golden Jubilee'

(Verse 1) Queen Elizabeth has reigned now for fifty years
Over this green and pleasant land.
She has smiled and I'm sure she has shed some tears
For reasons we can all understand.
The year of accession, 1952,
She took on this responsibility.
She has set the style for the longest while
Of just how cool royalty can be.
Now the whole of the Commonwealth
Wants to drink Her Majesty's health
Celebration of our unity.

(Chorus) Big party for your Golden Jubilee!
Everybody wishes Your Majesty
Health and happiness of the very best,
All around the world people saying 'God Bless'.
Big party for your Golden Jubilee
And long live Your Majesty.

(Verse 2) As young Princess Elizabeth she joined the guides
And won the Children's Challenge Shield aged 13.
She loves art, music, theatre and going for rides.
A fine horsewoman the Queen has always been!
She made her first radio broadcast – 1940,
Speaking to all children everywhere.
At 18 she stood in for her father the King
Addressing Parliament in a voice loud and clear.
She wed the Duke at age 21.
The following year she bore him a son,
Now it's four children and six grandchildren they share.

(Chorus)

(Verse 3) While on tour the princess heard of her father's failing health
And finally, that the King had passed on.
She was now Queen of Great Britain and The Commonwealth
And she took on what had to be done.
Hosting functions for big foreign dignitaries,
She's Patron of many an organisation,
Over 500 engagements annually,
Including having to meet politicians.
She is kept informed daily of the state of the country
And The Commonwealth for which she has such a passion.

(Chorus)

(Verse 4) Britain's Queen has been reigning for fifty years,
The last half of the last century.
In the art of statecraft the queen has no peers,
A true mistress of diplomacy.
She has seen so many prime ministers come and go,
With some big changes along the way.
At the times when she's suffered a personal blow
She would do her duty, anyway.
To show our appreciation we're having this celebration
And we wish Her Majesty a wonderful day. (Alexander D. Great 2002)

As a 'celebratory form of protest' (Kershaw 1992), masquerades in the spaces of the Royal Opera House, the Victoria and Albert Museum and the jubilee celebrations mark new contexts and new performance spaces and they draw new audiences. They point to the transformational powers of aesthetic experiences. They push against performance boundaries that are riddled with 'race issues'. The 'where' of music-making, following Herbst's suggestion that 'what' we generally think of as our object of study – music – 'is actually "where" it is happening' (Herbst 1997: xx) is vital to an analysis of British calypso that takes into account diasporic, postcolonial and national sensibilities. Carnival arts in these urban spaces indicate the social transformations that have taken place in the city over the past half-century, but they also display the traces of the places in which they have been produced. From Young Tiger's 'Coronation Calypso' to Alexander D. Great's 'Golden Jubilee Calypso', British calypsonians have been involved in the reinflection of 'Britishness'. They bring, as Welsh suggests in looking at other artists, 'new cultural valencies to the constitution of British identities, reinscribing and relocating the nation in terms of diverse and discordant new voices, bringing to bear new words and forms, opening up possibilities for a more complex sense of Britishness' (Welsh 1997: 61). Exploring the performance politics of British calypsonians, I have aimed at emphasising the extent to which the national is configured in diasporic and postcolonial projects and the need for adopting historical perspectives in the analysis of these configurations. The new performance spaces of British calypso confirm that this is music concerned with where it is happening. British calypso points to the possibilities of at least discursively refiguring diasporised sensibilities within national frameworks. While calypso may be a global form, widely practiced and disseminated, it is a British folk music for its British practitioners. And that perspective tells us about diaspora as locally configured, woven into the fabric of national life.

What do we observe when we shift our perspective? What does calypso as a global form tell us about the 'Britishness' of British calypso? To explore that question the next chapter turns to another musical example.

3
TOWARDS BEAUTIFUL COSMOS
Pan Perspectives on Musical Multiculturalisms and Diasporic Fusions

Walk along the River Thames and you might hear a steelpan musician busking outside one of London's main performance venues, the South Bank Centre. It is a scene that you could encounter in many cities. Steelpans have become a feature of such diverse musical landscapes as London, Plymouth, New York, Copenhagen, Paris and Johannesburg. They have become a global phenomenon. Talk to the busker and you might learn about the panyards in Trinidad where he or she first listened to and practised the steelpan. The musician might tell you about the history of the steelpan, about the musical activities of pan musicians who have contributed to the spread of these instruments, or about Trinidadian steelbands such as Desperadoes, Renegades, Exodus, Phase II Pan Groove, or Invaders. Telling stories about steelpan, about the practice and construction of the instrument in its island home of Trinidad and about the routes through which the steelpan has achieved a wide distribution, is an important aspect of the transmission of both musical and historical knowledge.

One of my first encounters with a steelband was as a student in a large Inner London school, one of those Victorian structures with long corridors and concrete playgrounds outside. The gleaming instruments were neatly presented in rows in the music room. The teacher was a steelband musician who had come to the school specially to run those classes. We learned to play tunes like 'Yellow Bird'. After learning a melody phrase by phrase, following the principles of oral transmission, notation was put onto the music stands in front of the pans. Lunchtime rehearsals took place once

TOWARDS BEAUTIFUL COSMOS 77

a week for a few months until the school concert. With around 20 members, the steelband performed to general acclaim and we all looked forward to progressing onto new pieces. The following term, however, we were disappointed. There was no steelband. Funding for the lessons had been discontinued.[1]

The images of the busker and of the school steelband sessions lend themselves to interpretations of different sorts. A lonely busker standing outside the Royal Festival Hall or discontinued steelband classes in an Inner London school seem to point to a multicultural politics of diversity and marginality. In contrast, these images can be interpreted in relation to more telling, connected images: of a 1951 steelband performance in that same concert hall, then newly constructed in the tide of postwar optimism, rendering this location as one of the sites of steelband history; of steelbands performing against the backdrop of Trafalgar Square's fountains or the leisure spaces of Leicester Square (Figure 3.1); of children learning to play steelpans in a variety of contexts that include those with no Caribbean communities as well as the urban spaces that boast well established ones. The contrasting interpretive moves to which these images lend themselves lead us into different routes through the multicultural maze. In emphasising the connections between steelband practitioners, such that the contemporary busker can be read in relation to a 1951 performance, this chapter aims to critically examine the ways in which steelband practices in various geographic spaces challenge anthropological, musicological, and everyday tropes of cultural boundaries. Such examination highlights the ways in which analysis of diaspora might be implicated in current moves to dismantle the anthropological and ethnomusicological investment in 'culture' that enables the neat delineation of various boundaries – cultural, political, ethnic, geographic or otherwise. Though hybridity has emerged as a main trope in explaining diasporic cultural practices that cut across boundaries, the dismantling project in this chapter suggests other ways of thinking about creative processes.

Let me begin with some remarks on the steelpan. Musicians play in rehearsal and performance spaces known as 'panyards'. The steelband is organised into sections: typically, although not

Figure 3.1 Ebony performing in Leicester Square, London

yet standardised, the tenor pans or 'soprano', cello pans, guitar pans and bass pans. (In the 1950s, the terms still in use were 'ping pong', 'alto pong', 'tenor boom' and 'bass boom'.) A drum kit and iron are often part of the steelband (Figure 3.2). From the mid 1940s until the early 1950s, musicians in Trinidad and Tobago identified with specific steelbands to the extent that there were violent clashes between bands arising from jealousies, musical rivalries and territorial loyalties. Gangster and wartime films inspired the names of the steelbands: Desperadoes, Red Army and Invaders, for example. Since steelbands were initially associated with some of the ghetto areas of Port-of-Spain, aspiring musicians from more privileged backgrounds were discouraged from participating. Having emerged as a distinct instrument in the 1930s, the steelpan has been transformed, however, from an instrument of disrepute to a national symbol, though carrying ambiguous national, ethnic and class significances (Steumpfle 1995: 225). Steelband repertoires are diverse. By the late 1950s, steelbands were 'reveling in the eclecticism of their repertoire' which included Latin popular songs, American film songs, classical pieces like Beethoven's Minuet in G as well as arrangements of Trinidadian calypsos (Dudley 2001:187–8). After Independence, steelbands were expected to promote calypso music during Carnival. Indeed, steelband competitions (especially Panorama) required arrangements of calypsos. Today, steelbands continue to rehearse diverse repertoires that include arrangements of calypsos, popular songs and the classics, as they prepare for competitions, festivals and Carnival.[2]

Figure 3.2 Salah and Family Steelpan Academy performing in Toronto, 2001

The steelpan has its origins in instruments that musicians made out of tin biscuit containers or oil drums discarded by oil companies when drumming was banned in Trinidad by colonial authorities in the 1930s. It has been heralded as an instrument that was invented in the twentieth century. To whom the invention can be attributed remains unclear and it seems that several people were involved with experiments to turn oil pans into musical instruments. Grant writes about the birth of the steelpan as a 'mythic story' with spiritual and healing dimensions. It is a story that deals with the transformation of industrial scrap metal into a highly sophisticated musical instrument, which has its origins in the African Orisha and the drum rhythms that evoked them (1999: 2–4). But the island space as one in which the imprints of various migrations can be felt also played a role in the forging of the steelpan. Grant observes that drumming had not been banned in Indian religious festivals and that 'the idea of firing the oil drums may have been copied from the firing of the clay for the tassa drum [a kettledrum]' (1999: 8). Similarly, the gongs and cymbals of Chinese music may have influenced the pan sound (1999: 8); indeed acoustic research suggests that these instruments share tonal qualities through a non-linear generation of harmonic partials (Kronman 1991).

Instrument makers have experimented with various methods but the basic processes have remained consistent since the early history of steelpan manufacturing technology. The first stage in making a steelpan is sinking the oil drum. This involves hammering the top of the drum to result in a smooth concave basin. The position of notes is marked (by measuring and drawing radial lines from the centre to the rim) and then grooved (hammering indentations that will separate notes). Only the bass pans use the full-sized oil drums. The other steelpans have to be cut down to the required sizes. Each note is hammered from the reverse side (a procedure called 'ponging up') and then the pan is heated over a fire and quickly cooled down to produce better tonal qualities. The notes are then flattened, in preparation for the final tuning, by tapping them into a convex shell and the drum is chrome plated. The final stage is tuning the pan, which involves intricate hammering and re-hammering. The tuning system follows Western temperament but the layout of notes is non-linear.

Winston 'Spree' Simon was involved in the early development of steelpan. He is sometimes credited as being the 'inventor' (see Jones 1973: 29), a claim that is made in his own account of the beginning of steelpan technology:

> In the year 1939 between the months of May or June, I cannot remember exactly which month, it happened one evening when the John John Band was parading the streets of the village in full force. I lent my kettle drum which had a special sound because it was made of a light soft metal, to a

strong friend of mine called Wilson Bartholomew alias 'Shaker' or 'Thick Lip', so that I could get a 'jump up' [dance] and rest from drumming. Upon my return I found that the face of the pan was beaten very badly, and the particular tone or sound that I had was gone. I also recognised the concave appearance. I then started pounding the inside surface of the drum to restore it to its original shape. I was using a stone. While pounding on different points with varying strength, I was surprised and shocked. I was able to get varying sounds or pitches. I then tried a piece of wood. The sounds or pitches were a little mellower. I was fascinated, I was able to get distinctly separated musical notes. Thereupon, I was able to knock four notes out. I turned my knowledge over to the other members of the band and pan was born' (Winston Simon, quoted in Jones 1973: 13–14).

Another instrument maker associated with the early history of steelpan is Ellie Mannette. He was leader of the Invaders steelband in Trinidad and developed steelpan technology by introducing pans known as double seconds, tenor bass and strummers (see Jones 1973: 29). While Winston 'Spree' Simon's pan was made into a convex shape, Mannette reversed this process and produced a concave-shaped pan. He also wrapped rubber strips around the ends of the beaters to produce a more mellow sound. Nowadays, Ellie Mannette is recognised as an authority on steelpan manufacture and performance. Through residencies in university departments (such as West Virginia), he has exercised considerable influence on contemporary steelband practices in the United States.[3]

Pan in Europe

The manufacture of and research into steelpan has extended far beyond the Caribbean island space. Much of this work takes place in European contexts. Some of the latest developments in steelpan technology have emerged from collaborative projects between pan-makers based in Switzerland and Britain, such as the three-octave range pyramid pans made by Esa Tervala (at that time associated with Cosmo Pans, Switzerland) and Dudley Dickson (Harpsi Drum, England). The Swiss group, PANch, played the pyramid pans at the 2000 World Steelband Festival in Trinidad and Tobago, and both the group's performances and the instruments they used attracted substantial media comment.

Fieldwork seems to haunt the researcher in unexpected ways; experiences remembered or replayed in variation in different geographic contexts have increasingly alerted me to the discomforts of some taken-for-granted paradigms and theoretical assumptions concerning the relation between music and place. Looking at one thing in one field context, I have found later on that I have actually been looking at it for another field project based elsewhere. Or perhaps those field locations have only seemed to be disparate. In the early 1990s, for example, I was in Finland exploring contemporary folk music, its engagement with the world music scene and modern forms of European nationalism. I went to interview Esa Tervala. At that time he was living in a wooden house in Espoo, in south Finland. The walls of his house were covered with posters of palm tree-laden beaches and calendars from Trinidad. Steelpans that he had made and his recording equipment were stored in the kitchen. The house reminded me of a Trinidadian shack. He played some calypso and steelband examples for me from his Trinidadian cassette collection. He had spent several months in Trinidad learning from composers and arrangers for steelbands. At first, people were surprised to hear about a Finn making his own steelpans and he attracted some publicity. On his second visit to Trinidad, Jit Samaroo, a well-known pan arranger, went to visit him. Esa Tervala was pleased for he had been studying Samaroo's work. Esa Tervala also composed his own songs, some of them in calypso style. One of his songs was influenced by West African genres, which he had been interested in before developing interests in the steelband. In his own compositions he often used steelpan as an accompaniment to calypsos. He expressed some regret in not finding enough people in Finland who shared his interest in Caribbean music and who would be able to form a band. In 1987 he formed a band called Steel Harps and in 1990 he tried to establish a Caribbean Club but did not have the resources to put on enough performances that might have secured public interest. Only a few years later, when

Esa Tervala was working as a successful pan-tuner in Switzerland, there was a growing steelband scene in Finland as well as in Sweden and Denmark. A Finnish steelband, Steel Pan Lovers, achieved third place in the European Steelband competition and won a place to go to the World Steelband Festival in Trinidad (2000). The leader of Steel Pan Lovers (Ari Viitanen) had been introduced to the steelband through performances given by the Swedish band, Hot Pans and had then spent a week in Denmark watching the virtuoso pan musician Rudy Smith making and tuning pans. Steel Pan Lovers was set up in 1992.

In Sweden, the physicist Ulf Kronman, who developed an interest in the instrument when he travelled to the Caribbean in 1979, undertook research into the acoustic properties of the steelpan. He published a volume, *Steel Pan Tuning* (1991) and became a founding member of the Stockholm based group Hot Pans. Ulf Kronman notes that knowledge about steelpan manufacture has traditionally been passed on through oral transmission methods and regards his study as a complementary aid to teaching the art of pan-making and to discussions on tuning techniques. His study did not aim at promoting a standardization of the crafting process but at presenting a resource for both skilled and beginner pan-makers (1991). Making the study available on the Internet has been a major contribution to the virtual community of steelpan practitioners. Since 1995, Kronman has maintained a website, 'The Pan Page – A Forum for the Steel Pan Instrument', with links to other steelband sites, directories of tuners and bands and news pages. This site, and others like it available to the virtual community, enables people to forge contacts and create new networks of practitioners. From Simon's and Mannette's early manufacturing experiments to Kronman's web pages, the twentieth century has seen a radical shift from oral transmission methods within the Caribbean island space to the use of global digital technologies in the dissemination of steelpan knowledge.

What other factors have shifted the trajectory of steelband from island experiment to global phenomenon? With the ties of empire providing an initial impetus, contemporary steelband projects in Europe can be traced to the Trinidad All Steel Percussion

Orchestra (TASPO) performance of July 1951 at the Festival of Britain celebrations at the South Bank in London. Musicians for TASPO were selected from various steelbands in Trinidad, raising funds for their participation in the festival through performances in Trinidad, and 'with a repertoire of calypsos, sambas, mambos, waltzes, marches and occasional adaptation of the "classics", they were a sensation' (Cowley 1990: 69–70). There were important consequences for the esteem in which the steelpan was held in Trinidad. The success of steelband performance in Britain, in 'the motherland', led to increased recognition in Trinidad. Members of TASPO were managed by Edric Connor and travelled via France where they made some recordings, which are amongst the earliest available of these ensembles. Amongst the twelve musicians selected for TASPO (ten arrived since one of them had to return due to illness and another deselected himself; see Appendix, Table A.1) were Winston 'Spree' Simon, who later spent eight months in Nigeria and Ghana teaching steelpan construction and tuning (in 1956), and Ellie Mannette.

Another TASPO musician, Sterling Betancourt, was to play a central role in developing steelband performance in other European contexts. He was born in the hills of Lavantille in Port-of-Spain in 1930. His family had a tamboo bamboo band[4] and as a child he tried to reproduce its sounds on milk tins and cocoa tins:

> At the age of fifteen, 1945, my mum said, 'Well listen, I'm going to send you to get some private lessons now'... and instead of going to my private lesson I'm under the tree tuning pan. So someone said, 'Sterling, look your mum coming up the road' and when I looked I saw her coming with her shopping and so on and the first thing I want to do is to get up and run because I don't want her to see me. So I got up and I started to run and I can hear in the distance, 'Don't worry to run. I've seen you already.' That's my mum! 'Come here. Is that what I'm paying my money for? I'm paying for lessons and you under the tree tuning pan?'... Then she put her hands on her hips and said, 'It's steelband you want? I'm going to buy steelpan for you.'... I remember those days were the riots which the steelband had bad publicity and my cousin is now saying to my mum, 'Stella, have you still got Sterling in that steelband? He's going to get into trouble and fights

and things.' And hear my mum now: 'Leave the child – you don't know one day it might take him to England.' Right? And by 1951 a band was chosen to come to England... I was chosen to be in that band. (Sterling Betancourt, quoted from a BBC radio interview, 6 December 2003).

Sterling Betancourt pursued a musical career in Britain, playing steelpans in clubs, a royal garden party (in 1955) and the Notting Hill Carnival. In the late 1970s, he ran workshops on making steelpan in Switzerland (in 1977), thereby appearing in narratives of the origins of pan performance in other European contexts. In 2000, a Swiss association to promote steelbands was established (Pan Confoederatio Helvetica) and by 2001 there were 150 steelbands in Switzerland.

From the 1960s, Trinidadian steelbands like the College Boys' Band Dixieland, who were competition winners, toured Britain, contributing to an increasing public familiarity with these instruments. Most steelband performance in Europe during the 1960s and 1970s took place in London, in venues like the Albany pub, the Colhern pub, Furlong Road pub and the Crucible nightclub (Francis 2001: 7, 20). Steelband musical scenes in other parts of Britain have included Coventry, Plymouth, Leeds and Leicester and, paralleling the Caribbean scene, competitions have provided a way of promoting steelband activities.

By 2001, the British Association of Steelbands listed 24 bands participating in the Notting Hill Panorama competition (see Appendix, Table A.2). London bands have not entirely dominated the steelband competition scene. The steelband Phase One from Coventry, for example, won the 1987 Panorama under the leadership of Victor Phillips, and I heard them performing at the South Bank Centre over a decade later, where they also sold CDs of a live performance that had been recorded at the Butts College Theatre in Coventry in 1999. As in Trinidadian steelband repertoires, these recordings present arrangements produced by the band's musical director, Stephon Phillip, of calypsos by Lord Kitchener and Shadow, popular songs by Bob Marley, Queen and Paul Simon, and items from the art music repertoire (Mozart and de Falla).

Not all British steelbands have participated in Notting Hill Carnival or Panorama performances. Educational projects have also contributed to the development of steelband performance. An important figure during the 1970s was Terry Noel (then general secretary of the Steelband Association of Great Britain), who was active in the Midlands, setting up the Leicester Melodians which performed at charity and church events. He wrote a booklet (Noel n.d.) on the steelband for the Commonwealth Institute; was described in a newspaper article in the *Evening News* of Trinidad and Tobago as 'the man behind "pan" in England' (16 November 1972: 2), and was involved in discussions on steelband both in Trinidad and Britain, recommending formal teaching with steelband programmes covering systematic approaches to steelpan playing; the historical development, economics and tuning of the pan, and musical appreciation (Noel 1978: 118). The association hoped that the integration of the steelband in the education system would result in greater appreciation of the steelband, continued development of the instrument, enhancement of the status of the pan musician and inclusion in music therapy projects.

In gaining peer recognition and being judged by Trinidadian representatives, however, competition winners are best placed to develop wide-ranging educational projects. The Mangrove Steelband, which developed from a small, pan-round-neck steelband to become one of the biggest steelbands in England under the leadership of Clive (Mashup) Philip, worked with a music school in Mauritius in 2000 to teach steelpan to young people who were excluded from mainstream opportunities. Ebony, another successful steelband in competitions, set up various educational projects in schools and has run community programmes in hospitals (as part of music therapy activities) and in a young offenders' institution.

In May 1999, as a result of a French initiative, a committee of steelband representatives from Britain, Denmark, Finland, France, Germany and Switzerland was established, called Pan European. The aims of Pan European are to offer opportunities for education and artistic exchanges and to forge a European network for steelbands. In 2000, the first European Pan Festival took place in Paris. This festival included the competitive element of steelband performance in which bands are placed in a ranking order in the Trinidadian Panorama, and the top European bands (PANch from Switzerland, Ebony from Britain and Steel Pan Lovers from Finland) were invited to participate in the Trinidad festival later that year.

Musical Multiculturalisms and the Politics of Steelband Pedagogy

Two contradictory ways of viewing the multicultural society are either to emphasise cultural exchanges resulting in various 'fusions' that characterise global cities like London or to foster a view of various cultural groupings maintaining distinct traditions. The former model contains an aspiration to inclusiveness but can also be linked to ideas about integration, homogeneity and the potential loss of cultural distinctiveness. The second model, by contrast, promotes 'cultural diversity' and a view of culturally separate groups inhabiting the same (usually urban) spaces. Both models rest on assumptions of difference. In fact, much multicultural discourse favours the second model. As Lundberg, Malm and Ronström note, the concept of multiculturalism stems from discourses in the USA in the 1960s which focused on ethnic groupings that were seen as being part of a 'mosaic' – and therein lies the contradiction of multiculturalism:

> Society and cultural life is seen as divided into clearly defined groups. The ideal is inclusivity at society level and exclusivity at group level. Ethnic activists, purists and the various groups' politicians guard the borders of the mosaic tiles. (2003: 42)

Strategies for inclusion and exclusion thus compete with each other, nevertheless having to co-exist. Lundberg, Malm and Ronström observe the effects of multicultural ideologies with reference to the Swedish case, but their observations can be usefully applied to other contexts too. There are 'troublesome' consequences to linking multiculturalism with ethnic groups. Diversity becomes both a 'diversity of expression' and a 'diversity of cultures', to the extent that differences between groups are over-emphasised, groups are rendered homogeneous, and the contributions made by members of one group to the cultural expressions of other groups are rendered invisible (see Lundberg, Malm and Ronström 2003: 43). Steelbands are not just played by members of Caribbean diasporic communities. Steelband membership emerges, in fact, as an important factor in thinking about analytical models of multicultural societies. What does non-Caribbean participation tell us about the restrictions of these models? Following the movements and musical activities of steelpan musicians and pan-makers like Winston 'Spree' Simon and Sterling Betancourt along diasporic routes gives visibility to the ways in which musical and cultural expressions are forged through interaction, through movements 'between' groups (in Lundberg et al.'s terms), and through shared experiences of musical practice. Such shared experiences compel us to critically assess the contradictions of 'multiculturalism' and rethink the epistemological ideologies – particularly the emphasis on discrete cultures – that underscore the 'multicultural'.

Musical pedagogy has provided a forum for much debate on the politics of multiculturalism, the terms of which often rest on 'race', or more recently, 'ethnicity', as the locus of cultural difference. Since the 1970s, practitioners have argued for the broadening of music curricula to reflect the social composition of the classroom. Discourses on musical multiculturalism have used narrative strategies that persuade readers of the social as well as musical worth of a multicultural music education. Elliott, for example, argues that music education should be directed toward 'being musical' rather than 'having musical understanding' and that this is best achieved through examining more than one set of musical practices: 'To deny a place in music education to the musical metaphors, forms and behaviours of other cultures is to deny students access to sources particularly qualified for and successful at integrating the prototypical experiences of human mental life' (1984: 7). He further points to the social advantages to be gained in a more comprehensive and global music curriculum: 'a dynamic multicultural music curriculum offers the possibility of developing appreciations and new behaviour patterns not only in relation to world musics, but also in relation to world *peoples*' (1989: 18). In contrast to arguments about social understanding generated through the musical curriculum, other pedagogues reveal the extent to which the multicultural urge is founded on the idea of difference. Walker, for example, provides an extreme expression of the underpinning ideology that 'race' is a basis for difference, which might be established through 'scientific' analysis of cognitive processes:

> answers to questions such as whether the physical, and therefore the mental processes of the human brain are the same for all races or different, depend on whether we can establish that there are clear physiological correlates for what we know as mental activity, and that these provide evidence for differences or similarities. The implications for either of these two alternatives are profound. If we all have similar, or the same basic processes why are we so obviously different in terms of what we call culture? (1986: 43)

We might pause when we realise how recently such an article has been published. Where does this view of human difference leave music education? For Walker, music education should 'be founded upon understanding of the profound differences which exist... we can do no greater good for the preservation of multiculturalism in music than to encourage all forms of cultural diversity across the world to flourish in their diversity' (1986: 50). In this argument for a multicultural music education in Britain, we glimpse traces of the nineteenth century science of 'race' permeating everyday understandings of music education. We glimpse a desire for musical diversity that rests on notions of 'cultural purity'. It is an approach to multiculturalism in music education that is underscored by the 'race-relation narrative' of British nationalism, which Hesse writes about, that 'questions the coherence and legitimacy of 'non-white' Britishness' (2000: 12).

More positively, moves towards multiculturalism in educational curricula have resulted, however, from a recognition that what is taught in schools reflects patterns of inclusion and exclusion. Whose histories, whose cultures, whose traditions are transmitted through institutional pedagogic practices? Why does curriculum content matter? Volk notes that in the case of American education systems, multiculturalism is based on acknowledging a diverse population and intending to help students understand their social environments. A multicultural approach takes into account changing demographic patterns and encourages world-mindedness. More specifically, support for multicultural perspectives in music education is based on ideas about encouraging knowledge of the role that music plays in society, broadening students' sound base by introducing compositional and improvisational devices from a variety of traditions and contributing to aesthetic experiences since musical expressions hold intrinsic value that can be appreciated to some extent by diverse audiences (Volk 1998: 3–6).

Critical challenges to multiculturalism include scrutiny of the ways in which multicultural pedagogic approaches interface with the politics of 'race' and the representation of cultures as static and homogeneous. The focus on issues of 'race' is evident in the descriptor 'multi-ethnic education', used from the late 1960s and preceding the current term 'multicultural education'. Volk notes that one radical criticism of multicultural education is that it does not go far enough in teaching against racism and discrimination and in discussing social empowerment (1998: 7). This is a charge that the Inner London Education Authority took up in the 1980s, resulting in conferences and the publication of a policy document (*Race, Sex and Class: Multi-ethnic Education in Schools*: see Inner London Education Authority 1983). The document situated education policies within the context of migration from around the Commonwealth but restricted discussion to the somewhat confining categories of 'black' and 'white'. It outlined three main perspectives, which respectively emphasised assimilation, cultural diversity and equality. To summarise, the Inner London Education Authority rejected the assimilation perspective (characterised by beliefs that race relations were largely positive, that curricula should reflect 'British' traditions and history, and that priority should be given to learning correct English) and the cultural diversity perspective (informed by beliefs that teaching about culture would promote positive self-images and that issues of racism should maintain a low profile). The Inner London

Education Authority chose the perspective emphasising equality as one that should inform pedagogic practices. The aims were to recognise racism and draw on Black perspectives.[5] These aims bring us back to a point that merits further comment as it refers to the entanglements of nationalism, diaspora, imperialism, postcolonialism and multiculturalism. The context that fuelled these policy-making initiatives was migration from the Commonwealth, a context that reveals a relationship between the multicultural and the postcolonial. It is in this relationship, in the migrations of people from the Caribbean, for example, that Hesse explains the fixations on 'race' in discourses on multiculturalism. The fixations that lend themselves to critical analysis of the politics of multiculturalism are the residues of incomplete historical transitions from 'western imperialisms to racialized liberal-democracies' (Hesse 2000: 13). While the policies of the Inner London Education Authority presented in the 1983 document raised further problems surrounding the configuration of 'race' (notably in polarising people into opposing categories of Black and white such that the multiple ways in which 'otherness' can be constructed are ignored), the Authority's proactive attempts to address questions about social inequality, culture and history provided a context in which steelband education projects could flourish. Crucially, for thinking about inclusion and exclusion in the curriculum, these projects were open to any interested participants; a pedagogic and political approach to membership that is reproduced in Brooklyn's steelbands (Allen and Slater 1998) and in Pan Québec projects. I turn to some ethnographic details concerning steelband teaching projects in two diasporic contexts (in Britain and in Canada).

Case Study 1: Steelband in London's Schools. Steelband projects were established in several Inner London schools due to reforms in the curriculum and moves towards introducing 'equality' in the classroom during the 1970s. Gerald Forsythe set up and taught the first school steelband in an Inner London school (Islington Green school) in 1969. By 1975, over 50 schools were participating in steelband projects, and by 1990, 160 schools offered some steelband training as part of the school music curriculum. School steelband education in Britain preceded similar educational initiatives in Trinidad and Tobago, where steelpan in school education was not introduced until the mid 1990s. Gerald Forsythe and Frank Rollock (who led London All Stars) established the Pan Teachers' Association in 1975. In 1972, the Trinidad and Tobago High Commission in London set up a group, Steelband Promotion, aiming to promote steelband in schools and more generally among young people. In the mid 1970s, the Commonwealth Institute (concerned with running museum displays, arts events and holding library resources on the Commonwealth) staged the Schools' Steelband Music Festival in Britain. The first Notting Hill Panorama competition was held in 1978. The winning band was Paddington Youth, established in 1974 by Frank Rollock.

One of the most important initiatives was the establishment of a steel orchestra that was open to students from across Inner London. Gerald Forsythe was appointed steelpan organiser for the Inner London Education Authority (ILEA) and director of the London Schools' Steel Orchestra (later known as the ILEA Schools' Steel Orchestra) in 1978. This steelband performed widely – for example, in a Caribbean Week at the University of Bremen (1980), at the World Wildlife Fund Conference in London (1981) and in a concert tour in Germany alongside the London Schools' Symphony Orchestra, the Symphonic Band and the Rock/Reggae group (Inner London Education Authority Music Centre 1982, Rawlins 1983). In 1986, Sally-Anne Spencer was course manager for the ILEA Schools' Steel Orchestra, observing rehearsals and writing a Masters dissertation about this experience. During the period of her research there were twenty-four members of the ILEA Schools' Steel Orchestra and they met every Friday evening in the Music Centre in Victoria for rehearsals. Attendance was voluntary although the orchestra performed at major concert venues: the Royal Festival Hall, the Queen Elizabeth Hall and the Royal Albert Hall. The orchestra also undertook a concert tour of Denmark (1985). The orchestra's repertoire included calypsos, film theme tunes and a Chopin Nocturne. Spencer's description of the teaching and rehearsal process reveals some fluidity within this formal context that can be compared to the approaches of Wilson in Canada (see case study 2 below).[6] Spencer noted that cello pan players were often expected to work out their own parts and would refer to the bass line in the process of arranging their parts. The tenors learnt their parts by remembering the movements of the teacher as he demonstrated and by learning from other players in their section. A new melody might be taught to some players outside the main teaching space or it might be played on the piano and later on tenors could introduce some improvisation in adding chromatic runs or harmonies. An important feature of these teaching sessions was constant sound and most learning involved repetition of phrases, sections and pieces in memorising the repertoire under study (Spencer 1986: 39–41).

Case Study 2: Pan Québec. In the mid 1980s, the steelpan musician Salah Wilson busked on the streets of Montreal, having migrated to Canada in 1973 and having previously performed with bands in Trinidad like Exodus and Desperadoes. He was a founding member and first president of the steelband organisation set up in 1990 in Montreal, Pan Québec. One of the organisation's first projects was to establish a steelband in schools programme. A pilot project was run at Coronation School and extended, amongst others, to Somerled Elementary School and John Grant High School. Teaching programmes for senior citizens were also run and two annual festivals were launched – Classics and Carols in winter and Pan Jamboree in summer. Eventually Salah Wilson set up his own steelpan teaching practice (1997): the Salah and Family Steelband Academy, occasionally returning to Trinidad to play with Exodus. As part of his teaching practice, he has written a book: *Steelpan Playing with Theory* (1999). This presents a formal approach to learning steelpan, in which the ranges and layouts of pan instruments, and exercises to help develop notation skills are given. Scales, chord and rhythm charts lead to four-part arrangements of pieces that include the theme tune of the children's television programme *Sesame Street*, and calypso and blues examples. Suggestions for jazz improvisation are included at the end of the book. This approach resonates with Salah Wilson's own informal and formal training experiences. Growing up with the steelband Flamingoes in his backyard, he had been the first pan musician to enroll on the jazz programme run at Concordia University.

I heard a group made up from members of Salah Wilson's teaching practice perform as part of Caribana (2001). The previous year they had won the Toronto Panorama competition. One thing that struck me about their performance was one of their items, which was an arrangement of Shadow's Soca Monarch winning song, 'Stranger' (see Figure 3.2). Snatching a few moments to talk to Salah after the performance, I asked about this arrangement, discovering that he had attended the same performance in Port-of-Spain ('Under the Trees') that I had, earlier that year:

> When I was in Trinidad I went to a show and Shadow was there and I saw him performing live. And I was really right up front so I was listening to all his diction and all the stuff so I said, you know, I can capture this. And that's what I did. For my arrangement, I looked at the artist and I formulated a concept of what he was trying to achieve. (Salah Wilson, personal communication, July 2001)

Beyond Multiculturalisms and Fusions: On the Moral Dimensions of 'Culture'

If the discourses of multiculturalism are preoccupied with smaller cultural units within larger ones, fusions play with ideas about the convergence of those units in new creative projects. Fusions also play with ideas about heritages but are usually analysed in terms of the 'mixing' of distinct musical traditions. Fusions do not represent new phenomena, as musicians have always experimented with musical sounds. As a descriptor, however, 'fusion' offers a way of talking about musical interactions and creative processes in contemporary global market spaces. Fusion is often used as a marketing label to identify musical interactions in a 'world music' arena and musicians themselves speak about undertaking fusion projects when they collaborate with other musicians. Recent theorisation of the kinds of processes that musicians might describe as 'fusion' has tended to favour the concept of 'hybridity', replacing earlier ones such as 'syncretism' and 'acculturation'. Ultimately, I aim to move beyond both fusions and hybridities to suggest other ways of understanding what is going on in these musical processes altogether. For now, I would like to hold onto the concept of hybridity, momentarily exploring it in terms of the musical fusion.

As an analytic category, fusions are interesting because they offer contradictions. They simultaneously alert us to the limitations of projects that map music onto society and maintain the possibility of such musical mapping in adhering to the notion of a meeting place for musical traditions. Elsewhere, I have warned against simple readings of musical practices at the poles of essentialism or creolisation and noted the hazards of misreading 'musical interaction' as the meeting of musical differences related to ethnic, political, social or cultural particularities, a caution that bears repetition here (Ramnarine 2004). The contradictions of fusions are apparent in Grant's account of the origins of the steelpan, which refers to African, Indian and Chinese models that render the instrument an apt national symbol because it seems to represent the diversity of the island's population. The contradictions are apparent too in the musical fusions that juxtapose the steelpan (as an island timbre) with other instruments to create textures that seem to draw attention to the different kinds of musical heritages that constitute the Caribbean island soundscapes.

An example can be found in the work of Mungal Patasar, who is famous in Trinidad for his experiments in fusing different musical traditions and instruments, combining steelpan and sitar. In the late 1970s, having trained as a classical Indian player, he was invited to a fusion workshop, fusing calypso and jazz. After studying sitar in India with the Visnupur gharana (a musical lineage for the transmission of performance style) of Bengal, he returned to Trinidad and started collaborating with steelpan players from the steelband Exodus. The group was called Pantar. They signed contracts with the recording company, Virgin, producing a second CD titled *Dreadlocks*. Although the album and title track evoked the symbols of Rastafarianism, it was marketed under Mungal Patasar's name, featured collaborations with the British-Asian musician Nitin Sawhney, and the steelpan had been given less prominence. The musicians intend, nevertheless, to continue experimenting with fusions. With a philosophy of experimentation, Patasar sees himself as continuing a trend first established by the sitarist Ravi Shankar, who was notable for collaborations with Yehudi Menuhin, The Beatles and Philip Glass. He explains this experimentation as having begun by chance, then becoming a philosophy 'of creating peace and harmony in the universe through music', and ending up as a fashion (Mungal Patasar, personal interview, February 2001).[7] Steelpan, dreadlocks, Visnupur gharana, Nitin Sawhney: Pantar's practices and discourses point to a complex sense of multi-locality that references the Caribbean, the South Asian and the African Diasporas.

These multi-local references, together with a conceptual framework of 'a society with a music', are similarly evident in the recorded repertoires of the steelband Skiffle Bunch. This is a steelband from San Fernando in south Trinidad, formed in 1976, which encourages experimentation with musical textures and eclectic repertoire choices:

> Our CD is a good representation. There is our band with an Indian singer. There's us with a classical singer. There's us with a violinist. You can mix with almost anything. We play Indian songs, we play Malaysian songs, African songs, classical pieces, church pieces. So it is a very dynamic instrument because you can play almost any type of music on the pan and incorporate other instruments with it as well. Our band experiments a lot with that. We don't just stick to calypso. We mix it up. We have reggae, we have Chinese pieces and we have classical pieces. (Leslie Anne, double guitar player with the steelband Skiffle Bunch, personal interview, July 2004)

Such fusions are encouraged through cultural policy-making processes, raising questions about the promotion and support of musical performances at government levels. In the late 1990s, Daphne Phillips (then Minister of Community Development, Culture and Women's Affairs of Trinidad and Tobago) argued for recognition of both the 'complexity of contemporary Trinidad and Tobago' and the 'profound cultural and political significance' of musical genres (Daphne Phillips, speech published in *Newsday*, 15 April 1998: 10–11). She outlined policies implemented with regard to the support of musical performance which included the provision of undergraduate scholarships, funding for lectureships, library materials and resources for a new Bachelor of Science degree in Pan at the University of West Indies. Such policy-making indicates awareness at government levels of the ways in which musical performances and institutional contexts shape concepts of national culture. Indeed Phillips noted that 'the state is aware of the role of culture in national development and ... it is willing to use its power and resources to influence efficiency, research, training, business development, people participation, self sufficiency, artistic integrity, equity and fairness' (Daphne Phillips, *Newsday*, 15 April 1998: 11).[8]

Various island debates have centred on which traditions are promoted through performance opportunities, pedagogic projects and state sponsorship. Offering the potential to reformulate representations of national identity, recent cultural policy-making trends in Trinidad and Tobago reveal an emphasis on representing the diversity of Caribbean island musical expressions in international spaces. In 2004, Skiffle Bunch was invited to take part in a music festival in London, the Diaspora Music Village. Wishing to highlight the two main diasporas that compose the island's population, the Minister of Culture for Trinidad and Tobago, Joan Williams, asked Junia Regrello, the leader of Skiffle Bunch, if a tassa group from Williamsville, Dynamic Tassa Group, could join the steelband for the festival performances in London. The groups performed at the October Gallery in a small courtyard setting for an audience enjoying a lunch break, and in the open-air spaces of the South Bank Centre and the Royal Botanical Gardens at Kew (3.3).

Although the project was undertaken at short notice, Regrello commented that the collaboration was very easy to pursue because the tassa is a percussion instrument:

So it is just the rhythm. You don't have to learn a melody so it's easy. You don't really have to rehearse. You just adapt to the beat. If they had to learn a melody it would be different because we have about sixty items. (Junia Regrello, personal interview, July 2004)

In the London festival appearances (and in contrast to what went on in informal playing apart from the performance contexts) there were only a few pieces that featured steelpans and tassa drums together and in one performance they were scheduled to play at different times in the programme, with the effect that they seemed to represent different musical traditions. Such an effect provides an

Figure 3.3 Skiffle Bunch (top) and Dynamic Tassa Group in performance at the October Gallery, London (2004)

important corrective to assumptions about musical practices in the Caribbean as *necessarily* being based on fusions and to theoretical models of creolisation processes in the Caribbean. Although there was a move on the part of government agencies to promote particular representations of national culture in international performance contexts, the principal aim of Skiffle Bunch for its London festival performances was to project the capability of the instrument; to show how it could be used in performing diverse repertoires. While the collaboration between Skiffle Bunch and Dynamic Tassa Group had been specifically arranged for the festival performances to highlight different diasporas in the Caribbean, this tassa ensemble is involved with more extensive musical fusion projects in Trinidad. The ensemble works with African-Trinidadian drummers in a group called Rhythm Section, and so its members were able to draw on their prior experiences of fusing 'Indian' and 'African' rhythms (personal communication, Darren Changoor, cutter with Dynamic Tassa Group). Their London performances nevertheless drew attention to the contradictions of fusions: mixes as musical meeting places for seemingly distinct traditions or as new musical expressions that represent and seem to emerge from new social configurations. In another event dedicated to the theme of music and diaspora, a chutney ensemble from Trinidad called D'Bhuyaa Saaj undertook a concert tour around India in February 2005 as part of the festival, Remembered Rhythms (see Ramnarine 2007). The group, representing an example of musical practice in one of the older Indian diasporic centres, notably included a steelpan alongside the traditional chutney instrumentation of *dholak* (double-headed drum), harmonium and *dhantal* (an idiophone made from an iron rod).

The processes that musicians describe as 'fusions', like the multicultural spaces from which they may emerge, seem to move between models of 'melting pot' (mixing it all up into a new creation) and 'mosaic' (maintaining boundaries between traditions). Neither model accounts convincingly for musical creative processes or for people's lived experiences. How else can we approach fusions? If we move away from 'a society with a music' as a point of departure, what does fusion seem to be?

Fusions show us how musicians are influenced by the sounds of their immediate environments and by working with other musicians. The timbres of steelpan and sitar, of steelpan and tassa drum, of steelpan and drum kits, reveal how the sounds of a place shape musical expressions in the diaspora. Fusions help us to move towards thinking about music not as a static practice but as a process, as a way in which musicians experiment with sonic possibilities and as a way of working with each other. Thinking about musical processes and interactions in terms of a 'sonic environment' is a description I use in trying to point to a view of 'fusion' that does not evoke ideas about separate and distinct musical cultures 'mixing' in a context of cultural contact. This is a view that demands a rethinking of some cherished theoretical perspectives within anthropology and ethnomusicology, as well as of popular, everyday beliefs about 'my music' and 'your music'.

Rather than look to musical fusions as providing appropriate examples of 'hybridity' (another concept that has been used by ethnomusicologists to describe 'cultural mixes'), I would suggest that they point to something else. In returning to the particularities of hybridity discourses, it might be instructive to note that Bhabha stresses interdependence and mutual subjective construction in a 'third space of enunciation', which 'may open the way to conceptualising an international culture, based not on the exoticism of multiculturalism or the diversity of cultures, but on the inscription and articulation of culture's hybridity' (1994: 38). In other words, all cultures are hybrid, or rather we're all in one global hybrid culture now, and it is in the Third Space – the in-between spaces – that we may, as Bhabha puts it, 'elude the politics of polarity and emerge as the others of our selves' (1994: 39). In moving beyond conventional understandings of hybridity we move towards politically articulated readings of social relations and creative processes.

Hesse proposes another descriptor that might be related to trying to make sense of the kinds of processes addressed by hybridity discourses – 'transruption'. This

> describes interrogative phenomena that, although related to what is represented as marginal or incidental or insignificant, that is identifiable

discrepancies, nevertheless refuse to be repressed. They resist all efforts to ignore or eliminate them by simply recurring at another time or in another place. Transruptions are troubling and unsettling because any acknowledgment of their incidence or significance within a discourse threatens the coherence or validity of that discourse, its concepts or social practices. (Hesse 2000: 17)

It is the persistence of transruption that I like. Musicians like Mungal Patasar and Junia Regrello who are involved in collaborative projects of musical experimentation with timbres, textures, instruments and forms that seem to combine elements from distinct musical traditions might be described as transruptive, as performers of 'culturally interventionist' projects, to borrow a phrase from Kershaw (1992: 245), unsettling the ways in which we describe, label and categorise music.

Unsettlement and transruption might also be applied to the concept of hybridity, as they certainly do in politically informed elaborations. The anthropologist Pnina Werbner notes the paradox of hybridity, 'celebrated as powerfully interruptive yet theorised as commonplace and pervasive' (1997: 1). What the practice of Pantar and Skiffle Bunch emphasises is the political capacity of hybridity to interrupt understandings of culture and cultural identities precisely because it *is* pervasive; not as a result of culture contact or contemporary globalisation processes, but as an everyday *expected creative process*. This is at once a more mundane view of what is actually going on in the practice of music and a statement about musical cognition, creativity and process that makes more radical theoretical claims. Viewing creativity as process in terms of the everyday or of the expected throws the theoretical apparatus of (ethno)musicological scholarship – the projects of musical mapping, of looking at music in culture and at music as culture – into relief, thus joining other interruptive paradigms such as hybridity, migration and globalisation that have gained currency in trying to account for processes across, between and beyond 'cultures'. Everyday, expected creative process, the ways in which musicians tune into all kinds of soundworlds, allows us to explore the dynamics between the creative and the political, just as hybridity and fusion do, but avoids the problems of hybridity; in fact it requires a re-reading of this pervasive trope (and for that matter of creolisation) as rooted in notions of breeding that map difference onto the body (see Chapter 4). Everyday process leaves us not always having to read the creative in conjunction with the political, even though the challenge to 'difference' that comes with looking beyond culture and hybridity is a profoundly political consequence. In understanding creative process as being indistinguishable from the everyday lies the 'volatility of the everyday' (Bharucha 2005). Everyday creative process takes us away from thinking about music and identity in static ways. Music emerges as a creative process that cannot be mapped unproblematically onto the political ideologies that underpin identity formations. Musicians collaborating to produce 'fusions' demonstrate that people do not want to be locked into the reproduction of identities, musical or social.

The notion of the everyday also fits well with that of the 'sonic environment', introduced earlier, fostering some kind of musical analysis of what is happening in the creative process that does not rest on the politics of creativity, on understandings of musical appropriation or musical exchange in unequal economic or power relations. The sonic environment and the everyday highlight shared experience, collaboration, the contemporary soundscapes that remember sounds from the past and experiment with new configurations. I am also partial to the idea of sonic environment because this is not restricted to place. The sonic environment can include the musical sounds that people tune into through mass media systems, the sounds from geographically distant places that feature in people's experiences of musical possibilities. Musicians experiment with and create new sounds with conscious intention as an aspect of creative processes; not just because historical and political circumstances have brought musical cultures together.

This leads to thinking about the moral dimensions of culture. I have been exploring the tensions between multiculturalism and diasporic fusions, and the challenges to the multicultural society posed by the boundary crossings of fusion practices. While models of fusion and multiculturalism provide ways into understanding both creative processes and the politics of creativity, I have called for an understanding of musical processes in terms of expected creativity that propels us towards a politics of creative practice compelled to deal with our common human capacities rather than with the perpetuation of creative practices as an integral dimension in the structuring of difference. The concept of 'culture' itself – pervasive, tapping into received understandings of the transmission of creative skills and knowledge, lying at the heart of thinking about multiculturalisms and fusions – is a powerful obstacle to the kind of politics of creative practice that is being proposed here. Let me turn to two ethnographic scenes.

Scene 1. Danielle LeMarinel told me about her experience as a tenor pan-player in a steelband called Pantastic in the town of Dorchester in Dorset. She joined the steelband, which had begun as a school project with around 15 members, at the age of 16. It was the first steelband in Dorchester, but as membership grew, it was divided into two: one for older students and the other for younger students. These occasionally joined forces. The high school steelband (for older students with a small membership of six or seven) was employed as part of various retail promotional events and appeared regularly on Saturdays at one particular shop. Although this steelband did not participate in any competitions, sufficient income was earned to embark on a tour around Italy where the steelband performed at hotels and busked on the streets. This is an extract from my interview with Danielle:

DM: We didn't really write anything down, the music we learnt was from CDs; we'd work out transcriptions and do it all orally because we thought that was really important. It was the only way that our school would get to learn traditions like that. We were like 'You've got to write it down' and our music teacher was like 'No you don't'.... We never performed from books or anything – just do it straight off from our heads – and we spent a lot of time improvising as well.... We did a combination of traditional pieces and then some that people would know, transcriptions and arrangements of modern day pieces. We did 'Under the Sea' from *Little Mermaid*, which everyone loved so much and especially the middle school band they did popular songs, The Beatles, and then more traditional songs like 'Wings of a Dove' and 'Yellow Bird'.

TKR: 'In your school were there any members of the band that had a Caribbean background?'

DM: 'No, unfortunately not'.

TKR: 'So the steelband wasn't used as a multicultural kind of resource?'

DM: 'No, it was just to learn.'

(Interview with Danielle LeMarinel, 22 November 2004)

Scene 2. This concerns what could be described as the transruption of timbres. The signifying strength of steelpan timbres and the historical recounting of the instrument as a twentieth century Trinidadian invention are sufficient evocations of Caribbean islands despite their elusive acoustic properties.[9] 'Pong and Chant' is a song recorded by the Antiguan group Burning Flames that juxtaposes African heritages ('we want to feel we from Africa') and Caribbean locations (with the use of steelpan in verse 4) to talk about a 'real culture' which turns out to be not just one thing:

> 'Pong and Chant'
>
> (Verse 4) (Steelpan plays the first part of the verse)
> We want to feel the real culture
> We want to feel we from Africa
> So when you stand to make your song
> Make a song we could sing along.

Pong and Chant reveals a response to Edward Said's questions, posed in thinking about the condition of exile, regarding what people would give up, recover and save of experiences that are about to disappear (1993: 407). Throughout the Caribbean and its Diaspora what has been relinquished, reclaimed and preserved are the performing and expressive arts. 'We want to feel the rhythm in the feet; pong iron and sing a song.' But, despite the rhetoric of 'from Africa', the 'real culture' in this song is revealed through vocal text and steelband timbre as being multi-referential, necessarily so for, as Said observes, 'no one today is purely *one* thing'; that it has been one of the legacies of imperialism 'to allow people to believe that they were only, mainly, exclusively, white, or black, or Western, or Oriental' (1993: 407–8). People follow the exhortation of 'Pong and Chant', making songs to which we can all sing along. Through perspectives on the steelband, I have tried to show that instead of viewing musical practices in terms of hybridity, acculturation, fusion and so on, we view them as everyday processes; not as evidence of one culture operating within and alongside another culture (a multicultural model) or of one culture interacting with another culture (a fusion model). This is an argument that is rooted in viewing music as a creative practice, as a process, and as human activity rather than as a commodity that brings into play dynamics of power and economy leading to different analytical avenues in exploring questions about social relations. An emphasis on musical process does not need to refer to ideas about separate cultures meeting, but does accommodate the different kinds of creative dynamics that we observe in analysing music in diasporic contexts – the continuity of preservation, the creative impulses that lead to new kinds of musical expressions, steelband projects that do not depend on Caribbean participation. As Danielle LeMarinel puts it, Pantastic was not a multicultural resource; 'it was just to learn'. Such an emphasis on process, on the encounters of the everyday, renders the celebration of 'culture' itself, not just of multiculturalism and fusion, problematic.

Culture has been, of course, the success story of the ethnographic disciplines. It is now habitual to talk about culture as a property and as an attribute, something that one has and that distinguishes one from another, or more precisely from an 'other'. Where culture has been refused, it is reclaimed with passion, as I noted at the Caribbean Soundscapes conference (Barbados, 2005), where much discussion focused on processes of appropriation, copyright and origins, deflecting attention from the 'everyday'. For Said, one would not

> deny the persisting continuities of long traditions, sustained habitations, national languages, and cultural geographies, but there seems no reason

except fear and prejudice to keep insisting on their separation and distinctiveness, as if that was all human life was about. (1993: 408)

Instead, Said writes about connections, as does the anthropologist Adam Kuper, who observes that a moral objection to culture theory is that it draws attention away from what people have in common. Although discourses on multiculturalism stress different cultures, these do not reflect people's experiences. People who move 'between cultures' generally seem

> to manage very well, given the chance, in their new homes – not forgetting their origins, but ever adaptable. They know what they are doing, they instruct greenhorns in tactics, and they write home to convey their experiences. (Kuper 1999: 243)

Kuper does not entirely escape from the idea of a home somewhere else, but he does point to the everyday experience of managing life in the environments in which one finds oneself. It is worth noting that earlier anthropologists have shared his suspicion of the culture concept. Radcliffe-Brown dismissed the idea of cultures interacting in 1940:

> what is happening in South Africa is not the interaction of British culture, and Afrikander (or Boer) culture, Hottentot culture, various Bantu cultures and Indian culture, but the interaction of individuals and groups within an established social structure which is itself in a process of change. (1940, Presidential Address to the Royal Anthropological Institute, cited in Kuper 1999: xiv)

Not many cultures interacting, but individuals interacting. If Radcliffe-Brown's views on change were shaped by the evolutionary thinking of that time (societies progressing from the simple to the complex), the critique against cultures in interaction is a current one.

A Question for a Topical Show. Appearing on a topical television show, Aunty Nansi asks the host:

'Now Mr Kilroy, you tell me
Am I Afro-Celto-Euro-Indo
Or just beautiful byproduct of cosmos?'

> And with her question spiralling like a ghost
> Aunty Nansi took the opportunity
> To wave hello to her folks across the galaxy.
> ('How Aunty Nansi Singularly Widened the Debate on Plural Identity', John Agard (2000: 75))

This chapter has focused on how critical perspectives on culture theory raise questions about musical multiculturalisms and fusions that interface with hybridity discourses in interesting ways. If musical multiculturalism depicts a context in which several musical scenes co-exist, fusions seem to describe the interactions between them. 'Fusion' thus challenges concepts of bounded, discrete cultures in focusing on musical interaction and the inspiration of diverse soundworlds. Yet, fusion also reinforces the boundaries of the 'multicultural' through the persistent ideology of fusion as a creative space in which musical traditions or bearers of distinct traditions meet each other. Multiculturalism and fusion are also connected in their capacity to shape state policy-making through education and performance projects. Neither 'multiculturalism' nor 'fusion' are unproblematic concepts. Both are ambiguous, containing contradictory moral dimensions. Both multiculturalism and fusion hold the potential to develop and foster diverse creativities as well as forge new creativities and new identities. Both are only conceptually possible if one's point of departure is the celebration of cultural distinctiveness, of cultures as discrete and separable – a subscription to culture theory (from which hybridity discourses also spring) in which multiculturalisms and fusions become aberrations, special features of modern global cities and current creative conditions, theoretically untidy, spillages over cultural borders.

'Am I Afro-Celto-Euro-Indo?' It seems to be a simple question. One that many might ask. It is a question that resonates with my arguments against the incessant configurations of the politics of ethnicity in relation to the politics of culture that confine us within the trenches of multiculturalisms and fusions. It is a question that reminds us of the struggles over 'race', 'culture' and 'identity'. It compels us to think holistically, making it nonsensical to attempt to identify the separate elements that make up the whole. It turns our attention to the conceptual constraints against which thoughts about plural identities, double consciousness, two histories, and multiple subjectivities have emerged in negotiating the political polarities of 'home' and 'diaspora'. 'Am I Afro-Celto-Euro-Indo?' The analytical models that divide are ill-equipped to provide any responses to this question. Too often the discourses of fusion, hybridity or multiculturalism that grapple with the complexities of Afro-Celto-Euro-Indo have been unable to either escape the limits or resolve the discrepancies of those analytical models. To understand those complexities we need the close-up view offered by musical analyses of how musical sounds are put together and ethnographic descriptions of musical practices in their social contexts. To escape the limits of analytical models that divide we might have to take the long-distance vantage point, to embrace the encompassing context of the global and hybrid culture (interaction and process writ large) in which we all find a place; that is if we cannot reject culture, too prone to division, altogether. In a global arena the everyday fits well, for there is plurality in the everyday as well as commonality, so that this politics of creative practice does not have to entertain the dull prospect of all musical expression just sounding the same. If there are signs of such a politics in steelbands – in their membership and in 'just learning' – they have little impact on the politics of today. In her perplexity, arising from her own subjective experiences, Aunty Nansi addresses the moral dimensions of culture, asks about multiculturalism and hybridity, and offers an alternative vision. She does so from the spaces of diaspora, for Aunty Nansi is John Agard's transformation of the West African trickster spider, Kwaku-Ananse. As a transformation of the spider of West African stories that continue to be narrated in the Caribbean and its Diaspora you might expect that she would offer a view close to the ground. On the contrary, she presents us with liberating tools that resist the divisive labels of culture and identity and confuse the borders of multicultural and of fusion to move to an appreciation of everyday process and/or individual subjectivity as 'beautiful byproduct of cosmos'.

4
DANCING DIASPORA

'I've got rhythm in my blood' the salsero tells me as we whirl and twirl to Dark Latin Groove's 'Muevete' (Sony Discos 1996, track 5). The DJ is busy spinning track after track, taking us from the classics of Cachao's virtuoso double bass playing and Celia Cruz's popular 'Tamborilero' (originally recorded for the New York Latin record label, Seeco, 1959–65) to the latest sounds of ragga-influenced salsa from New York. The dance floor is crowded and negotiating spins requires an eye on where a space might temporarily open up for more elaborate movements. This is a crowd of serious salsa dancers. Some of them have been participating in the intermediate and advanced-level dance classes that run just before the club opens and we can see them practising the new steps and sequences that they have just learned. There are regular participants too. After a few sessions, people recognise and forge friendships with each other. For respite, dancers gather at the bar seeking refreshments. But no one stays there too long. The DJ chooses a catchy track and they are back on the dance floor.

Dance forms an integral part of many Caribbean popular musical performances. In Caribbean diasporic contexts too, various communities gather together for an evening of music and dance as a way of celebrating and reinforcing a sense of 'community'. In the celebration of 'community', recent dance scholarship has been productively engaged in tracing the origins of dance styles and reflecting on the body's capacity to remember through aesthetic movement. This is an idea that Wilson Harris explored in considering the limbo as a dance that takes us through the 'apparent void of history', and in so doing, opening 'gateways between civilizations' and reflecting the 'long duress of the imagination' (Harris 1999 [1970]: 166). The dancing body allows us to look into the past. Thinking about the dancing body as a site of history, the origins of salsa, for example, have been traced to the Congo (Crowell 2002, Daniel 2002). But in this ethnographic moment, the group is diverse, as in many of London's salsa clubs. As Sloat observes, 'the world dances to Caribbean beats. From Sydney to Helsinki, Tokyo to Abidjan, salsa and reggae call out to aficionados' (2002: vii).

What are the relations between contemporary, global salsa practice and salsa as a dance that provides insights into histories now being reclaimed through the study of the body as a 'primary text' (Desmond 1997)? A difficulty with reading dance styles as historical texts is that dance movements change. We might note the stylistic differences in salsa dancing in clubs in Cuba, Colombia, Puerto Rico, New York, Miami, London or Barcelona. Within these contexts we can observe further levels of stylistic difference. Classes in London's salsa clubs offer different perspectives on this dance depending on the teacher and the participants' levels of skill. On one hand, such stylistic differences may assist in distinguishing between salsa in the world's clubs and salsa performance read as history. On the other hand, the differences in dance styles facilitate the mapping of dance movements onto social groups, a theme that has been taken up by dance scholars and anthropologists. Developing a kinaesthetic semiotics to place dance research on the agenda of cultural studies, Desmond writes about movement codified in dance serving as a marker in the production of identities. Where dance movements become stylised in different ways between social groups, it seems that dance may be, as Desmond notes, 'especially vulnerable to interpretation in terms of essentialized identities associated with biological difference', particularly in the categories of gender and race (1997: 43). Recognising the vulnerability of dance style to the ideology of essentialism provides a corrective to current fascination with the 'embodiment of difference' (a way of reading culture, experience and perception through the body – thereby acknowledging the 'body' as something we all have but maintaining cultural differences through the processes of embodying). Between

Congolese origins and aficionados throughout the world dancing to salsa we find the embodiment of memory and the embodiment of difference brought into a complex relationship. The aficionado plays a crucial role in mediating the tensions between these modes of embodiment, allowing us to see a way to rejecting one yet retaining the other. Through the aficionado we may criticise the view that difference is mapped onto the body yet retain an understanding of the body as a site of historical memory. The aficionado who acquires requisite levels of dance skills does what the dancer who is remembering through the body does: practice. In practice, one appreciates the time devoted to preparation, the process of learning and the attainment of skill that enable a critical scrutiny of the embodiment of difference.

At the outset, it is worth noting that while this chapter presents an argument about skill and practice as ways of challenging difference mapped onto the body, those same parameters have been used in the assertion of difference through perceptions about the body's innate attributes. For example, in a study of dance and song amongst enslaved women in Jamaica during the period 1770–1830, Altink analyses colonialist accounts as providing both picturesque images of dancing enslaved women (praised for their grace, form and discipline) and negative images in which differences (regarded as 'natural and self-evident') between enslaved women and white women were emphasised. Yet colonial writers were observers of practice. Edward Long, in his volume *The History of Jamaica* (1774), wrote that 'the right execution of this wriggle, keeping exact time with the music, is esteemed among them in particular excellence and they practise this from an early age onwards' (Long cited in Altink 2000: 9). Altink (2000) suggests that the language of difference applied to dance and song performance was as much a way of establishing relations of power as violence and control over labour, and that such discourses were linked with both notions of sexual purity and colonial desires.

Why should the idea of the 'embodiment of difference' make sense to anyone? What does it mean to think difference through the body? Partial responses may be found in Caribbean and Caribbean diasporic contexts, in which the 'embodiment of difference' is rooted in colonial history and is further complicated by hybridity discourses, themselves offering critical perspectives on difference mapped onto bodies because of encounters between them. Aptly expressed in Aunty Nansi's question: 'Am I Afro-Celto-Euro-Indo?' which reminds us of unrelenting theoretical problems in descriptions of Caribbean 'hybridities', we move away from understandings of hybridity embraced by music researchers that are solely concerned with cultural production and creativity. Aunty Nansi's question moves us away from a Bhabhian notion of culture at the borderlines encountering newness, thereby creating transformed spaces that renew the past and innovate the present (Bhabha 1994: 7). While hybridity discourses in analyses of cultural production can be critiqued for presupposing anterior purities, contact zones and processes of borrowing and mixing such that fixations with origins and borders can be maintained, there are more invidious political applications in moving from the realms of cultural production to reproduction of people. Here we find that these discourses have their origins in the biological sciences marked by the urge towards classification, and in the fictions of race politics fostered by colonial enterprises and, in turn, fostering colonial anxieties about sexual border crossings. Given these historical dimensions of hybridity talk, what are the political stakes in musical designations of hybridity in contemporary constructions of identities or in analyses of dance styles centred on the embodiment of difference? Hutnyk observes that 'the discursive replication of hybridity-talk deserves the critical attention it receives, if only to make explicit what is not being said' (2005: 97).

Contributing to a move away from the comfortable zones of a contemporary musicological celebration of hybridity, two central and interrelated issues are discussed in this chapter. What is the relationship between musical/dance performance and body politics? How has musical scholarship acted as an agent in the attribution of musical authority to the body? I wish to explore what, for example, the salsa dancer means when s/he says 'I've got rhythm in my blood.' Who is being included and who excluded by such a statement? How is difference asserted through the body in biological terms in music and dance performance analyses? How is the body being represented such that how it looks – and I do not mean just the visual aesthetics of dance performance – seems to tell us who people are, what their histories are, and where they are from? In exploring these questions, the theoretical paradigm of hybridity is further interrogated and juxtaposed with notions about 'embodiment'. Drawing on the ambiguities of what is seen in music and dance performance, I am referring here to the notion that 'as a bodily and performative practice, music enters a very public and contested sphere, in which the political nature of its discourse can be hidden from no one' (Bohlman 1993: 432). By way of illustration, I refer to salsa, based on Cuban and Puerto Rican dance styles, which emerged in the 1970s in New York but now inhabits global spaces.

Rhythm

'Step, two, three, tap. Step, two, three, tap.' These were the verbal instructions given to members of a beginners' salsa dance class, which I joined. The class, like many dance classes offered in London's suburbs, was held in a large church hall. Around the corner were the local newsagents and grocery stores, a Chinese herbal medical practice and a Thai restaurant. The teacher was not from the Caribbean or Latin America, but from Yemen. He had developed an enthusiasm for salsa and travelled all over London to teach such classes. He had distributed leaflets advertising the classes in various neighbourhoods. It was through such a leaflet that newcomers to this dance form gathered cautiously around the church hall for the first session. Many did not return for the second session, but those who did became regular members of the class, persisting with their dance practise over the cold and dark winter months. Over several months, we spent hours practising dance steps to salsa tracks played on a small ghettoblaster. The teacher suggested readings for the class so that we could learn more about the history of salsa and also recommended recordings. The class progressed and our teacher urged us to try out our dance skills in a salsa club, La Finca, near Angel in central London. Teachers at this salsa club organised beginners, intermediate and advanced classes, and had a team of assistants who helped to demonstrate and correct each student's steps so that more polished dancing could emerge. A salsa aficionado there instructed me to 'Lose the tap! You can't do anything if you keep the tap.' What he pointed to were the dance gestures centred on 'freedom of the body' in which 'dancers may move to a more fluid, less determinate free play of responses to the music' (Concepción 2002: 173). Concepción notes that the basic salsa steps might be mistaken as simple, but that dance skill is dependent on appropriate musical understanding:

> to be able to dance in rhythm with the music and in synch with a partner, a complex combination of musicality and virtuosity is required, as well as a great deal of versatility. One can dance salsa according to one's own rhythm, that is to say, not everyone dances on the same note. But, at the same time, it is essential to step in tune within a variety of possibilities. (2002: 173)

Crowell makes a similar point about rhythmic complications in salsa footwork, elaborating the possibilities by noting that dancers 'generally begin on beat one, but aficionados may start on two; many insert a hesitation, and the dancers may be dancing in syncopation to the rhythm' (2002: 13). Free play of responses to music and rhythmic complexity in dance footwork in this context is a result of developing sufficient skill. Where does this attention to skill feature in discourses about rhythm in the blood? The simple answer is that it does not. Rather, having rhythm and not having rhythm often play on commonplace stereotypes about the innate attributes of bodies, revealing the ways in which performers are pre-located in and circumscribed by a set of perceptions inflected by socio-political discourses and images. Salsa, like other dance styles, has inspired debate in relation to the body politics evident in the mapping of dance styles onto 'race', a point that Desmond similarly notes in observing that in North America 'it is no accident that both "blacks" and "Latins" are said to "have rhythm"' since the supposed connection between 'race' and rhythm 'rests on an implicit division between moving and thinking, mind and body' (1997: 48). Aficionados and salsa dance teachers are just as likely as anyone else to promote these stereotypes in their discourses about dance styles, even if the configurations of 'having rhythm' vary. In the advanced dance class, one aficionado told me that I should dance with a straight back to dance in a proper 'Latino' style and with a slightly curved back to achieve an 'African' style.

Music scholarship has played a part in investing musical authority in the body. In fact, it has been an inventing agent in the attribution of musical authority to the body, particularly in relation to constructions of the body in terms of gender and 'race'.[1] We can turn to music scholarship to trace some of the ways in which 'having rhythm' has gained currency both within and beyond the academy, but it is worth noting that the idea of the experience of the body in music has been 'enormously difficult for many musicologists to accept' and that 'rejection of the body has long characterized musicology's historiography' (Bohlman 1993: 431). This is in contrast to scholarship on African musical traditions dating back to the early twentieth century. Historical perspectives on the musical analysis of rhythm and motor function provide a context for understanding the emergence of current concepts regarding dance as the cultural embodiment of difference and as the signalling and negotiation of social identities through bodily movement (Desmond 1997). One of the key figures in the Berlin school of comparative musicology, Erich von Hornbostel, presented an influential theory of African rhythm in an article in 1928. The article was concerned with comparing 'African' and 'European' music in order to establish that they were constructed on different principles. For Hornbostel, European music was grounded in hearing and mental concepts while psychomotor considerations generated African music. Modelled on drumming, Hornbostel regarded African rhythm as being generated through motion and muscular sensation, illustrated through lifting the arm to beat a drum, thereby creating a 'motor accent'. Christopher Waterman comments that this hypothesis, formulated through the study of recordings deposited in the Berlin archives rather than through observation in situ, 'discloses a leap of logic, an internal gap that invites external explanation' (Waterman 1991: 172). Waterman explains that the opposition that Hornbostel proposed between hearing and body motion was produced not only in relation to historical circumstances, which fostered a separation between Africans and Europeans, but also to a concern with preservation that has marked much twentieth-century salvage ethnomusicology. Noting processes at work in the New World, Hornbostel suggested that African music might disappear with the encroachment of European styles, writing that:

> It is therefore to be feared that the modern efforts to protect culture are coming too late. As yet we hardly know what African music is. If we do not hasten to collect systematically and to record by means of the phonograph, we will not even learn what it was. (Hornbostel 1928, cited in Waterman 1991: 172)

In looking at musical processes in the New World and fearing that similar processes in Africa would lead to the erasure of musical systems still relatively uncharted in European scholarship, Hornbostel reproduced modes of thinking within musical and psychological discourses that had been rehearsed within the complex dynamics of Caribbean plantation societies and that have also marked Caribbean diasporic experiences. The wish to find and preserve musical 'purity' complements and reinforces colonial preoccupations with difference.

This early insistence on difference has been one of the factors conditioning later ethnomusicological understandings of 'African' musical practice and perception (Waterman 1991: 179). Hornbostel's work selected rhythm as a key musical parameter in the analysis of 'African' music. As Agawu suggests, though, 'African rhythm' is 'an invention, a construction, a fiction, a myth, ultimately a lie' (2003: 61) in which even African scholars, operating within 'an intellectual space defined by Euro-American traditions of ordering knowledge', have been complicit (2003: 58). In highlighting rhythm as a focal point for musical analyses contributing to the conceptualisation of difference, it is worth noting, as both Waterman and Agawu do, that much work within ethnomusicology has contested such analytical conclusions, that

Hornbostel's work has contributed valuable insights into musical practice, and that rhythm is a musical parameter that requires analytical investigation. The preceding discussion is merely by way of providing contextual perspectives on a music scholarship that has contributed to the mapping of 'rhythm' onto 'race'.

This context also provides a cautionary note to a dance scholarship that now invests authority in the 'text' (resonating with previous models in anthropology of 'culture as text' and in musicology of 'music as text', in which notation has been privileged), such that bodies can be 'read'. How do these readings conform to the distinctions between subject and interlocutor? The body as text model runs the 'risk of "writing" persons who do not wish to be written' (Battaglia 1999: 117) and leads to theoretical oppositions between the body viewed as being either shaped by social conventions ('body as text') or as an intentional agent, engaging intersubjectively with the world ('cultural embodiment'; see Csordas 1999).

Practice

Once the members of my dance class had started participating in the salsa sessions held at La Finca, our teacher ended his classes held at the local church hall. It was time for us to study more complex choreographies with other salsa aficionados. Our new teachers were from Colombia, Bolivia and Cuba. This development meant that we lost the convenience of a local class and started commuting into central London locations, often two or three times a week, staying up late despite early morning work commitments. Our salsa circle expanded and in our classes we often compared the details of different salsa dance styles. Through salsa newsletters, more information about classes, recordings, teachers and teaching videos was disseminated. We observed the salsa dance competitions held at these central London locations and got excited about the films and television documentaries that were made at these clubs about London's salsa scene. This was a scene that was the city's latest craze. Anyone could join the dancing; it was not restricted to members of any particular 'community'. In addition to the clubs, there were big salsa parties in London's parks and private parties in the city's town halls. The shift from local hobby to more committed participation in London's salsa dance scenes took us through the interlocking networks of salsa practice and salsa as an industry (promoted, advertised, sold).

Practice fits well with theorisation of the body in terms of intentionality and agency. My emphasis on learning process and the development of skill accords with insights about musical and dance performance as embodied practice. The significance of practice is that it points to a learning process in which descriptions of 'having rhythm' or 'not having rhythm' emerge not from innate, embodied qualities that might reveal or be confined by the inscription of the social onto the body, but from human actions led by the aesthetics of choice and judgements of style. A dancer chooses which dance style to learn and is evaluated as having attained sufficient skill according to the frameworks regarded as appropriate within a particular dance performance domain. From this perspective there is nothing that prevents a dancer from learning any dance style. Practice and the attainment of skill point to the impossibilities of suggesting that social groups dance salsa in different styles because of fundamental bodily differences. Practice – as a way of looking at choice, motivation, intention, deliberation and becoming skilful – emphasises process; not predetermined possibilities but determined aspirations.

Practice and aspiration are precisely what emerged in interviews with members of the London-based salsa group Salsa y Aché. Román-Velazquez notes that musical understanding and perception rather than ethnic background guided their salsa musical practice. Band members described transcribing from recordings, listening and learning about salsa rhythms. Acknowledging that playing salsa is a learning process, musicians tended to conform, however, to stereotypes about 'Latins having the rhythm and Europeans having the melody' (Román-Velazquez 1999: 120), and vocalists were expected to sing in Spanish as a way of signalling Latin musical identity. The ways in which these performers constructed 'Latin' musical identities supports Desmond's suggestion that dance is a way of looking at the cultural embodiment of difference given that some of the most tenacious categories of social identities are mapped onto the body (Desmond 1997: 57). At the same time, the musicians in this salsa group challenged the constraints of 'essentialist beliefs about a natural Latin body and musical abilities' (Román-Velazquez 1999: 128). Another example of simultaneously supporting and rejecting essentialist beliefs about the body is found in the testimony of a salsa dance practitioner who stated in a newsletter interview:

> When I first went to Latin America to do research I was told by the dance academics over there that I could never achieve the multi-rhythms of a Latino because I was English. I was told that the internal flow and freedom in the Latino body was impossible for Europeans.... Interestingly, what I did find is that Latinos who moved into the cities led a lifestyle that affected their ability to feel and express the rhythm and dance... this gave me the clue that Latino rhythmic grace is an acquired skill, rather than inborn. (Kerry Ribchester, salsa dance teacher, featured in *Salsa World*, n.d., issue 3, c.1997)

Re-inscriptions and Radical Articulations

Whilst embracing the insights of thinking about embodiment as process, there are troubling dimensions to the view that dance is the cultural embodiment of difference, which I would like to explore through considering 'hybridity' further. In his letters from London, written and published in the *Port-of-Spain Gazette* in 1932, C. L. R. James noted his observations on ongoing colonial preoccupations and anxieties surrounding encounters between 'different people'. He wrote:

> I have been to two dances here. There were heaps of nice girls, really nice people, well-educated, good manners, and some of them quite beautifully dressed.... But there were very few English *men* there. Those present were either connected with the giving of the dance, or friends of those who had given it. At one dance in particular there were no more than about five men under thirty, one might almost say under fifty. And these five sat in corners

and glowered, and looked as unpleasant and as dissatisfied as possible. That tells its own tale. (James 2003 [1932]: 84)

The tale to which James refers is one that points to earlier nuances of hybridity discourse, the anxieties over 'race', which might make us pause in our contemporary celebrations of this trope. The ethnic stratifications and complex hierarchical relations that James describes would have been familiar to him from the Caribbean as well as the British context.

Lo identifies two contrasting approaches to hybridity. One approach is celebratory, in which cultural barriers in an age of transnationalism are viewed as becoming increasingly permeable. Lo calls this 'happy hybridity', a description that celebrates 'the proliferation of cultural difference to the extent where it can produce a sense of political in-difference to underlying issues of political and economic inequities'. Lo contrasts this way of thinking about hybridity with what Bakhtin calls 'intentional hybridity' (Bakhtin 1981: 361). For Lo, intentional hybridity is distinguished from happy hybridity by

> its motivation and location within an identified field of contesting power relations. The happy hybridity model celebrates the proliferation of difference as unbounded culture. The end result is harmonious fusion whereupon difference is reabsorbed into the status quo. In contrast to this, intentional hybridity stresses its strategic use as a mode of intervention and politicisation. (Lo 2000)

Like Lo, Hutnyk makes a similar argument about hybridity offering a 'rerun of cultural relativist unities', but he does not distinguish between 'happy' and 'intentional' versions. For Hutnyk, 'correct theory' does not lead to 'adequate politics' and he suggests that it would be 'a more practical and political choice to begin with the terms which practitioners, and their audiences, deploy themselves in explanation of what they are doing' (1997: 123). Given that performers and their audiences do not necessarily perceive performance in terms of the social contexts of its production and in relation to the political strategies of identity formation, 'happy' and 'intentional' forms of hybridity might not be as apposite as they seem. The rhetoric of harmonious fusion has a political edge that is asserted in a range of contexts, often in an attempt to address power inequities. In Lo's formulation of happy hybridity as a celebration of global difference that is reabsorbed into an unchanging political order of inequality, it is worth asking about the inconsistencies that arise from thinking about the uniformity of difference in an unbounded culture. These 'harmonious fusions' are analysed as cultural processes in global terms without striving for the kind of global political action that challenges inequality. In other words, 'happy hybridity' as merely a celebratory trope is nowhere near the visions of a global culture that recognise hybridity as a pervasive and everyday process and that might make us revise our ideas about the nature of 'culture'. In the absence of such revision, Lo's assessment of the reabsorption of difference in an unchanging political order and Hutnyk's observations on the limits of hybridity-talk to carry out the political work that would organise political alliances across the differences celebrated by hybridity are compelling.

To reiterate a question posed in the previous chapter, what does it mean to think about hybridity in relation to the mundane of the everyday? Perhaps, if we thought that we were living in a global, hybrid culture there would be no need to think about 'fusion' (presupposing separable elements in combination), harmonious or otherwise. By adhering to the rhetoric of fusion in which cultures meet and to seeing the world in terms of uniformities of difference, happy hybridity loses an opportunity for revealing its potential transformation into 'intentional' hybridity on a global scale. Thinking globally is, after all, a contested political stance, too.

Paradoxically, thinking about hybridity only in relation to the cultural makes it more complicated to think globally (for we always encounter the borders of cultures), but easier to talk, even innocently, about the embodiment of difference. If the rehearsal of cultural relativisms provides one kind of obstacle to thinking globally it reinforces the model of embodiment as a process through which cultures are experienced in their variety. Cultural relativism is necessarily a plural proposition, through which difference must emerge; and if bodies living in particular cultural contexts are shaped by their cultural experiences, where does that leave us in terms of theoretical constructions? Reclaiming earlier understandings of hybridity in biological terms reveals more directly what is at stake in the notion of the cultural embodiment of difference. Viewed through the lens of hybridity, this kind of 'embodiment' looks like another way of renewing hierarchies of human relations and difference. There is an irony in using a trope (hybridity) that has itself been critiqued for celebrating difference to criticise another trope (embodiment) that demonstrates some shared assumptions. But it is through descriptors of hybridity in terms of the biological that some discomforts with embodiment as the persistence of difference through the body can be presented.

If hybridity is nowadays theorised in relation to culture, so too is the body. As Csordas explains, 'culture and self can be understood from the standpoint of embodiment as an existential condition in which the body is the subjective source or intersubjective ground of experience'. This is a theoretical move to which the distinction between body and embodiment is critical: 'of course we have bodies, but there are multiple modes of embodiment, and it is the modulations of embodiment that are critical for the understanding of culture' (Csordas 1999: 181–2). In the extract from the letter cited above, C. L. R. James was referring to the anxieties that have plagued Caribbean colonial societies, and resonated through postcolonial Caribbean diasporic experiences, surrounding 'Afro-Celto-Euro-Indo'. Those anxieties lead us to wonder about embodiment across culture, an implicit critique taken up by Gilroy in considering the theoretical distinctions between the cultural and biological that are the legacies of enlightenment anthropology. He writes:

> Secreted inside the dazzling rhetoric of universal inclusiveness and limitless variation within humankind, there is another pragmatic and hierarchical anthropology that can recognize a degree of injustice in imperial conquest but be comfortable nonetheless with the commonsense wisdoms that produce race as a deep fracture in culture, capacity, and experience. (Gilroy 2005: 63)

The effects of 'ethnic absolutism' (and the cultural embodiment of difference could be seen in these terms) is to 'freeze us in our cultural habits' from where 'there seems to be no workable precedent for adopting a more generous and creative view of how human beings might communicate or act in concert across racial, ethnic, or civilizational divisions' (Gilroy 2005: 63).

The difficulties with working across those divisions are that they are set up on all sides, not just in the theoretical legacies of the human and ethnographic sciences. People assert their differences in everyday life and are anxious to highlight the particularities of their experiences. The ethnomusicologist Ted Solís reports a variation on the statement 'I've got rhythm in my blood'. He tells his salsa partner, a member of the Puerto Rican community in Hawai'i, how much he enjoys the dance despite some ineptness, to which she responds: 'You have good rhythm but shake your hips too much', a comment that leads to his reflecting on the ways in which dance and music intertwine with the 'complexities of self-image' (Solís 2005: 75). There is a broader relevance in Solís's anecdote, however, which returns us to the aficionado.

The aficionado turns attention away from narrow representations and expectations of the body towards thinking about the capacities of dancers and musicians to achieve skilled levels of performance. Drawing attention to the levels of skill required for successful dance performance challenges the idea that the body passively embodies 'cultural difference'. Moreover, skill as an achievement that works beyond the borders of culture reveals that an emphasis on embodiment as cultural experience deserves some critical commentary. But some of the analytical insights that have been gained in relation to thinking about musical choreographies should be recuperated. In looking at dance *to* music we can also consider dance *in* music – the choreography of musical skill as part of musical cognitive processes. From this angle, the analytical insights of earlier researchers (concerned with what should now be regarded as an indefensible project of establishing fundamental differences between African and European musicians by separating, for example, the physical and mental processes of musicianship) can be revised and partially reclaimed. Like dancers, musicians move through, to and with music. The musical gesture is an aspect of the musical thought. The choreographies of dance and music turn our attention to practice and skill, which allow us to recognise attainment, deliberation and decision. Without having to think in terms of different people having different cultures and different bodies (the mapping project plagued by the certainties of the relation between performance, place and 'race'), practice and skill enable an appreciation of creativity as a process and as a choice. Performance traditions, then, can be evocative and identifiable as the practices of certain places, but are not restricted to being so identified. Process, manifested over time, encourages nuances in readings of hybridity, politics and power. Practice, deliberation and skill, together with creative and historical processes, forge alternative paths to thinking through static modes of cultures, hybridities and bodies.

The notion of cultural embodiment (experience of the world) has largely replaced textual models (culture to be read and interpreted) within ethnographic disciplines. For Csordas, textuality benefits from a dialogic partner, in the phenomenological tradition of Heidegger. He writes:

> semiotics gives us textuality in order to understand representation, phenomenology gives us embodiment in order to understand 'being-in-the-world'. This understanding in turn requires that, when we once again focus on the body *per se*, we recognize that it can be constructed both as a source of representations and as a ground of being-in-the-world. (Csordas 1999: 184)

This seems to be close to Desmond's 'kinaesthetic semiotics'. The emphasis on dialogue also returns us to earlier meanings of 'text'. As Schechner suggests,

> in its earliest and most active meanings, a text is the product of a skilled joining of different materials to make a single, supple, whole, and strong stuff. Those who make texts are both artists and craft persons.... Although today text implies writing, the earlier meanings continue to operate – behind the scenes, as it were. Texts are synthetic, constructed, crafted,

made up, invented: sites of interpretation and disagreement, not fixed canons. (2002: 193)

My emphasis on skill enables a dynamic and process-orientated reading of the 'body as text', which highlights choice and practice, as well as experience and representation. The main reason why I dislike the 'cultural embodiment of difference' is that it offers a variation of the political body that has been marked out as different through parameters such as 'race'. In the 'cultural embodiment of difference' an assumption of cultural essentialism replaces biological essentialism. At worst it can be mistaken as a euphemism, as another way of continuing to talk about 'race' by following a train of thought that acknowledges that we all have bodies but insists we are different, nevertheless, because we perceive and experience life differently according to the dictates of the cultures within which we are located. It is another way of categorising, pre-circumscribing, and setting boundaries around people and their experiences.

Instead of being analysed through the confines of our subjective perceptions and cultural experiences (so that we can culturally embody difference), the body as text metaphor at least offers the hope of alternative readings. In discussing Jamaican dancehall in terms of 'race' and gender, Cooper notes that it is 'disparaged as a homophobic, homicidal, misogynist discourse' but may be understood as a 'potentially liberating space' for women escaping social conventions in which the celebration of female sexuality and fertility is ritualised. Dancehall constitutes a social space in which the sexualisation of the female body paradoxically re-inscribes and subverts racial and sexual stereotyping. It draws attention to the moral frameworks around discourses on the body and to the tropics as a trope for passion. Referring to an eighteenth-century Jamaican popular song recorded in print by Moreton, 'Me Know No Law, Me Know No Sin', an early literary example of 'subversive noises', Cooper suggests that dancehall can be theorised as an act of self-conscious female assertion of control over the representation of her person. Dancehall culture permits its participants 'to enjoy the pleasures of release from the prison of identity that limits the definition of the person to one's social class and colour' (Cooper 2006).

I return to the salsa aficionado, for skill is something that leads us to alternative ways of understanding the body (as represented by others as well as selves) and embodiment (as the experiences that shape our engagements with the world). In bringing skill centre-stage, a different reading of 'body as text' is suggested, but more importantly the possibility of moving beyond 'race' discourses is brought into view. If 'race' has become a 'canon' – a fixity of the body, a trope that continues to pervade everyday discourses of difference manifested in the social and political effects of marginality and racism – it is nevertheless one that can be read anew. The 'body' does not have to be read in terms of 'race'. Rhythm does not have to be mapped onto some bodies but not others. A text 'invites being remade into new texts' (Schechner 2002: 193), and bodies as texts lend themselves, as Cooper suggests, to re-inscription.

At the outset, I stated that while rejecting a categorical notion of the cultural embodiment of difference, it might be useful to retain an understanding of the body as a site of memory. Inscription and re-inscription occur over time, returning us to readings of dance performance that are framed by both kinetic knowledge about the past and the socio-political projects of historical reclamations. Although salsa emerged as a commercial venture in the 1970s, marketed by the record company Fania, it was based on 'layers of traditions' (Concepción 2002: 172). These included Cuban, Puerto Rican and African American music and dance traditions, some of which had been mediated by the American entertainment industry, the cha cha cha shows directed by Xavier Cugat in the 1950s, for example. Quite apart from the marketing strategies of the entertainment industry, the 'embodied meanings' of these dances, unknown to some salsa practitioners, include religious ones (Concepción 2002). The dialogue between drummer and dancer is a significant feature of ritual practice that points to both the religious, musical and kinetic memories of enslaved people in the Caribbean and to cultural connections with Africa. Delgado and Muñoz suggest that the cultures of Africa survived the institutions of slavery and colonization and continue to survive, despite the institutions of capitalism and so-called development, in the sounding of the drums. In the times of our ancestors, the drums invoked the gods and the gods dwelled within the body of the duration of the dance. And they still do. (Delgado and Muñoz 1997: 11)

Thompson similarly writes about the spiritual aspects of mambo music and dance as well as about the ways in which meanings are either understood or not, noting how he often saw Tito Puente tracing a circle around his head with his drumstick and a dancer on the dance floor mirroring the movement: 'To Anglos in the house it was "showmanship". But to knowing Latinos, it was self-purification, a *limpieza*, in the name of God and the spirits' (Thompson 2002: 344). The layers of traditions that make up contemporary salsa performance alert us to the complexities of the body as a site of history just as hybridity-talk points to the politics of difference at work in the distinction between the understanding of 'Anglos' and 'Latinos' of Tito Puente's actions. 'Why talk hybridity now rather than a more explicitly radical language?' asks Hutnyk (1997: 122). If hybridity itself 'stops short of political action' even as it draws our attention to the maintenance of exclusion though cultural constructions (Hutnyk 1997: 131), tracing the spiritual aspects of music and dance performance in relation to salsa begins to move us towards considering a more radical articulation of political action. For this tracing of ritual significance parallels the tracing of performance traditions mediated through the world's most powerful entertainment industries. The latter mediation offers a salutary reminder that choice, practice and skill might challenge difference mapped onto bodies but that the real problems in the politics of difference lie in access, control and resources. Where the aficionado shows us that it is impossible to think in terms of cultural embodiments of difference, the routes whereby salsa has been made accessible to aficionados globally tell us something about the dynamics of corporate marketing power that underlie musical practice in the marketplace. Musicians are not necessarily helpless participants in market ventures. In remembering dance and music in diasporic contexts as a ritual and spiritual practice and participating in the mediations of entertainment industries we find performers reconciling the disparate modes of salsa as embodied memory and salsa as global practice. In the next chapter we will find performers committed not only to revaluing the past but also using the structures of music industries to preach a global politics of equity.

5
RIDDIM IN LYRICS
On the Insurgency of Musical Creativity

'The only bomb we need is love', sings Sheldon Blackman. A small audience, mainly friends and acquaintances, listens attentively, feeling privileged to be present at this performance in a café in Tobago. The dog on guard at the entrance has stopped barking. The steelpan tuner opposite has closed his store. It is late. Mosquitoes hover in a cool sea breeze.

'The only bomb we need is peace' – we hear the second line of the refrain. Across the table I notice Brother Resistance, a pioneer of rapso, a commentator on postcolonial politics. We nod at each other in greeting.

Tossing his dreadlocks, Sheldon sings into the microphone, accompanying himself on the guitar. Some of his siblings, all of them members of the group Love Circle, provide vocal backings. We hear voices in thirds for the choruses and rich instrumental textures of electric with acoustic guitars and drum kits. The live performance tempos are much faster than the recorded ones. The volume output from the microphones is high. This is jamoo (Jahovah's music), promoted by Sheldon Blackman's father, Ras Shorty I (who started his calypso performance career using the stage name, Lord Shorty, changed his name on experiencing a spiritual revelation, and pioneered soca during the 1960s and 1970s). Soca had drawn on Indian-Caribbean rhythms and instruments like the *dhantal* (struck iron rod) and *dholak* (small barrel drum), the sounds that Ras Shorty I had heard growing up in a predominantly Indian village in the south of Trinidad. It was originally known as 'sokah' (an amalgam of calypso and kaherwa taal). The spelling was important because it pointed to the different diasporic histories that forged the genre.

Ras Shorty I's spiritual revelation and promotion of sokah/soca alerts us to moments of revelation in diasporic consciousness. The language of revelation was used in Ras Shorty I's description of soca as the 'soul of calypso'. Similarly, he considered jamoo to be the 'gospel of soca'. Working on this music he focused on the spiritual aspects of calypso and soca, reminding listeners of the many diasporas inhabiting a shared Caribbean island space, and offering musical visions of social unity. The jamoo sound was distinct from those genres because the tempo was generally slower. Ras Shorty I's children continue to experiment with this musical form, holding his ideas of musical inclusiveness in mind. Sheldon Blackman has been developing ideas about jamoo as music 'for edification' that expresses pan-Caribbeanness, and he regards African Caribbean and African American musical expressions like calypso, dub, rap and reggae as manifestations of African heritages interplaying with other artistic influences around the Caribbean from the colonial era onwards (Sheldon Blackman, personal communication, November 2002) (see Figure 5.1). The recorded repertoire of Love Circle includes jamoo, soca and 'conscious chutney'.

'Don't tell me that war is a solution'. We reach verse 1 and I imagine that this must have been what it was like to hear Bob Marley under the shadows of Caribbean island palm trees in the days before he achieved superstardom.

The messages articulated through the texts of song genres like jamoo, reggae and rapso are often explicitly political and spiritual. This chapter is concerned with song in and as politics, with song texts, or lyrics, as I shall henceforth refer to them, which comment on power inequities, engage with postcolonial discourses, and call for an activist stand on political issues. Through an ethnographic experiment in 'chatting', this chapter reflects on political activism through creative procedures, on what I call the insurgency of musical creativity. The ethnographic experiment involves collaborating with other commentators so that different perspectives can be presented alongside each other, lending themselves to comparison,

Figure 5.1 Alexander D. Great (right) and Sheldon Blackman teaching at a music workshop

reflecting different articulations on a theme, questioning the need for others to be spoken for. The experiment stems from concerns with the construction of authorship and authority in ethnography. As Trouillot comments, 'anthropologists never give the people they study the right to be as knowledgeable or, more precisely, to have the same kind of knowledge about their own society as ethnographers' (2003: 129). In its control over 'native' voices, ethnography not only seems to summarise these voices but also claims to encapsulate the lived experiences, which those voices represent, in such a way as to make a 'reading' of the original voices redundant (Trouillot 2003: 130). The ethnographic disciplines have not been oblivious to this charge, recently experiencing a crisis of confidence in such narrative strategies, turning inwards to ask questions about the privileging of one set of discourses over others and uncovering the theoretical and ideological assumptions that have informed the production of ethnographic texts. Yet, ethnography has emerged relatively unscathed from this crisis, retaining its former privileges within the academy with the ethnographer now re-cast as the 'interpreter'.[1]

Through my experiment in 'chatting', I argue that others do not always need to be spoken for or interpreted, that they are far more eloquent and more widely heard than much ethnography might allow us to believe, and that ethnography, in fact, can be read in ways to highlight the 'original' voices. The mode of presentation thus addresses two concerns: the singing voice in political articulation and the singer's voice as a contributor to, and/or critic of, ethnographic discourses. I invited three singers/writers to collaborate with me to produce performance-orientated, analytical and reflexive perspectives on the insurgency of musical creativity. It is difficult to distinguish quite so readily between the 'native's discourse' and the 'ethnographic interpreter' in this collaborative enterprise. One contributor is Wayne Marshall, who is an ethnomusicologist based in the USA and also a hip-hop/reggae performer. I heard him present a conference paper in 2003 and was struck by our parallel interests in the traffic of musicians, musical ideas and musical products between the Caribbean and its diasporic centres. Another contributor is Alexander D. Great, a British calypsonian and educator. (I wrote about him in Chapter 2. He writes about himself in this chapter.) The third contributor is the sociologist W. A. Henry also known as the British dancehall DJ Lezlee Lyrix.

This ethnographic experiment is not without precedents although it is a variation on other collaborative writing projects.[2] In 'chatting', I follow the form of one voice followed by another and another. Moving between voices in this way, it is the task of the reader to read the chatting as a series of interconnected and interweaving lines. Chatting is not just about having your say. It involves listening and responding to what you have heard. Through chatting, a series of assumptions about 'others' being spoken for, which accompany debates on ethnographic authority and authorship, will be critiqued. I have in mind Battaglia's suggestion that 'the far shores of ethnographic enquiry are the regions of the marginalized, the subaltern, the otherwise authoritatively de-centred human subject' (1999: 119) and that there 'is nothing that improves upon the ethnographic method for drawing out and drawing into relationship the thoughts and feelings of the invisible and unheard people of these regions, whom anthropology seeks to make visible and heard – to "write" – in its capacity as a counter-hegemonic practice' (Battaglia 1999: 119). In contrast, Trouillot observes that ethnography 'matters more in the world of the ethnographer than in the world that it supposedly describes' (2003:132). Through chatting, this chapter presents analysis from within the 'field' (such that ethnographic and academic shores converge upon each other), questions the privileging of ethnographic authority in counter-hegemonic practices, and critiques the ethnographer as interpreter who might be able to say more about 'others' than they themselves can. The ethnographer-performers here emerge as individual voices in heterophonic debates (simultaneous, many sounding, each voice rendering its articulation in its own time), and it is in heterophony that I find chatting-listening-responding such a useful model. The form of chatting allows a narrative unfolding of voices, but my intention is that they should be imagined as a simultaneous expression (they were written in this way) – a heterophonic texture that an edited text does not easily reproduce. It is in heterophony that I would claim a space for ethnographic writings: as voices in a chorus of many, where the debates do not have to be presented in unison or in harmony, where a statement does not require a response, where someone does not need to be spoken for, where the listener can shift attention from one articulation to another.

While ethnography can certainly be a counter-hegemonic practice, particularly as a tool in what has become known as 'engaged' scholarship, it does not always escape the assumptions of prevailing hegemonies. Indeed, in its origins as a descriptive tool for the administration and exploration of 'others', and in its persistence in creating 'others' and labelling 'cultures', we find ethnography as an agent in the establishment of those hegemonies. To claim too much for ethnography as a counter-hegemonic practice, therefore, without acknowledging a multitude of such practices is to diminish the political capacities of ethnographic writing. Counter-hegemonic practice lies in those radical alternatives that take us out of familiar understandings and we can find examples in performance as well as in ethnography. I began with Sheldon Blackman's 'Love Bomb'. Another excellent example from the world of musical performance lies in the songs of Bob Marley, articulator of the political philosophy of Marcus Garvey. He became a global icon in singing about resistance to the politics of oppression. His legacy in different locations highlights the ways in which a genre identified as 'Jamaican' is mediated locally and globally. His counter-hegemonic practice offers perspectives on the tenets of ethnography.

'Chatting': Bob Marley and his Legacy

In 1979, Vivien Goldman remarked to Bob Marley that his new tunes were becoming more direct and militant. She was interviewing Marley in New Kingston for an article that would appear in the magazine *Melody Maker*. Bob Marley responded:

> Sometimes you have to fight with music. So it's not just someone who studies and chats, it's a whole development. Right now is a more militant time on earth, because it's Jah Jah time. But me always militant you know. Me *too* militant. (Marley, cited in Goldman 1997 [1979]: 40)

Marley's lyrics, dealing with oppression and injustice, were shaped by the political philosophy of Marcus Garvey (1887–1940) who promoted pan-Africanism, established the United Negro Improvement Association in the USA in 1917, believed in 'redemption through repatriation' for Africans in exile and prophesied the crowning of a king in Africa. For Garvey's followers, the prophecy seemed to be realised in the crowning of Ras Tafari Mekonnen as Haile Selassie I, Emperor of Ethiopia. The Rastafarian movement was born, with its adherents viewing Haile Selassie as the Conquering Lion of the tribe of Judah (in resisting Mussolini's advances) and themselves as captives in Babylon looking to a homeland in Zion (Ethiopia). Lyrics such as: 'get up, stand up, stand up for your rights', 'rebel, rebel, Babylon system is a vampire', 'free yourself from mental slavery', 'iron, lion, Zion', 'Africa unite' express the politics of freedom struggles, the pan-African political philosophies of Garvey and the religious beliefs of Rastafarians. They have also had a much broader impact on popular music in the global market, speaking of resistance and justice to diverse audiences.

It is worth bearing in mind Marley's self-assessment as being militant given that, as Cooper notes, revisionist readings of his work in Jamaica have focused on the 'One Love' message: 'These days it is easy to forget the blood-and-fire, lightning-thunder-and-brimstone Bob Marley. The revolutionary Tuff Gong Rastaman has been commodified and repackaged as our "One Love" apologist for the Jamaican tourist industry' (Cooper 2004: 179–80). Becoming the global symbol of 'conscious' reggae has resulted in an ideological divide between reggae and its offspring, dancehall, to the extent that Cooper suggests 'we must rehumanize Bob Marley by taking him off the pedestal on which he has been firmly fixed and thus made inaccessible to the present generation of ghetto youth at ground level' (2004: 19).

In an assessment of Marley as a 'world' musician, Gilroy asks:

> Do people connect themselves and their hopes with the figure of Bob Marley as a man, a Jamaican, a Caribbean, an African, or a Pan-African artist? Is he somehow all of the above and more, a rebel voice of the poor and the underdeveloped world that made itself audible in the core of overdeveloped social and economic life he called Babylon? (2000: 132)

The latter question seems to come closest in looking at his legacy in contemporary musical practices. If Marley's reggae has been stripped off its militant Ethiopianism, the messages of justice and peace have continued to provide models for diverse groups beyond Jamaica, such as the Australian Yothu Yindi, the Serbian Eyesburn, the Russian ДЖАнгл (JAHngle), and reggae musicians and groups in various parts of Africa.

The 'rebel voice' singing messages of 'One Love' has been interpreted in different ways. Malm and Sarstad (1997) found that reggae, ragga and rap were heard in the East African centres of Nairobi (Kenya), Dar es Salaam (Tanzania) and Lusaka (Zambia) despite the emphasis on media transmission of local musical genres. Kenyan musicians cite Bob Marley as an important influence, even if, like Titi Solomon and his band Jami Moja, they disapprove of the demand in clubs for the 'Bob Marley' sound. The band Them Mushrooms, included the first reggae song recorded in East Africa in their 1981 album (*Mama Afrika*, CBS Kenya Records). Their reggae performances did not achieve any wide success until they began to introduce local music styles like benga. Them Mushrooms laid the foundations for the popularity of reggae with the 'reggae on benga' songs that they began performing in the mid 1980s. Kenyan musicians have also taken into account more recent Jamaican musical styles. Jah-Mbo Rebels Band, for example, use Jamaican dancehall tapes to learn Jamaican patois, which they use in their song texts alongside Swahili.

The reggae scene of Dar es Salaam has been shaped by nostalgia for Jamaica since a Jamaican promoter, Ras T, has been pivotal in organising reggae concerts in memory of Bob Marley. But this is not Bob Marley interpreted as the bearer of a universal or at least pan-African message. As in Nairobi, reggae musicians in Tanzania stress the local variants and specificities of their practice. Ras Inno states that his reggae music 'sounds different from Jamaican reggae and European reggae, even different from South African kind of reggae. If you listen to my songs they have something Tanzanian in them' (Ras Inno, cited in Malm and Sarstad 1997).

Ras Inno's views about Tanzanian reggae can be compared with the contrasting claim of a pan-African musical expression. Ras Pompidou, for example, claimed: 'A lot of people wondered what is the style [ragga] this guy is playing. They don't know that this style comes from Africa, from tradition' (Ras Pompidou, cited in Malm and Sarstad 1997). Jah Kimbute spoke about his reggae music in terms of both pan-African and local expressions:

> my music is black music. It has an influence of all black sounds.... There is a line of jazz in my music to put more flesh on the music. You can get the soul feeling in my music. There is a traditional touch in my music. I just try to blend. I find it hard to come out with just something like.... This is Tanzania and it should be like any popular style. (Jah Kimbute, cited in Malm and Sarstad 1997)

In Zambia, reggae has had a large following since the 1970s and since 1983 a Bob Marley memorial concert has been held annually. DJ Mike Tabor noted:

> Bob Marley is kind of a semi-god in Zambia. His following cuts across class, occupational, regional and tribal lines. Anywhere you go in Zambia you will hear Bob Marley. A lot of people in Zambia have a moral philosophy and also political ideas that derive from Bob Marley's songs. (Mike Tabor, cited in Malm and Sarstad 1997)

There's a 'listening-in-writing and a writing-in-listening', observes Bharucha (2003: 2), and as I write this chapter I am listening to one CD over and over again. The title of the album is *Reggae Around the World* (Putumayo 1998). There's an Australian Aboriginal band that was formed in 1986 in the Northern Territory town of Barunga, called Blekbala Mujik. A track of a song they recorded ('Drang-kinbala') features on the CD. It is about the creation of the world and it features a didgeridu in a sonic texturing of cosmological, historical and revolutionary themes. It is followed by tracks that tune us into reggae in Brazil, Sudan, Mali and Nigeria. We end up with Peter Rowan's 'country' version of Bob Marley's 'No Woman, No Cry'. There's an instrumental interlude with a display of virtuoso pizzicato (plucked strings) technique on the fiddle, played by Mark O'Connor. What intrigues me about this recording is the interplay between the local and the global and between musical styles: a Jamaican genre performed and recorded far beyond the Caribbean island space. If the reggae of Bob Marley has come to be identified as one of the most recognisable Jamaican sounds, the island's soundscapes provide insights into the wide circulation of music and musicians connecting the Caribbean with other parts of the world. Musical performance in circulation constantly prompts us to reconsider the ways in which we try to contain music within geographic, cultural and political borders, within 'ethnic' groups, and within styles and genres. Perhaps the creative processes involved in producing reggae might not be confined by attending political discourses of adding something described as 'Kenyan', or 'Tanzanian', or 'country'. Witmer's analysis of written historical sources shows that from the late nineteenth century to the independence and national movements of the 1950s, the urban popular music in Kingston was closely connected with theatre orchestras playing for North American silent films and with military wind bands that were trained by European bandmasters. Radio programmes of Trinidadian calypsos and classical music were amongst the most popular in the mid 1950s. Thereafter, Jamaican popular music saw the emergence of genres that were to be identified as local: ska, rocksteady and reggae that must have had their origins in undocumented traditional styles that ran in parallel to documented urban popular genres and that connect the island's soundscapes with those of Africa (Witmer 1987). These historical soundscapes tell us something about creative processes in contemporary political and ethnographic soundscapes.

'LISTENING 1': WAYNE MARSHALL

I first travelled to Jamaica in the fall of 2001 as part of a team organised by Harvard Law School to observe a rehabilitation program in Kingston's prisons. Asked to play the role of 'musicological consultant', I eagerly boarded a plane that took me to Norman Manley Airport, where we were picked up by a bus and driven straight into Tower Street, aka GP, or General Penitentiary – Kingston's largest, most overcrowded and most violent prison. It was a unique introduction to Jamaican society and culture, fi true. As I sat in the van and looked around, I saw men in mesh-marinas milling about, smoking ganja, and looking just as curiously at me. We were treated that morning to a concert put on by a group of inmates who had earned themselves distinction as men devoted to the rehabilitation process and as accomplished musicians. A band comprising a drummer, bassist, guitarist, and keyboardist accompanied various singers and groups who performed in the vast array of styles that fill Jamaica's soundscape: roots reggae, dancehall, gospel, R&B, pop, rock, dub poetry, Rastafarian chants, syrupy ballads and various hybrids. Introducing the rehabilitation program to a bunch of (presumably resource-rich) foreigners through music was clearly an explicit, and effective, strategy. I felt like yet another tourist being seduced by Jamaica's music, and in spite of my critical proclivities I found myself admiring the expression and emotion of the performances, even when a voice went out of tune or a Paul Simon cover failed to impress.

It was not the music at Tower Street, however, that drew me into what would become a serious engagement with Jamaican culture and society. It was the hip-hop playing in cars, clubs, and just about everywhere I turned. As someone with his ears tuned to hip-hop's global resonance, I was struck by the music's ubiquity in the land where reggae is king. I was introduced to a young producer named Makonnen who, before I left, handed me a CD containing 'underground' recordings by young Kingstonians who rapped in patois over the latest hip-hop beats – some of which had only been released in the US the week before. The CD also featured a number of songs by an upcoming DJ named Wayne Marshall, which explained why the customs officials were laughing at my passport. My namesake had been making a name for himself by recording witty, localised versions of popular hip-hop tracks. I laughed at his translation of Ludacris's 'Area Codes,' which substituted Jamaican phone numbers for American ones, and my head spun at the rapidity of circulation and the possibilities for appropriation and identification presented by hip-hop's reception in Jamaica.

Shortly thereafter, I abandoned 'hip-hop in Germany' as a dissertation topic for 'hip-hop in Jamaica' and set about getting up to speed with the world of Jamaican music. Fortunately, I had a lifetime of encounters with reggae to provide me with reference points as I began to wade through the dense reggae literature, so full of names and dates and 'big chunes' that I had never heard of. I *had* heard of Bob Marley, of course, and the usual roots suspects: Toots and the Maytals, Jimmy Cliff (via *The Harder They Come*), Burning Spear, Black Uhuru, and so on. I had heard or heard of many of these acts through their regular tour-stops in Boston. I had been turned off, however, by a Jimmy Cliff concert where the audience of drunk, white yuppies went wild for a less-than-rousing cover of 'Hakuna Matata' from *The Lion King*. Of course, I revered Bob Marley as much as any music-lover, though my acquaintance with his work did not extend much beyond the *Legend* compilation. My familiarity with reggae was much stronger when it came to dancehall. I remembered fondly our high school dances at Cambridge Rindge and Latin, where the student DJs inevitably segued from R&B and hip-hop to dancehall at a certain point in the evening. As Mad Cobra's 'Flex' or Chaka Demus's and Pliers's 'Murder She Wrote' blasted across the cafeteria, my peers transformed into a mass of gyrating bodies, winin' and grindin' like they knew they were supposed to when reggae came on. As a devotee of hip-hop, I knew Shabba and Super Cat, having seen their videos during BET's 'Rap City' and 'Yo! MTV Raps'. From the occasional coverage of contemporary dancehall in hip-hop magazines, I knew that Beenie Man and Bounty Killer were the big men of latter-day dancehall. And as I reached back further into memory, I became more and more aware of how much reggae had infused hip-hop over the years. I remembered the patois stylings of KRS-One, Special Ed, Shinehead, Das EFX, Fu-Schnickens, Smif'n'Wessun, and many more. The deeper I dug into Jamaican music, the more I realised that the links between hip-hop and reggae ran deep – deeper than Kool Herc's translation of sound-system style for his Bronx peers, deeper than the early 1990s crossover moment, and deeper than the latest Stateside successes of Shaggy and Sean Paul. I decided that Jamaica would make at least as interesting a place to study hip-hop outside the US as Germany, and I made plans to spend some time there as soon as I could finish my coursework and take my exams.

The following summer, I returned to Kingston to spend a month conducting 'preliminary research'. I arranged to live with Makonnen and his mother, sleeping on a couch in the small room he used as a home studio. We were visited daily by a number of DJs and singers who came over to vibe with Mak's beats, to hear the latest hip-hop he had downloaded, and to record demo versions of their latest tunes. In this way I met several young Kingstonians who had devoted their lives to music and who had grown up as much with Tupac and Biggie as with Beenie and Bounty, never mind Bob. My entry into this scene was greatly facilitated by my ability to build reggae riddims and hip-hop beats, which I had been doing for the previous five years, and to rap, which I had been doing since about age 13. On many occasions I watched as my rapping worked a kind of social alchemy. It was clear that by rapping in what seemed to Jamaican observers to be an 'authentic' and 'original' manner that I was able to demonstrate a depth of engagement – not to mention cultural cachet, since many of these young men attempted, in vain, to sound like an American rapper – that immediately changed people's perceptions of me. 'The man sound real,' was a common response to one of my tirades of rhythmically-right-on syllables.

By rapping and producing riddims with Jamaican artists, I developed relationships that no mere observer could ever develop. Although I was often dismayed by my new collaborators' affinity for lyrics that focused on violence, conspicuous consumption, and objectification of women, I attempted to meet them on their own terms, showing by example rather than passing judgment, and maintaining in my own lyrics the critical-comical, self-reflective stance that I learned from 'Golden Age' hip-hop. In some ways, I had less to prove as a white American rapper than these youths did as black Jamaican rappers. To many, it seemed more incongruous, and perhaps inauthentic, for them to be rapping in a Brooklyn accent than for me to be rapping at all. (I had not yet picked up enough patois to bother the purists, perhaps.) As an ethnographer, I had been steadily recording my collaborators' tastes and 'influences,' which were utterly catholic: from Bob Marley, of course (always first, even if not really an audible presence in contemporary Kingston), to Nat King Cole, Nas, Celine Dion, Admiral Bailey, and just about any other pop, rap or reggae artist you could name. For most Jamaicans, such an ecumenical approach to music comes rather easily – just flip the radio dial to behold a musical diversity unheard on the corporate-consolidated radio of the US. At times, however, people draw stark lines of community around sound and sentiment. I witnessed these tensions firsthand when, along with Makonnen and a musician named Kazam, I visited the house of Buju Banton and participated in the following exchange, which I recorded in my blog (thus the lower-case letters, which I employ to differentiate my blogs from other forms of writing):

> whereas mak was deep into hip-hop, kazam played guitar and spoke glowingly of sam cooke, nat king cole, whitney houston, and shakira. at one point, i was standing on the porch while kazam played guitar. buju, his back toward us, ate dinner. kazam got his courage up, made his quiet strumming more audible, and began to sing a song he had written. (he told me later that he had walked past buju's place many times as a youth and vowed that one day he would go in and sing for the dj.) when kazam finished the song, buju, who had yet to turn around, addressed him:
>
> *buju*: 'who are your influences?'
> *kazam*: 'influences?'
> *wayne*: 'that's the same question i asked him.'
> *buju*: [turning] 'that's the same question you asked him?' ... [to kazam] 'you sound like a white punk-rocker. who you like? green day?'
> *kazam*: 'i like everything. bob marley first.'
> *buju*: 'you sound like you're from southern california.'
> *wayne*: 'if he sounds like a white punk-rocker from california and makonnen sounds like a puerto-rican rapper from the bronx, what do you make of that?'
> *buju*: 'i'd say they're both pretty strange.'
>
> kazam was pretty devastated by the exchange and i was pretty annoyed at buju's lack of kindness. kazam muttered to himself for a while, including such phrases as, 'music has color. yeah.' i did my best to convince him that he'd laugh about it someday.

What most struck me about this exchange was the way that music could so powerfully represent one's community relationships. While Kazam sought to express a kind of universalism, no doubt inspired by Bob Marley, Buju sought to police the boundaries of Jamaican expression, invoking a racialised norm from which, at least in Buju's mind, Kazam and Mak both departed. From my perspective, the rift seemed to run along generational lines, with Jamaica's 'hip-hop generation' embracing sounds and styles that, while foreign for older Jamaicans, constituted a familiar and compelling set of resources for the expression of a new kind of Jamaican-ness, one that did not abandon a stance of 'modern blackness,' as Deborah Thomas puts it, but expanded it through trans-national articulations of sameness. Having developed these relationships in the late summer of 2002, I returned in January of 2003 and spent a solid six months living on Hope Road (just a few blocks from the overly commodified Marley museum, which I could never bring myself to visit), where I turned my apartment into a recording studio and invited my friends over for recording sessions. Here we would negotiate the very sonic signifiers that seemed to connote such things as Jamaican-ness and American-ness, blackness and whiteness, reggae and hip-hop, a 'local' sound and an 'international' sound. I attempted to observe as I participated and, as a good producer, to do my best to realise my collaborators' visions even as I attempted to bring my own creative and critical ideas to bear on our co-productions. I produced gal tunes and gun tunes, weed tunes and reality tunes, party songs and Rasta manifestos. And when it was time to collect all of these together, I presented the tunes alongside interview segments with the same artists, songs of my own that I composed upon returning to the US and reflecting on my experiences, and collages composed from recordings of Jamaica's varied soundscape, making riddim-centric compositions out of stray dogs, taxi transmissions, radio fragments, waterfalls, crickets, and cocks. I invested hours and hours into making my collaborators sound as good as I could, and I attempted to make the riddims signify on the songs: a badman tune with a Spaghetti-Western backdrop, an ode to conspicuous consumption over beats that bling-bling with shiny timbres. In my own songs, I attempted to make jokes and wry observations about Jamaican mores, from fundamentalist Christianity to homophobia to the national love of KFC. I called the album *Boston Jerk* to pun on a Jamaican phrase and acknowledge my position as a critical outsider. When I shared the final product with my collaborators, I was relieved that they and their friends not only approved of the project but were surprised and impressed by its scope. They were, of course, also hopeful that it would bring them some recognition, some opportunities to advance their careers, and some shot at the mobility so sought after by so many Jamaicans.

Outside of Jamaica, the response to *Boston Jerk* has been more varied. I have witnessed, on the one hand, how the sound of Jamaican voices and dancehall riddims carry an aura of authenticity outside of Jamaica that is practically unrivalled by any other 'national' music. Hip-hop heads dig it. Jungle DJs flip for it. World music enthusiasts find the syncopations and exotic sounds they seek. In a kind of funhouse-mirror manner, considering how my performance of (African-)American-ness worked wonders in Jamaica, I have accrued a kind of cultural cachet back home based on my ability to perform Jamaican-ness. I have connected my collaborators to reggae selectors and record-label owners in the Boston area, who enjoyed the Boston-Kingston link-up and have helped to spread their names and their music. Having put the music, and a large amount of reflective text about it, on the Internet, I have been contacted by delighted listeners from England, Germany, Australia and other far-flung spots with a love for reggae and hip-hop. I have also, however, encountered occasional resistance from certain reggae lovers – almost always non-Jamaicans – who disdain what they hear as an irreverent or impure version of the music they elevate to righteous heights. For me, they represent yet another audience whose assumptions I seek to challenge. Still, I am often struck by the irony of such a position. Anyone who spends a little time in Jamaica today should realise that it has little regard for such conceptions of purity, despite the roots'n'culture emphasis on Ital living.

When it comes to music (and media of all sorts), Jamaica is one of the most omnivorous places in the world. This is not to say that boundaries are not important – and my musical collaborations and academic investigations continue to explore the way music draws the lines of community in Jamaica. But I am as likely to return from Jamaica with mixtapes of the latest R&B and hip-hop hits as dancehall tunes. And young artists continue to record their patois-patter over the latest hip-hop beats in order to capture the imaginations of their peers in Jamaica and, they hope, their peers overseas. Kinda like Bob Marley singing like Curtis Mayfield over some James Brown-inspired roots riddims, innit? Or the Skatalites versioning Johnny Cash with their jazz-derived chops, see me a say? Or Welton Irie versioning the Sugar Hill Gang's 'Rapper's Delight' only months after it brought recorded rap to the world, you see me? Or Boogie Down Productions representing the Bronx to the fullest through thick patois and borrowed melodies from the day's dancehall hits, you knomesayin'? Or Chinese-American rapper Jin resignifying Yellowman's 'Mr Chin' while Haitian-American producer Wyclef tells us we're gonna 'Learn Chinese' or dem a go 'shot the bloodclaat,' knamean? Or some Boston Jerk rapping in patois and 'acting Jamaican' in order to raise the question of what that means and how music makes it mean, seen?

'LISTENING 2': ALEXANDER D. GREAT

Calypso was something I heard very early in my life. I was born in Trinidad and lived in Jamaica from the age of six months until I was two and a half. I returned to Trinidad, thence to England. However, between the ages of three and five I was sent to live with my paternal grandmother in Germany while my parents did postgraduate studies in London.

I remember my father singing folk songs and Jamaican mentos like 'Linstead Market', 'Fan Me Soldier Man Fan Me', 'Hill And Gully Ride – oh, Hol' im Joe', also calypsos from Trinidad like 'Matilda' and Roaring Lion's 'Ugly Woman' which were hugely popular and sung by both my parents and friends who came to the house. Certainly by the time I was six or seven I was well aware of the music and loved it. I heard 'Jean and Dinah', Sparrow's brilliant but vengeful attack on prostitutes and the American presence in Trinidad throughout the 1940s and 1950s. In England, Lord Kitchener made me sit up and take notice with 'Doctor Kitch', the wittiest rude record I had heard up till then. In 1957 some visiting relative brought the calypso album of that year with them which contained 'Carnival Boycott' by Mighty Sparrow. Even at the age of nine I knew there was something special about that calypso, not only its great melody but also its anger. I did not realise it at the time but I had heard my first protest song, long before I got into James Brown, Aretha Franklin, John Lennon, Bob Dylan, Stevie Wonder, Nina Simone or Bob Marley.

'Carnival Boycott' concerns Sparrow's refusal to sing at Carnival in 1957 because of the measly prize money given to the Calypso Monarch and the winning steel band, as compared to the new car and fat cheque presented to the Carnival Queen. (Until the 1960s this was always a white or very light-skinned girl from the upper middle class.) In the last chorus he changes the third and fourth lines to 'Let the queen run the show, Wid she fridge and she radio'. This was heady stuff to a nine-year-old who thought the queen being referred to was Elizabeth II. I was intrigued and excited by this Mighty Sparrow who could snub the Queen in a song.

My father had a younger brother and sister, then in their early twenties, who lived with my grandmother in Gottingen, about an hour's drive from Hanover. My aunt and uncle were both fairly good pianists and played Mozart, Haydn and Scarlatti sonatas. They were also very fond of Baroque music and put the radio on in the evenings to listen to Handel, Bach or Purcell. In addition they had what they called 'Italian Musical Evenings' which involved one or two friends coming round with violin or clarinet for a meal and an evening of live music. Apart from the two years I spent there as a toddler I went back several times for summer holidays and these musical evenings awakened a strong desire in me to play the piano.

I grew up in England, not taking much interest in popular music (which was Tommy Steele and Alma Cogan) until The Shadows came along. I liked the way they all moved the guitars up and down together and the sound of the tremolo and echo boxes but Cliff Richard left me cold. Then in 1963 The Beatles arrived, self-made, *senza* strings and lush orchestras, gritty and with outlandish harmonies in 4ths and high quasi-ululations (learnt from Little Richard) and I was forever hooked. A few months after hearing The Beatles' and Rolling Stones' first albums, Booker T. and the MGs LP *Green Onions* tipped me over the edge and made me a disciple (and later exponent) of 'the devil's music'. From the age of 13 I began to listen to Ray Charles, Chuck Berry, Buddy Holly (who sang Berry's 'Brown-eyed Handsome Man') and Bo

Diddley. Bo Diddley's songs used a beat that sounded like a mix of soca and Rhythm 'n' Blues, which Holly used in 'Not Fade Away', later a big hit for The Rolling Stones. Both my parents fed my interest in the Blues and Jazz, my father introducing me to Sonny Boy Williamson, Little Walter, Sonny Terry and Brownie McGhee, Etta James, Sister Rosetta Tharpe, Howlin' Wolf et al., while my mother sang songs by Gershwin, Verdi and Ellington with equal brilliance. It seems funny now, but my Black Caribbean mum sang classical and American music and my German dad sang calypso and mento as well as folk songs from around the world. Between the ages of eight and twelve I had classical piano lessons but did not understand theory. I hated practising but liked exploring different sounds on the piano, without knowing what I was looking for.

Like many West Indians, my parents let a room out for a while to people who came to study or find work. One of these who stayed with us for about three years was a calypso singer. He sang all the good calypsos around at that time by Melody, Sparrow, Cristo and Kitchener. He also taught me a couple of chords on his guitar. Another Irish folk singer friend of the family taught me a couple of other chords and I began to try singing songs like 'Down by the Riverside' and 'Amazing Grace' as well as Sparrow's 'Sailorman' and Melody's 'Mama Look a BooBoo deh'.

When I left school, Motown and Stax soul were all the rage. I had formed a band at school and we set out to conquer the world. I became the keyboard player and ceased playing guitar on stage for 30 years. I spent the first ten years of my professional life as a gigging/session musician, touring America once and Europe several times with a variety of different artists and bands. I was also involved in several original band projects of a bluesy/jazzy/ rock nature. I made various recordings with several bands writing our own stuff but without commercial success. By my mid twenties I felt a desire to learn as much about formal music as I could and went to college, first to the West London Institute and then to Dartington in Devon.

Apart from writing a Boney M style sort of Euro-Caribbean song, which became a single release in 1979 for RCA in Germany,

I did not record any calypsos until 1994 when cricketer Brian Lara broke two world records in the same month. My sister said we should write a calypso to celebrate the event and the result was 'Lash Dem Lara'. In 1995 I went to Trinidad (where incidentally there were 34 other calypsos about Lara) and sang it on stage and TV at the Carnival. From then I never looked back and decided that I would go right back to my roots. I went to see DJ Martin Jay, who did a calypso/soca show on Choice FM and we devised a weekly slot for me to do a song. This ran for over two years with me singing about any current news subject I liked. In February 2000 I began doing the same thing for the BBC.

In 1997 I formed a record label to record my own brand of calypso, which I call SocaBlues. I wanted the name to suggest soca, with conscious subject matter, but also more complex and interesting chord progressions and arrangements. When funds allow I tour with a nine-piece band, consisting of guitar, bass, drums, steelpan, percussion, keyboards, and three brass, trumpet, sax and trombone. Ideally, I would like a larger brass section, at least one more trumpet, but the tight finances in the calypso arena in Britain means that three horns are the norm.

All my arrangements are handwritten in short score (see Figure 2.1, pp. 58–60 for the handwritten and printed versions), one stave for trumpet and tenor sax (already transposed up a tone), one for trombone, one for the vocal line and one for bass. Chord symbols are written over the bass part. Until about ten years ago I have always written out the parts by hand. As I usually arrange when I am fresh and tend to do the copying late at night when I am tired, I minimise possible mistakes in transposition later on, by doing it at the beginning as I arrange. My brass lines are almost always in harmony. Unison lines sound good used sparingly and for effect, but to give three instruments the same lines to play all through a song seems to me a waste of resources. Many soca arrangers do this either out of laziness or because they do not know how to arrange and do all their stuff on synthesisers, where many brass samples are blocks of unisons. The brass should not obscure the vocals so I generally have them doing answering phrases in the gaps (bars 48 and 62). In bar 60 where the brass doubles the vocal line they are all in unison for a moment. My favourite voicing consists of the trumpet at the top, playing the prominent line, with the tenor a 6th below and the trombone a 5th below that. This creates a warm but powerful sound. Writing in thirds with the trumpet only works in lower ranges because the tenor's highest note is E flat a 10th above Middle C and tenor players do not like to spend all their time playing up in the rafters pretending to be 2nd trumpets.

My musical style is influenced firstly by the Baroque, particularly Bach and Handel. This shows up most in my contrapuntal arrangements and bass lines ('Monsanto's Law' and 'Black On Black' – the latter written for 2003 UK Calypso Monarch Sister Sandra). Second, classic calypso, particularly Kitchener and Sparrow with their excellent brass arrangements, has shaped my style. Motown, Earth, Wind and Fire, Steely Dan – these have all had a strong effect on my arrangement ideas.

Many years ago I read that David Geffen, manager of The Eagles, had told the band members not to be influenced by any other artists, to lock themselves away, watch no TV and listen to no radio – just write. To an extent that is an approach I have taken. I admire other calypsonians' work, particularly David Rudder's and Shadow's, but I never try to copy their style. When I was in Trinidad during the 1990s I would call on Roaring Lion, Kitchener and Chalkdust to pay my respects and talk but rarely to swap ideas on composition. The Roaring Lion told me (in 1993) that to be a great calypsonian you had to have Shakespeare, Milton, Byron, Tennyson, Wilde and T. S. Eliot under your belt as well as knowledge of all the great French dramatists. Bob Marley, too, had an influence on my thinking and choice of subject matter in terms of black consciousness.

Notes on the 'Afrika Suite'. On my *Panorama Attack* album, four songs comprise the 'Afrika Suite'. Although the suite is a European Baroque device for linking dance movements to make a satisfactory large scale work, it seemed appropriate to use it to have my say on things African. I do, after all, have a foot in both camps (according to one of my uncles, a lawyer in Trinidad who has extensively researched the family tree, we are descended from a Foulani slave from Mali). I use different rhyme schemes in each song. The first song, 'Wake Up Afrika', is a plea to Africans to give up fighting amongst themselves thereby playing straight into the hands of imperialists who would divide them and rule.

> (Chorus) Wake up Afrika,
> No more eye for and eye
> No more tooth for a tooth
> It's time to face the truth.
> Wake up Afrika
> Spread your wings, you can fly
> Cease the war and the strife
> And wake up to your life.

The murder in Nigeria of griot and human rights activist Ken Saro-Wiwa by Sani Abacha sparked the second song, 'Prayer for Nigeria'.

> (Chorus) Say a prayer for Nigeria,
> A country where life is considered inferior
> To the oil and the cash
> Which the politicians stash
> So the land which once was rich
> Is just a shell
> It's a living hell
> Say a prayer for Nigeria.

'Heart of Afrika' was my response to the news of an exhibition of African art at the National Gallery in London. I felt it was ironic that Black people should be paying to go and see Benin royal masks in the land that had stolen them. The verse scheme is simply two pairs of rhymed lines followed by a chorus where all the line endings are to the sound of 'er' or 'a' which sound the same.

> (Verse 1) National Gallery been playing its part
> Putting on a show of Afrikan art.
> Our forefathers sweat produced what we see
> Yet we stand in line paying money.

(Chorus) Bring back the heart of Afrika
Give back the art, which belongs to her.
Bring back the soul of Afrika
The wealth they stole she must recover
Re-light the flame of Afrika
Let us reclaim the diaspora
Bring back the art, which has gone so far
Bring back the heart of Afrika.

'Amandla Mandela' was actually the first of the suite to be written (commissioned by the BBC for Mandela's visit to Britain in 1996) and was first sung outside the Roxy in Brixton with a crowd of Mandela well-wishers. The last part of the chorus is my own take on the African Anthem 'Nkosi Tsikileli Afrika'. The chorus is pairs of rhymes but the verse is in a deliberate pattern, which rhymes line 1 with line 4, lines 2 and 3, and lines 5 and 6. The assonance of 'Mandela' and 'together' is a ploy to make the hearer believe there is a 'half-rhyme' technique being used, although this is not the case.

(Verse 1) The Queen of England has met with Nelson Mandela
They shook hands together
To signify there's a change in the weather.
This man spent a third of his life in a cellar
With stale food and water
While South Africa was a welter of slaughter.

(Chorus) Nelson... when you came before
They make you stand by the door,
Now that you have come so far
They're treating you like a star
But Nelson... with all that they do
There is no bitterness in you,
You keep your faith with who you are
Nkosi tsikilele Afrika.

Amandla Mandela
Nkosi Tsikilele Afrika (3 times).

'LISTENING 3': W. A. HENRY

Giving voices to the voiceless: an 'insider' perspective on ethnographic writing

> We are the best ones to deal with Reggae because we are what the music is about and I am writing a book on it myself. Cos when I read some of the stuff that has been written, chuh. When we were out there chatting all over the place, trying to uplift the youths, the press and them people deh was not interested in what we had to say. In fact nuff of them were fraid fi come ah dance fi see what did ah gwaan, which is why them used to write and chat so much rubbish bout we ah thief, murderer and criminal. Or just chat about the eediot one them (Deejays) who weren't saying nut'n. (Asher Senator, cited in Henry 2006: 84)

The above reasoning from one of Britain's premier Reggae Dancehall DJs, Asher Senator, captures the ethos behind why I deem it necessary to offer an alternative insight into the culture, from an 'insider' perspective. An insight that makes known how black youth during the mid 1970s to the late 1980s, documented and articulated their experiences of racial discrimination in a unique and highly intelligent fashion. By recovering this aspect of British Black oral history I generate a new empirical discussion about identity formations around recognisably Black cultural forms, which provide a mechanism for coping with the multiple and ever-present forms of popular racism. For this reason in my work I present detailed accounts of what happens within a space where those that are excluded from a public sphere which renders them voiceless, do in fact engage in discussions that concern very public issues from an alternative black perspective. These discussions and articulations are voiced within the unique cultural sphere of the Reggae Dancehall event that provides an autonomous space for a counter narrative to be forthcoming. Therefore the Reggae Dancehall becomes a site where ordinary people get to air and discuss their innermost concerns and engage in cultural and political dialogue publicly, without fear of reprisal and sanction. It is a site that not only features the voices of the voiceless, but equally provides an amplified 'public' platform for them to articulate their oppression.

The reason why I document and disseminate the worth, role and purpose of this manifestation of Jamaican expressive culture in the UK context is linked to the fact that I was born in Britain of Jamaican parentage and have never felt like I belonged to Britain. I felt like Black youth were excluded from engaging in any meaningful dialogue with the people who seemed to want to control our thoughts and actions, without perhaps appreciating that for us they represented an enemy presence. Hence the spaces within which I could really discuss the reality of being Black in Britain with others who shared a similar outlook on the experiences of being discriminated against were in fact the Reggae Dancehalls where I used to DJ and also be exposed to the lyricism of other DJs. Furthermore, for as long as I can remember my main source of an alternative identity has come from black music, especially Reggae music and the messages that chant down Babylon and extol the virtues of Rastafari livity (all aspects of everyday being). Simply put, by embracing an alternative idea of what it means to be black in a white world where you have a history that is meaningful and uplifting, I gained a sense of belonging and community which countered the exclusion I felt from white society in Britain. Therefore, once I began my studies as a mature student at university I decided to analyse the lyricism of the DJs as a way to research and map an alternative history of the Black British experience that had a 'sound' empirical base. Of equal importance I wanted to offer a corrective to much that was written about a cultural form that was responsible for keeping me in tune with what was going on in the black communities in the UK, Jamaica and other places across the Afrikan Diaspora. I make this claim because as a DJ who has read much of the material written about this verbal art, I find it difficult to recognise myself in many of these accounts. More importantly my philosophy is that if you see a problem and you have the tools to fix it then do so, which is what I hope I have achieved in my writings on the seminal role that Jamaican culture and Reggae music played in the formation of this form of black cultural expression in the UK.

One main failing with many of these accounts was the fact that they relied on recorded released material, which can never fully explain the profound influence Jamaican Sound Systems, their singers and DJs had on Black youth in the UK, North America and other parts of the globe. It is therefore my placement as a pioneering figure in the Reggae Dancehall scene in the UK, coupled with my knowledge of the live recordings that were known as Yard (Yard = Jamaican) or Session (tapes from Britain or the US) tapes that makes my contribution unique. In fact these recordings of the 'hidden voices' are crucial to my work as they contain the alternative perspective on what it meant to be Black in Britain and throughout the Diaspora, which details this alternative history of the Black experience from a grass-roots perspective. Therefore my methodological approach considers the practical worth of knowledges that are generated within the culture and uses them as conceptual tools to create bridges of meaning that enable me to stake my alternative claims. One reason for this is that many of these accounts are, as suggested above, written from the 'outside' by ethnographers who come into the field, gather their data over a given period of time and then leave the field once the project is completed. Therefore, I argue for an account that uses my knowledge and experience of the cultural form under consideration to demonstrate the validity of the observer position from the 'inside'. This is because it was the lyricism and rhythms of Jamaican performers in the first instance that inspired many Black youth in the UK to overstand their social predicament and more importantly do something about it. So when we heard tales of everyday life in Jamaica, such as how 'soldier tek over an ah curfew the area' in the lyricism of the late great DJ General Echo, it opened up a whole new world of appreciation for the vibes and inspiration we received from that small island in the Caribbean Sea. That is why it is necessary to appreciate all aspects of the culture from the inside because the loudest voices that seemingly have the most 'authority' are generally commenting from the outside.

Let me provide an example to make this point clearer. Bob Marley is universally known as the 'King' of Reggae and is generally associated with a 'One Love' mentality that filters his works significantly as he is packaged and repackaged to a global audience. Yet the Bob Marley that strengthened many of us during our youth was the hell-fire prophet who was just as much of a 'fire man' as the much vilified Capleton or Sizzla. Now the point is that for us he was not the 'King' of Reggae but another soldier in Jah army who recognised that his mission alongside Peter Tosh, Bunny Wailer and the I Threes, was to rise up and wise up the people. Especially Black people through the teaching and preaching of Rastafari fuelled by the power of His Majesty, Emperor Haile Selassie I, mediated through Marcus Garvey's prophetic words that we must 'emancipate ourselves from mental slavery for none but ourselves can free our minds'. I am not suggesting that Marley did not sing about love, but what has happened is that he has become reduced to this in the minds of many of his fans, which is why it is often suggested that Reggae music died when he died. Now whenever I hear such a claim I point out that Reggae music comes out of Jamaica and so did Bob Marley. A point that was made clear to me during a reasoning session I had with Jah Shaka and a Jamaican producer called Leggo, who when I challenged the idea of Bob Marley as the King of Reggae, he suggested:

> Many people call Bob the King because of record sales and don't understand why we in Jamaica call him the King. It was not just that he took our music to a global height and made people recognise what Jamaica has to offer the world. He never forgot where he came from. So whenever he returned to Jamaica he would bring back things for his people and just 'gi them weh' and mingle with the I them as an ordinary man. And that is why we call him the King. (Leggo, personal communication in London, 1999)

I am arguing that because I was socialised as an indigenous member of the black community, I have access to, and a greater understanding of, certain knowledges that an 'outsider' would not. Equally, by presenting the insider perspective that I bring to the academic table, I practically demonstrate the value of an ethnographer who can truly bridge the divide between theory and practice (Henry 2006).

'Response': The Struggle for 'One Love'

The practices of Boston Jerk rapping in patois to raise questions about what it means to be 'Jamaican', of Alexander D. Great composing a text dealing with themes of African political consciousness using the structure of European Baroque dance suites, and of W. A. Henry in bridging the divides between theory and performance, insider and outsider, provide examples of insurgency in musical creativity. They challenge stereotypes and preconceptions about what might be musically appropriate for musical agents. They raise questions about the politics of identity, mediating between the contradictions in thinking about a spectrum that ranges from the small-scale (that is, the individual) to the large-scale (that is, planetary humanism). Turning to Bob Marley and his legacy, to the testimonies of Boston Jerk and Alexander D. Great, I have been layering the performance spaces between shifting island, national, pan-African, pan-Black and global expressions of identity, and would like to add a further layer (in the counter-hegemonic practices of performance, ethnography, postcolonial discourses and oral histories) to think about the voice, power and representation in relation to 'One Love'.

It would be disingenuous to read ethnography only as a narrative form that privileges the author's interpretations. Ethnography usually depends on and includes statements of people in the 'field' context. These are selected and edited, of course, but they give us the possibility of reading voices other than the author's. The polyphonic dimensions of ethnographic narrative reveal power relations that have been examined in reflexive scrutiny of ethnographic production, raising issues of authority and voice that intersect with postcolonial discourses, oral history projects and performance lyricism in interesting ways. Postcolonial discourses, oral histories and lyricism – like ethnography – have emphasised the decentring or reinterpretation of dominant narratives to enable people who have been 'hidden' from accounts of 'history' to be 'heard'. In listening to people's stories and memories, postcolonial and oral history projects invite alternative readings of historical documents, reconsideration of 'history' and 'historical knowledge' and recognition that the everyday memories of people have historical and political importance.[3] This shift in attention to what is being said and who is saying it corresponds with a heterephonic approach to writing and reading ethnography as a medium that holds the potential to respond to calls for a postcolonial polyvocality, which allows narratives to be retold from different subject positions.

The decentring strategies of ethnography, oral histories, postcolonial discourses and lyricism share attempts to uncover different voices and layers of meaning. The interrogation and interpretation of different voices can lead, however, to very different conclusions, which is why W. A. Henry insists on bringing 'an insider perspective to the academic table'. Manuel (2000) and Stolzoff (2000), for example, dismiss the lyrics of chutney and dancehall respectively as containing little substance. In contrast, I have suggested (2001) that it is through musical lyricism that we find some of the most forceful political statements, that seemingly trivial lyrics (for example, 'Little Jack Horner sat in a corner' or 'I have a ragga dulahin') hold deep historical and political significances that are understood by their audiences. What does widespread familiarity with an English nursery rhyme tell us about musical life in colonial societies? What does the 'ragga dulahin' tell us about postcolonial social organisation? The lyrics of genres like reggae, rap, rapso, dub poetry, reggae poetry and calypso emphasise the capacity of oral tradition to interrogate history, to comment on society and to offer alternative political visions. The insurgency of lyricism, even in what might appear to be trivial, is recognised by performers. Members of the rapso group 3Canal talk about being 'soldiers' and the genre is described as 'the power of the word in de riddim of de word'. 3Canal describe themselves as a group with 'a mission to spread the power of the word, the message of Peace, Love and Possibility'. As one of 3Canal's members, Stanton Kewley, says, 'we are on a musical adventure and the Rapsoman's mission is to educate and entertain. We have the freedom to "make a statement", while "riding" a powerful infectious riddim' (www.3canal.com>, accessed 27 March 2005). Lloyd 'Bread' McDonald, a member of the duo

Wailing Souls (with Winston 'Pipe' Matthews), now living in the United States and practising reggae as an ongoing spiritual and political message, says:

> I definitely think of myself, and other Jamaican musicians, as warriors. We're soldiers, even now. You have a work to do, so you keep soldiering on... The music can change the politics. The music makes people more aware of what is going on outside. The music works on the soul. (Matthews, cited in Foehr 2000: 51–2)

While the political and spiritual messages of lyrics are explicit, language is not always used in ways that can be easily interpreted. 'I need a hammer to hammer them down', sang Bob Marley. The poet John Agard writes that 'human breath is a dangerous weapon' in his poem 'Listen Mr Oxford Don', observing: 'I don't need no hammer to mash up yu grammar' (Agard 1985). Henry makes a similar point in his contribution above and in his analysis of dancehall lyrics as presenting alternative ways of understanding. British dancehall DJs choose to express themselves in Patwah rather than Standard English:

> The 'conscious' Deejay realises that white supremacist thinking permeates the culture of the English language, thus perpetuating black inferiority as natural... As a Deejay one of the strongest ways to counter the legitimacy of the 'language of instruction' is by demonstrating how the enemy distorts 'truth' in your own usage and manipulations of words and sounds. For instance, the Deejay can take a word like 'education', explain what it should be based on, our commonsense assumptions of a meritocratic 'learning' process, and then provide what they deem to be a more accurate description of this process from a blak perspective; 'head-decay-shun'. By doing so the Deejay draws on cultural knowledges that purposefully challenge the neutrality of the English language, in this case the term 'head-decay-shun' stems from a Rastafari notion of 'brainwash education'. This means that Rastafari has evaluated the notion of what it is to be 'educated' by your enemy and concluded that what occurs is decadent and something to be shunned. (Henry 2002: 37–8)

Lyrics, like ethnography, are polyphonic in the sense that they contain other voices. To hear them well one has to have heard

other sources on which they draw. These include references to the
Bible, to political statements, to the lyrics of other singers, and to
the narratives 'preserved in oral traditions'. Such multi-referentiality also points to hearing lyrics in relation to related African
Diasporic genres that include reggae, calypso, dub, rap, zouk,
ska, jamoo, gospelypso and that connect people across Africa, the
Americas and Europe – Gilroy's *Black Atlantic* (1993b). When
we add genres like chutney soca, jamoo chutney, rajamuffin and
bhangramuffin, we also have to hear lyrics in relation to other
global diasporas, in these instances, the Indian Diaspora.

This kind of hearing plunges us back into the dilemmas of trying
to think both locally and globally as well as beyond the maps of
music and place. I would like to illustrate this point briefly with
reference to particular lyrics, written and recorded by around
twenty musicians as a tribute to the power of rapso, 'Rapso
Nation'. 3Canal, Brother Resistance, Sheldon Blackman, Black
Lyrics, Sister Ava and Lady Spencer are amongst the performers
singing in the chorus: 'The rapso nation, it have no boundaries,
no segregation'. Verses refer to the power of rapso: 'the lyrics
in me mouth is like a bullet from a gun', and to its spiritual
dimensions: 'we come with a message for all the world, we come
to tell that Jah in control'. The sonic effects of different vocal
deliveries contribute to the widespread appeal of these lyrics ('the
power of de word in de riddim of de word'). Layered on top of
bass lines, the voice(s) use a variety of rhythmic-melodic configurations. Three distinct kinds of rhythmic-melodic delivery in this
song are spoken lines with speech-tones, sung lines (especially
for the chorus) and rapid, staccato spoken lines. A loose call and
response format can be heard in the textural distinctions between
solo vocal spoken lines and choral sung lines and in the contrasts
between non-rhyming and rhyming lines.

The lyrics of 'Rapso Nation' are concerned with a spiritual
politics underscored by an appreciation of historical specificities
and the legacies of the past that shape people's experiences
('Rapso rhythm is the manifestation of the perpetuation of the
oral tradition'), but avoiding the prisons of boundaries and
segregation ('rapso soldiers coming round the corner, getting

out of order, crossing your border'). This is a spiritual politics expressed using the language of violence ('love bomb', 'lyrics like bullets', 'soldiers') to convey a message of people connected globally. Such language emphasises the struggle involved in this kind of political vision. I use the word 'struggle' advisedly. In a world of border controls and boundary maintenances, 'Us' and 'Other' labelling in the everyday and invidious production of difference, 'race' discourse and racism, violent confrontations, this political vision assumes a spiritual aura, offering glimpses into other kinds of possibilities that might, nevertheless take us some way towards formulating a theory of global political action that challenges inequalities. This is diaspora as a stance that 'does not so much *describe* the world as seek to *remake* it' (Brubaker 2005: 12). Reminding us that music does not provide a cosy haven from the traumas of difference, One Love lyricism stands in stark contrast to the 'hate' lyrics (homophobic and misogynistic) of genres like reggae, dancehall and soca. In the lyricism of 'One Love', (just as in ethnographies that make it possible to think of engaged scholarship and counter-hegemonic practice), we hear singers affirming the merits of struggling for a global political action of respect, of thinking in terms of planetary humanism. From the perspective of struggle, the 'revolutionary Tuff Gong Rastaman' is still here. For that kind of spiritual politics is also the insurgency in Bob Marley's 'One Love' lyrics. One Love, then, is not about happy affects and affectations. It is about the struggle of thinking beyond difference and of working through histories of colonialism, genocide and exploitation. Yes. You hear what I'm saying? One Love Tina.

6
'I'M A STRANGER'
Musical Spectacles I

This chapter questions the common depiction that diasporic communities are 'minority' groups within nation-states by looking at an island space in which different diasporic experiences emerge as being central to national politics. What is the relation between diaspora and nation when almost everyone within the nation is diasporised? How are musical memories and marketing strategies linked in postcolonial debates about national development? Focusing on musical spectacles (Carnival and Phagwa) in the twenty-first century in Trinidad, this chapter is linked with the following one on British and Canadian Carnivals (Notting Hill and Caribana). While interactions between audiences and performers in the Caribbean island and its Diaspora are a feature of these musical spectacles, especially in the transmission of repertoires and in the circulation of participants, Carnival provides variations on the play of 'home' in each of these geographic settings. I hope to indicate the extent to which the play of 'home' revolves around local political concerns, many of which have been expressed in relation to Carnival development strategies and tourist economies. The play of 'home' is also expressed in terms of a preoccupation with questions about to whom Carnival belongs, which have been debated in relation to issues over control, containment and ownership. The control of Carnival through policing and route setting has been a central theme in the ethnographic contexts considered here, and contemporary discussions reproduce those documented in nineteenth-century sources.

In focusing on discourses of locality we find that 'home' is played out in relation to the concept of diaspora, in the island setting as much as in metropolitan sites in Britain and in North America. Some commentators in Trinidad and Tobago posit Carnival performance histories and origin theories in Africa or in India. Carnivalists in Caribbean diasporic contexts, by contrast, have begun to speak about the rather specific 'Trinidad' model, instead of Carnival as a generalised Caribbean expression. By drawing on an ethnographic view of Carnival 2001 in three geographic locations, my aim is to track debates about Carnival in relation to a transnational performance politics that involves aesthetic considerations and ideas about cultural industries. For now, it can be noted that for all three contexts, Carnival 2001 provided a forum for discussions centred on histories, heritages, performance authenticities, repertoires, and the potential for developing Carnival as a tourist and cultural industry.

Contested Carnival Histories, Performance Politics

In 1932, Joseph Belgrave contributed his reflections on Carnival to a Trinidadian magazine, *The Beacon*, in a description that is pertinent to the contemporary festival:

> There is an atmosphere of pleasure and anxious expectation throughout the whole island. Dances take place every night all over Port-of-Spain, whilst the bands feverishly prepare their costumes.... On Shrove Sunday night the whole air is filled with music and singing. The streets are thronged with people, bands of masqueraders are parading, some going to dances, everywhere singing and dancing predominates. (1978 [1932]: 43)

Belgrave pointed to the national significance of Carnival and to its potential to represent the island. His hope was that 'Carnival in Trinidad might become one of the most beautiful in the world and one of the best means of advertising the Colony' (1978 [1932]: 44). His ambitions for Carnival have been realised. While there are a number of festival traditions throughout the Caribbean, the pre-Lenten Carnival of Trinidad and Tobago has become one of the region's major musical spectacles. It provides one of the most well known representations of island performance traditions in the international forum, contributing to the tourist economy and attracting research attention (for example, van Koningsbruggen 1997, Riggio 2004). Such is its significance that in contemporary Carnival literature today, writers assess the Trinidad and Tobago Carnival as being 'the best folk festival in the western world, and the best show on earth' (Claude Clarke in a publication of the National Carnival Commission: NCC 2001: 2) and 'the Mother of all Carnivals' (Nurse 2001: 5).

While many commentators extol the wonders of Carnival as a performance spectacle, others point to the season's frictions, hostilities and clashes. Van Koningsbruggen interprets Carnival as a 'search for national identity' but notes the 'dynamic interplay of conflicting orientations' that surrounds this performance arena (1997: 192). In fact, descriptions in Trinidadian news reports dating back to the early nineteenth century reveal Carnival as a long-standing forum for highlighting the island struggles that resulted from the efforts of colonial authorities to control Carnival performance. The 1833 Carnival marked one such struggle. Against the backdrops of British legislation reducing the powers of slave owners and of enslaved people questioning their social status and working conditions, the premature celebration of Carnival was regarded as a 'disturbance' by colonial authorities. The arrests of two carnivalists led to violent protest (*Port-of-Spain Gazette*, 22 January 1833, cited in Cowley 1996: 25). Another example concerns the 1858 Carnival. In accordance with the anti-masquing lobby, the newly arrived Governor, Robert William Keate, issued a proclamation forbidding the wearing of masks at Shrovetide, which resulted in confrontations between Carnival participants and the police.[1] In 1898, Carnival songs were criticised by the press. The *Gazette* (8 February 1898) commented:

> These songs are for the most part intended to bring certain persons into ridicule, and if rumour speaks correctly some of the respectable persons do not think it either undignified or as setting a bad example, to attend some of these rehearsals and openly evince their approval and appreciation of these mountebank proceedings which were they lovers of order and public decency they would use every effort on their part to stamp out of

our midst as a disgrace and scandal to our boasted civilisation. (cited in Cowley 1996: 143)

Carnival 2001 provided several opportunities to observe the playing out of 'conflicting orientations'. It was dedicated to honouring one of the legends of the calypso world – the Mighty Sparrow, who made headline news with awards conferred on him and by his angry reaction to a photographer snapping shots during a performance. Denyse Plummer, having won the Calypso Monarch competition, entered into dispute with the songwriter Kurt Allen over the 'ownership' of one of the winning songs. Soca parties kept non-participating residents awake until the early hours of the morning. In the newspapers, people debated the appropriateness of Orisha (an African religious movement) themes in mas (costume) bands. Television coverage drew my attention to a collection of essays about Carnival in *Ah Come Back Home* (Smart and Nehusi 2000), in which conflicting orientations are revealed in interpreting the historical, the mythical and the 'time beyond recall' (Naipaul 1984). The volume is an exploration of Carnival in relation to African Diaspora studies aiming to explore radical and new perspectives on Carnival. These include historical reclamations characteristic of much diaspora discourse in the form of the 'new' African histories. In *Ah Come Back Home*, paralleling Naipaul's insights in *Finding the Centre* (1984: 51), we find interplay between two ideas of history. The received historical narratives of the kind learnt through formal education systems, at school, are thrown into question by the newly reclaimed histories that look at Carnival as the presentation of alternative historical narratives that have survived in performances despite repression from colonial channels.

Within this framework of the reclaimed past, Smart and Nehusi posit an ancient history for Carnival. For them, the Trinidad Carnival is a New World reorientation of a festival that began in the Nile Valley, in Kemet (Ancient Egypt). Drawing on the work of a former keeper of antiquities in the British Museum (Budge 1973 [1911]), Nehusi examines details found on an Egyptian stele of the Wosirian drama, a central part of the Festival of Wosir (a variant of the ancient Egyptian deity, Osiris). In these details he finds similarities to contemporary Carnival practice: crowds in procession, a float sailing on the river or pulled along the streets, a sham stick fight, masks, music and dancing. In these details, he concludes that we have the 'first description in the world, at its very birthplace, of what is today called Carnival' (Nehusi 2000: 85). Of significance to Nehusi as a contemporary commentator with aspirations for the development of the modern Trinidad Carnival was the huge expenditure and preparation necessary to realise the Kemet festival (2000: 82). For Adeyinka, rejection of the African origin of Carnival thesis is a 'modern falsification' and a 'desecration of the sacred memory of the African Carnival pioneers' (Adeyinka 2000: 129).

While Carnival is usually analysed in relation to its African or European origins, a challenge to the African origin thesis – as well as an alternative connection via ancient Egyptian festivals – is offered from a surprising source. Persad argues that Carnival has its origins in Saivism. In 2001, Carnival coincided with the Hindu (Saivist) festival of Shivratri and the Islamic period of Hajj. These occasions, Persad wrote, 'are strong reminders that we are an ancient people, that we have brought customs and traditions from the "old world", which survive in Trinidad and are in effect Trinidadian' (Persad 2001: 16). This claim leads to an exposition on the origins of Shivratri in Hindu India and the spread of Saivism in the ancient world, including through ancient Egyptian festivals and Islamic Hajj. Persad concludes that the Saivist origins of Carnival and Hajj have been forgotten but that Hindus should remember this history (2001: 16).

Contributors to these debates seem to be concerned with the different ways in which memory flows through performances and with the recuperation of Carnival history, cultural heritages and knowledge about origins. Yet, these discussions of Carnival performance as a remembrance of an ancient past and as a testimony to cultural survival despite enforced displacement also pay attention to contemporary Carnival politics in Trinidad and Tobago. Uncovering the origins of Carnival turns out to be more than an exploration of historical sources to provide new interpretations of diasporic African or Indian histories. Exploring the 'time beyond recall' is an exercise in political activism that emphasises the importance of Carnival celebrations in its modern contexts. There is nothing new in this. Carnival has long been a political forum, especially as a site of resistance during the colonial era. In re-interpreting historical materials such as the Egyptian stele in the British Museum and Carnival performances, Smart and Nehusi write against 'Colony' but nevertheless affirm, like the 1930s writings of Belgrave, the centrality of Carnival in island performance. Springer describes Carnival as being at the centre of 'the cultural confidence of Trinidad and Tobago' (Springer 2000: 17). For Nehusi, Carnival is 'an important representation of home' (Nehusi 2000: 1); it is a 'treasure' that provides people 'with the deepest memories of where we come from, where we have been and therefore who we are, and where home is and could more often be found' (2000: 3). Yet, because Carnival cannot be a simple reproduction of the ancient Wosirian drama, it is also an 'exercise in cultural innovation; never merely a perpetuation of cultural memory' (Springer 2000: 17).

In these commentaries we find diasporic and national sensibilities cutting across each other, intersecting and featuring in discussions about cultural continuity and change. These narratives about Carnival histories highlight the ways in which the island space has been intimately connected with other spaces across the globe through population movements since the fifteenth century. Ultimately, the principal aims of *Ah Come Back Home* and of Persad's hypothesis are to reclaim the past and to posit its relevance in the present by suggesting practical strategies for the development of Carnival. Suggestions for the development of the Trinidad Carnival include Springer's call for the formulation of formal strategies that focus on education systems and national policies. She writes: 'schools must teach our children that the energy and intensity they display at Carnival time can be harnessed to ensure their success in other facets of their lives' (Springer 2000: 26). Smart believes that Carnival should be controlled within national spheres for the economic empowerment of the makers of Carnival. He calls upon the government to invest further money in the development of Carnival (Smart 2000: 86) referring to Nehusi's historical analysis, which provides an indication of the extent to which state support could extend.

Whether Carnival is 'we thing', an African and pan-African memory (as Smart and Nehusi 2000 emphasise), or a Saivist remnant (according to Persad 2001), it is a performance arena that exposes the fragilities of island consensus and the multitude dramas of current disputes to a wide forum. This is a forum that includes the Carnival tourist, a visitor considered by Smart. He refers to ecotourism initiatives in proposing 'a cultural phenomenon like the Carnival can be considered to fit under the rubric of human ecology. And on this basis an authentic "humanoecotourism" could be developed' (Smart 2000: 36).

Carnival Tourism

The centrality of Carnival to Trinidad and Tobago's tourist industry is recognised by the island's political and policy-making units. A National Carnival Commission (NCC) was established by an act of Parliament in 1986 and grew from the Carnival Development Committee (1957). It includes the associations for calypsonians, carnival bands and the steelpan industry. In the opening pages of its Carnival 2001 publication, *Before and Beyond Mas*, the NCC enters into discussion on the ambiguities surrounding the origins of this event. The two main schools of thought are outlined: Carnival as a celebration brought by European settlers, or as an African street festival. Rather than supporting any one of these origin theories, the NCC concludes that both of these views

> together contribute to the building of an edifice of knowledge which probably makes the celebration the grand occasion it is today. So when searching to understand Carnival, it is best to compare it to an intricate tapestry. Carnival is blessed with a culture and history so tightly interwoven as to blur the lines of its true origins. (NCC 2001: 9)

In addition to the National Carnival Commission, the government established a National Carnival Institute in 1999. It provides education and research facilities, but one of its main aims is to develop Carnival into a year-round industry.

The tourist is important to this industry. Tourists arrive in Trinidad booking Carnival accommodation packages at higher than usual rates. Hotel and guesthouse managements comment that this is the one time in the year when they can earn extra income (personal communications, February, March 2001). Statistics published by the Tourism and Industrial Development Company (TIDCO) of Trinidad and Tobago show that tourism contributes $1.3 billion to the economy and that Carnival is an increasingly important income generator. Numbers of visitors during the Carnival period increased rapidly over a three-year period (from 46,773 visitors in 1998 to 340,659 in 2000; statistics are published on the TIDCO website, <www.tidco.co.tt>).[2]

Calypsonians also comment on Carnival and tourism. They have composed well-known songs exploring the theme of the tourist. Lord Kitchener won the 1968 Road March (the people's choice of the winning song of the year) with 'Miss Tourist', Short Shirt won in 1976 with 'Tourist Leggo' and the most recent win was Shadow's 'Stranger' in 2001. Shadow sang about a tourist

> eager to get in the groove; music fever had her on the move... (verse 2). I said welcome to sweet Trinidad, to have you here, I am very glad. Let me wish you happy holiday, I do hope that you enjoy your stay (verse 3).

An impromptu performance by a tourist, who jumped on stage as Shadow competed for the title of Soca Monarch 2001 (which he won), added extra visibility to this aspect of Carnival. The impromptu appearance was formalised for the Calypso Monarch competition (won, however, by Denyse Plummer). The tourist appeared alongside Shadow as an integral part of the performance. 'Do your thing', sings Shadow. One thing that his song does is to teach the tourist what to do. It is the narrative voice of the tourist that we hear in the first verse: 'I'm a stranger... I came down here for the Carnival. Kaiso music have me in a trance, want to play mas, teach me how to dance.' Shadow responds: 'Buy a little rag and put it in your pocket. Buy a little flag, that's the way we do it. Find yourself a band and find a good position. When the

'I'M A STRANGER' 169

music blasts you'll find out how to play mas [carnival].' His dance instructions sung in the chorus are 'when they say rag, pull your rag; when they say flag, pull your flag and wave it. When they say wine, you got to wine; when they say wine roll your waist; jump up; wine up.'[3]

Walking towards Woodbrook and St James in Port-of-Spain, looking out for the panyards, I came across another example of teaching tourists what to do in Carnival 2001 activities. Entering the panyard of Phase II Pan Groove, I heard the rehearsal of short repeated phrases (Figure 6.1). This was a class in progress, tucked away in a corner of the panyard, and the majority of students were Carnival tourists (Figure 6.2). Around them, pans were being polished and painted in preparation for the National Panorama Finals (the island's major steelpan competition). Members of the band were preparing for a jam session that afternoon, tuning instruments, arranging the performance space and laying out food stalls (Figure 6.3). Amidst these preparations, a founding member took time to tell me about the band's history and about its current Carnival activities. Phase II Pan Groove is a steelband that emerged from the group, Starlift to explore new pieces and arrangements by Boogsie Sharp, ('a phenomenon' and one of the

Figure 6.1 The panyard of Phase II Pan Groove

170 BEAUTIFUL COSMOS

Figure 6.2 A steelband class for tourists

most well-known of contemporary pan arrangers). For the 2001 Panorama, the group prepared a tune called 'Freedom', which was about the World Steelband Festival, a celebration of the global pan attended by bands from different countries (Michael Philips, founding member, personal communication, February 2001).

Celebrating the global pan was also evident in the arrival of Trinidad Diaspora pannists who joined the band for Carnival rehearsals, jam sessions, competitions and concerts. Some of these musicians had played with the band before migrating elsewhere and have maintained contact through Carnival pilgrimages. Other players are members of steelbands in Trinidad Diaspora centres. Their pan proficiency enables them to augment the regular membership of Phase II Pan Groove during the Carnival season. Phase II members similarly augment steelbands during Carnivals in London, New York and Toronto (Jamal, member of Phase II, personal communication, February 2001).

Pan musicians draw a distinction between the interchange of pan skills through these diasporic performance networks and the development of the pan abilities of other kinds of transient Carnival visitors like the tourists attending the pan class. The

Figure 6.3 Preparations for Panorama

pan lessons for tourists were offered by and were the initiative of a German-born Dutch music teacher and pan player, Frauke Luhning, herself a 'Carnival tourist', who had become a student of pan with this group. She hoped that tourists would develop an appreciation of pan proficiency by experiencing the learning process themselves, and that by offering lessons that utilised existing resources band members would be further empowered:

> I bought myself a little tenor and started to play. I bought it back to Holland and started to play with other pan players. I decided after I finished my studies at the Rotterdam Conservatoire to come back here for three months and find out for myself how it is to work in such a big orchestra in an oral tradition – in the auditive learning way – because as a music teacher I'm very interested in auditive learning: learning music by ear. So I came here

in the winter of 1996. I try to introduce steelpan to schools in Holland, and I saw many tourists come into the yard [in Trinidad] and look at us. They don't really understand what is going on and I thought probably a lot of these people get a little itchy in their hands and want to try it as well, but they wouldn't dare to come into a band. So I said, 'Let's put all these factors together: we have so many good pan players who don't have an income out of their playing (and often they don't have a job at all); there's a band that has space and the instruments, that needs money, and there are a lot of people who want to try it.... So when I put all this together, I organized this [lessons for tourists] for the first time in 1999 and it was really a big success. Every day we had 15 to 20 people coming and some came every day for six weeks in a row to learn as many tunes as they could. (Frauke Luhning, personal interview, February 2001)

Frauke Luhning noted that amongst the positive benefits of offering steelpan lessons to tourists were greater appreciation and respect for the skill involved in playing pan and the generation of income, which had resulted in the issue of a CD recording. In 2001, she hoped to raise enough money to purchase a fax machine for the band and to encourage band members in developing teaching skills relevant to tourist learners (personal interview, February 2001). Panyards are open public spaces, and Luhning has found a role in Phase II Pan Groove as an interested pan student who is involved in implementing grass-roots level economic developments. Such empowering strategies take into account the symbolic importance of the steelpan for tourists as well as for islanders. Positioned as a tourist, Luhning's engagement in developing Carnival as a tourist enterprise adds further layers to the debates about to whom Carnival 'belongs'. Her experience is relevant in thinking about musical ownership and performance exclusivities. Luhning's involvement accords with Smart's notion of developing 'humanoecotourism', but a consequence is that this performance forum moves away from being 'we thing' (Carnival as cultural property) and towards non-islander inclusion, a move encouraged in Carnival development debates. The narrative voice of the tourist in Shadow's song 'Stranger' and the tourist dancer who became part of the song's performances in competitions similarly open up the Carnival forum. The tourist takes centre-stage. Yet, the tourist's presence is both desirable and undesirable. The tourist may help the island's economic development and visibly contribute to performances in public spaces, but is cast nevertheless in the role of an outsider – Shadow's 'Stranger'. This stranger is seen also as someone who may bring dangers. Shadow's second Carnival 2001 song, 'HIV', urged precaution, including in pursuit of relationships with Carnival tourists. At this point I shall shift attention to another kind of musical spectacle to further explore the musical narratives of diaspora, the politics of island identity, and to consider what these tell us about the island home.

Phagwa Performance

A chutney stage had been set up on the Brian Lara Promenade for Carnival (Figure 6.4). Once it had been dismantled, empowering strategies and performance politics continued to be evident in the post-Carnival musical and religious spectacles of Phagwa. 'Empowerment through culture' – exploring the full cultural potential of Trinidad and Tobago – was echoed by one Phagwa celebration organiser, Ravi Ji (Ravi Ji 2001: 21). Although the 2001 celebration of Phagwa in Trinidad followed Carnival, most of the tourists had departed before this festival began. The tourist, then, is a transient visitor who might momentarily become a part of Carnival performance, but misses the intricacies of national political debates centred on Carnival and Phagwa performances in juxtaposition.

Phagwa is a religious (Hindu) festival celebrating spring. The Hindu text *Vishnu Purana* tells the story of King Hiranyakashipu who aimed to destroy his son, Prahalad for worshipping God before his father. Hiranyakashipu plotted with his sister, Holika, to destroy his son by fire. It was Holika, however, who perished. This is a moral tale about the triumph of good over evil. As part of Phagwa celebrations an effigy of Holika continues to be burnt on a bonfire.

Figure 6.4 Rikki Jai performing on the chutney stage, Brian Lara Promenade

Phagwa (like Carnival) commands much media attention because it generates aesthetic and ideological controversies. In March 2001, these controversies focused in the form and legitimacy of Phagwa performance. Two principal organisers of Phagwa celebrations in Trinidad, the Kendra Phagwa Festival and the Sanatan Dharma Maha Sabha (the major Hindu organisation in Trinidad and Tobago formed in 1952 and now running around 150 mandirs (temples) and 50 schools), debated the appropriateness of performing pichakaaree songs (a new genre) in preference to the traditional chowtal song repertoire (songs sang in praise of Krishna). The central point of contestation was that some commentators saw pichakaaree in Phagwa as being little more than encouraging an 'Indian' Carnival, while its proponents saw this repertoire as being an innovative continuation of traditional Indian practices (Figure 6.5).

Resonating with Springer's views on Carnival as involving both innovation and preservation of tradition, Ravi Ji, the founder of pichakaaree, aimed to encourage innovative as well as traditional song performances during Phagwa:

Figure 6.5 The stage of the Kendra Phagwa Festival (2001)

> pichakaaree is a new way of recording the Jhahaji [brotherhood of the boat] experiences of the Indian community.... It records our Jhahaji experiences in the Caribbean and how we feel about the events we experience. (Ravi Ji, cited in Doodhai 2001: 5).[4]

Ravi Ji introduced pichakaaree (a term that refers to both the genre and the festival) as a student-centred initiative but soon realised its potential for social commentary:

> The whole thing arose from a group of students I have who were taking to composing and they had no forum to express themselves. On the other side, there was a need for a voice – an instrument to expose the voice of a people who were saying things from the Indian side. (Ravi Ji, personal interview, July 1996)

Although objections were raised against putting pichakaaree on an Indian religious festival day, Ravi Ji argued that

> Anytime the Hindu civilization wanted to do something they always found a religious centre for it.... Divali is so austere, fasting and all that, it [pichakaaree] wouldn't fit into that – it would be too dissonant for that. But Phagwa permits that type of thing because although there is a religious

centre in it there is enough of a kind of free expression. Apart from that, poetry recitation is also an important part of Phagwa – the poetry that they recite is social commentary, political commentary, recording events, very obscene poetry too. I thought this was important. (Ravi Ji, personal interview, July 1996)

In their song texts, pichakaaree singers refer to topics such as domestic abuse, alcoholism and drug problems, nation-building and current politics. They sing in English with a few Hindi or Bhojpuri phrases, draw on Indian folk melodies or film songs and are accompanied by instruments such as the *dholak* (double-headed drum), *dhantal* (struck iron rod), harmonium, *jhaal* (cymbals) and electronic resources.

Representatives from the Hindu organisation Sanatan Dharma Maha Sabha denounced pichakaaree performances organised by Ravi Ji and the Kendra Phagwa Festival on the grounds that an inappropriate song repertoire was being used. Moreover, pichakaaree was seen as reducing Phagwa celebrations to a mere emulation of Carnival. As in the calypso competitions, pichakaaree competition singers are evaluated in several different categories including pichakaaree champion, best social commentary, best composer and most imaginative use of Hindi.[5] One representative of the Sanatan Dharma Maha Sabha stated:

Pichakaree is essentially the singing of Indian calypsos on stage while a crowd sprays each other with abir [red powder] associated with Phagwa. The traditional song for Phagwa – the chowtal – has been abandoned by the organizers of this event, who instead appear to have taken a cue from the Calypso Tents of Port-of-Spain. The entire show is merely an Indianised version of what goes on at the Spektakula Revue. (P. Maharaj 2001: 10)

Another representative of the organisation referred to repertoire choices in relation to ethnic politics:

Phagwa, or the Hindu festival of Holi, is not an extension of Carnival, nor is it the Indian/Hindu response to the innumerable attack calypsos that denigrate Hinduism and Indians every Carnival season.... The singing of chowtals better represents Phagwa (than pichakaree) and that is why it remains on the Maha Sabha's programme. (S. Maharaj 2001: 1)

The Maha Sabha were further disenchanted by the media coverage accorded to pichakaaree, claiming that community-based activities were being threatened by a single large-scale operation:

> The Maha Sabha over the years has fostered the village mandir to become the focal point of religious celebration and purposefully moved away from a centralized celebration. This de-centralising will ensure that Phagwa is felt on a national level beyond a mere television and radio broadcast from one site. (P. Maharaj 2001: 10)

Ravi Ji believed that he was able to give a voice to singers through pichakaaree performance to reflect the concerns of Indian-Trinidadians. The Maha Sabha on the other hand, perceived the introduction of this repertoire into Phagwa as evidence of a Carnival ideology (implicitly understood by this organisation as a predominantly African-Trinidadian expression) infiltrating an Indian sacred space. Accusations that the Kendra Phagwa Festival was using Carnival models extended beyond artistic and organisational considerations. They were related to the contestations over 'African' and 'Indian' cultural spaces that have also been played out in Carnival and in debates about education curriculums. The objections of the Maha Sabha to pichakaaree repertoire were reminiscent of those raised by this organisation to initiatives proposing to introduce the steelpan into schools as part of the national school curriculum during the mid 1990s. In the pages of the local press (1994), S. Maraj argued that if steelpan were to be represented at this level in the national curriculum, then Ministry of Culture support should similarly extend to the harmonium, an instrument important in 'Indian' musical practice. These arguments did not take into account the involvement of Indian musicians with the steelpan (such as the well known pan arranger for the steelband Renegades, Jit Samaroo, and Mungal Patasar's combinations of sitar and pan timbres with his group Pantar). Neither did they take into account Carnival as a performance space that has long included Indian as well as African participation (Cowley 1996).[6] The steelpan and harmonium controversy was resolved by 1995 by state agreement to purchase harmoniums for schools too. In both the pichakaaree versus chowtal and the pan versus harmonium debates, the Maha Sabha articulated an extreme position on the politics of ethnicity and on the protection of 'Indian' musical spaces. In this respect, this discourse parallels that of Carnival assessments that repudiate non-African influence. On the surface, these formulations seem to emphasise issues of ethnicity that feed into well-known island debates and social analyses of inter-ethnic conflicts. As with debates about Carnival history, however, the important point here is that the pichakaaree versus chowtal and the pan versus harmonium controversies had been targeted at national policy-making processes.

The debate over Phagwa between the Maha Sabha and the Kendra Phagwa Festival was one that revealed contestations about performance practice and song repertoires that were related to different ideas about the place of 'Indian' communities in Trinidad and Tobago. Expressed in terms of musical repertoire choices, it was a debate that focused on musical and aesthetic legitimacy, competition over resources, ideas about tradition and the appropriateness of performance genres in sacred and secular contexts.

'Ganges and the Nile'

Through the ethnographic details and historical narratives discussed so far, I have aimed to provide a portrait of complex musical and social island negotiations. One further thread that impacts on Carnival and Phagwa can be briefly considered here. While diaspora invokes history, albeit contested histories of the kinds that have been explored above, it is also an idea through which people think and perform postcolonially. Central to a postcolonial view of diasporic performance is a reinterpretation of colonial history that allows us to consider the contemporary consequences of a colonial policy of 'divide and rule', and look for the ways in which performers seek to overcome the frictions of ethnic politics. The presentation of alternative histories provides a starting point with its insistence on knowledge of history as being implicated in political projects. These reclaimed, alternative histories can be interpreted as a form of 'empire writing back' (Ashcroft, Griffiths and Tiffin 1989) to those texts that all too easily dismiss them (see for example, Van Koningsbruggen 1997: 202–3).[7] They raise a series of questions about the relations between history, power, truth and agency. Whose history? What kind of story is history? Which histories are left unexplored? Which histories are silenced, dismissed? How are histories linked to the legitimisation of political power? What does the status of historical knowledge tell us about remaining authoritatively decentred in a postcolonial state? These are questions raised by the rapso singer Brother Resistance in observing 'is a lie so big, even history believe it':

> Is a big dirty lie, tell Columbus could die, tell me the cause for the celebration when all he bring the Caribbean was aggravation, the lust and the greed and the destruction, disease and distress to the population...
>
> They willing to forget about the days of slavery, five hundred years of colonial agony, I have a duty to tell the true story.... Is a lie so big even history believe it. ('Goodbye Columbus', Brother Resistance, 1995)[8]

The replacement of one kind of history with another – Brother Resistance's 'duty to tell the "true" story' – does not resolve the problems of historical interpretations. But with such replacements we become attuned to the possibility of new stories waiting to be offered. The 'writing back' histories, writing from the so-called margins of former Empire, bring to our attention other historical voices and the possibility of reading historical narratives, to use a phrase from Stuart Hall, 'against the grain'.

Smart and Nehusi (2000) and Persad (2001) rethink historical narratives and propose development strategies that are linked to the concerns of island political discourses framed in terms of distinct ethnicities and separate histories. Their narratives are unified, nevertheless, in their response against the legacy of colonialism. They argue against white supremacy (as in Brother Resistance's line, 'tell Columbus could die') and in doing so introduce a further layer to discourses on island ethnicity and history without escaping the confines of oppositional relations between people. How might we think of both diasporic and postcolonial belongings beyond difference and marginality?

How can we move beyond the lingering dichotomies of 'white supremacy' and 'ethnic Others'? The problems with an uncritical acceptance of the categories 'white' and 'ethnic Others' are reproduced in Caribbean Diasporic performances, as we shall see in the following chapter. What are the alternatives? How can musical spectacles be understood as performances of being at home even if they contain and display the dramas of difference?

A postcolonial imagining of African and Indian Diasporas in Carnival and Phagwa performances, drawing on different historical narratives and musical repertoires, references 'the theme of location'. This is a point which, as Avtar Brah observes, 'warrants emphasis because the very strong association of notions of diaspora with displacement and dislocation means that the experience of location can easily dissolve out of focus' (Brah 1996: 180). A focus on contested musical practices and discourses (as in origin theories of Carnival and steelpan versus harmonium debates) can lead to a misrepresentative emphasis on island differences configured in terms of ethnic divisions. The 'experience of location' in Trinidad moves beyond the 'struggles over ethnicity' (Yelvington 1993). In reconciliatory and encompassing modes, singers often reinforce the notion of national unity and sing of the experience of a common belonging. Rikki Jai, Ella Andall and David Rudder all sang about the drum as an instrument that brings people together. The chorus to one of Rikki Jai's 2001 competition songs is 'I'm Rikki Jai, I sing chutney and calypso for I'm a Trinbagonian.' The Orisha-influenced calypsonian Ella Andall talked about her familiarity with Indian film songs. David Rudder composed a song about 'a magic island full of magic people':

> (Verse) Many rivers flow to this naked isle, bringing fear and pain but also a brand new style. And of all these rivers that shape this land, two mighty ones move, like a sculptor's hand. And today those hands across the land are still landscaping, and there's no doubt if the work is out there is no escaping.
>
> (Chorus) See how we moving, watch how we grooving. See how we step in line. One lovely nation.... Ganges has met the Nile.

The stories of 'histories' are vital to people's sense of home. The past matters to people. Yet, through musical expression and song text, David Rudder's, Ella Andall's and Rikki Jai's performances are the new creative expressions that confirm the historical ties of diasporised peoples to the Caribbean as much as they foster memories of homes elsewhere. I have turned to Andall, Rudder and Jai, and have juxtaposed details about Carnival and Phagwa in Trinidad, to add emphasis to the point that these performances draw from the diasporic imagination but are predicated on a politics of belonging, rather than of marginalisation, exclusion or social difference. Island musical practices and musical discourses analysed in terms of the frictions of difference turn out to be, then, an expression of a common island experience.

The insights of Wilson Harris provide an apt framework through which new ideas about Carnival history, refuted repertoires and instruments, and songs for national unity may be understood. For Harris, a 'philosophy of history' may 'lie buried in the arts of the imagination'. It is in the arts of the imagination that 'the possibility exists for us to become involved in perspectives of renascence which can bring into play a figurative meaning beyond an apparently real world or prison of history' (1999 [1970]: 156). The diasporic imagination is global in scope, it is sparked by ideas about histories, traditions and innovations, and it brings into play past and present. In their creative endeavours, musicians are involved in the exploration of histories and places remembered, forgotten and reclaimed. Carnival and Phagwa performances tell us about the island's sonic environment and cultural landscape, as well as about a diversity between islanders that is not reducible to simply conceived notions of inter-ethnic conflicts. Carnival 2001 raised questions about historical knowledge, cultural ownership and tourist economies. In the same year, Phagwa raised questions about tradition, musical choices, the legitimacy of creating new genres and adopting Carnival performance models. These are themes that continued to be explored in subsequent years, becoming central to political discussions on the region's economies, resources, markets and future sustainability. Song texts provide some of the most potent examples of discourses on locality. Beyond song texts alone – in timbres, rhythmic and melodic features – one can hear the musical narratives of place and time. Necessarily indeterminate. Narratives that question, as much as they affirm, geographies and temporalities. These are the musical narratives that reveal the centrality of performance in the economies of diaspora – from the labour of plantation production that forged the modern Caribbean to the tourist industry of the postcolonial nation-state.

7
REACHING FOR THE TRICKSTER GATEWAY
MUSICAL SPECTACLES II

This chapter is concerned with Carnivals in the Caribbean Diaspora. Insofar as the Trinidad and Tobago Carnival provides a model for Carnivals in London and Toronto (the examples discussed here), Nurse's claim that it is 'the mother of all carnivals' is an apt one (Nurse 2001: 5). Carnivals are the biggest musical spectacles found in the Caribbean Diaspora. They provide celebratory performance spaces. They have marked Black solidarity and been amongst the most visible arenas of political dissent and ethnic conflict. They have taken on the mantle of multicultural display.

The ethnic politics of the Notting Hill (London) and Caribana (Toronto) Carnivals reproduce and offer a variation on the musical spectacles of Trinidad. For the founder organisers of Caribana, this Carnival was not just a Caribbean celebration that marked the Caribbean community's contribution to Canada's centennial celebrations. It was to be a 'distinctive Canadian carnival' that drew on both Caribbean and Canadian models, including the Emancipation Day parades of African-Canadians (Foster and Schwartz 1995: 24–5). It was organised against the background of civil rights movements, which had been given impetus by speakers like Malcolm X and Martin Luther King Junior who had given talks in Toronto. The chairperson of the organising committee, Charles Roach, commented that at the time,

> There was a feeling of consciousness of race and racism. The '60s was really a time when there was a lot of openness in confronting racism, especially towards the end of the '60s going into the '70s. This openness came as a

kind of relief from that kind of tension that was the general mood of not just us here in Toronto but in the whole of North America. (Charles Roach, cited in Foster and Schwartz 1995: 29-30)

The route of the first Caribana included two of Toronto's busiest streets, Bloor and Yonge. As Foster and Schwartz observe, there was a political dimension to this choice of route: 'By closing off activities on these streets for the hours allowed for the parade, a group of immigrants with seemingly little political clout could bring life to a standstill in the heart of the city', and ending the parade route in front of the city hall was an assertion that 'Blacks and Caribbean people were an integral part of the new Canada' (Foster and Schwartz 1995: 34). Tensions over 'race' issues have led to hostilities over Carnival and to discussions about its 'containment'.

In Britain, too, the Notting Hill Carnival emerged from the 'race riots' of 1958, which also marked Carnival 1976, and which have framed subsequent discourses about Carnival. These have ranged from complaints about Black 'noisiness' to one of the latest variations on the theme of 'race' discourse (expressed in 2001): the complaint, voiced through several media channels, that the 'new' white audiences participating in a Carnival that has outgrown its traditional location were the ones compromising public safety. Two murders at the 2000 Notting Hill Carnival and ongoing concerns about public safety, the rise in crimes committed and overcrowding prompted the Greater London Authority to set up an independent Carnival Review Group to address public concerns, safeguard the future of Carnival and explore ways in which Carnival could be developed. The main issues considered by the Notting Hill Carnival Review Group focused on practical arrangements and Carnival content. In the Review Group's consultation document, the issues outlined were public safety and density of people; Carnival location and route; travel to and from Carnival; policing; Carnival content; facilities; and communication and signage (Greater London Authority 2001). Similar kinds of organisational discussions have been a feature of Caribana.

The Notting Hill Carnival

I wish to resume the theme of Carnival tourism and indicate the ways in which talks about developing Carnival as a tourist spectacle in Caribbean diasporic contexts mirror those discussed in the previous chapter. As in Trinidad, discussions about developing the tourist potential of Notting Hill Carnival were framed by historical narratives, particularly those relating to past Carnival performance practices. Performers who were interested in promoting their own specific Carnival genres turned to the trope of performance authenticity. Strategy formulation for the development of Carnival in London and in Toronto has generated tensions between participants who view Notting Hill, and to a lesser degree Caribana, as either major 'multicultural' tourist attractions or as a year-round commitment to the art form that is rooted in traditional Trinidadian models. Adherence to Trinidadian models and the terms in which performance authenticities are framed reveal layers of complexity in the diasporic imagination. While musical spectacles in the Caribbean context provide a medium through which ideas about African and Indian as well as other heritages can be expressed, in the following Caribbean Diaspora examples, musicians more often refer to a homeland in the Caribbean – one increasingly identified as an island home.

Repertoires, Authenticity, the 'Regeneration of the Past'. What is involved in claiming performance authenticity? The 'disgraceful' and 'scandalous' songs so decried in Trinidad in 1898 for being 'intended to bring certain persons into ridicule' were being put forward by the Association of British Calypsonians, in its submitted recommendations to the Greater London Authority Carnival Review Group, as 'the traditional and official music of Carnival' which should 'therefore be recognised and promoted as such' (2001). This claim was supported by the British Association of Steelbands, which recommended to the same Review Group that 'efforts be made to bring steelbands and calypsonians back onto the route and to incorporate their presence into the

Carnival scene' (2001). The British Association of Steelbands (BAS), more specifically concerned with promoting steelband activities, suggested that a large-scale event should be hosted to commemorate the 50th anniversary of the first performance of a steelband in Great Britain. Members also wanted to see the reintroduction of a Steelband Music Festival for UK bands. Such a festival was seen as having the potential to 'provide a platform for British bands to clearly demonstrate the versatility of the instrument and the dexterity and undeniable talent of the people involved'. More than just displaying talent, the British Association of Steelbands hoped that such exposure would 'serve to raise the profile of the steelpan and integrate it into mainstream music in the UK', ambitions that go beyond Carnival as a way of coming home 'only in play' (Alleyne-Dettmers 2000: 139).[1]

Association representatives at the Carnival Review Group public meetings debated audience responses to other Carnival musical genres. Some representatives claimed that certain Carnival repertoires merited greater attention because they were more 'authentic'. Others argued that audiences should decide what should be heard. Calypsonian and steelband association representatives thus argued for resources for their art forms on the basis of performance authenticity and traditional repertoires, and they were united in their critiques of a 'newer' Carnival art form: sound systems on the move as part of the Carnival parade. The British Association of Steelbands noted: 'Urgent consideration must be given to the size and output of mobile sound systems. BAS recommends that the size of the lorries and output of sound systems be limited.' By contrast, the British Association of Sound Systems (BASS), also presenting recommendations to the Carnival Review Group, argued for further resources on the basis of positive audience reception: 'The services... could do more to embrace BASS members at Carnival. We play music extremely well – the public says so.' Moreover, this Association departed from the general emphasis on returning to 'traditional' and 'Trinidadian' Carnival models, preferring to view the Notting Hill event as at least a pan-Black, if not yet a completely multicultural, spectacle: 'There should be a recognition that BASS members provide a variety of music for Carnival whilst still promoting and remaining within the genre of Black music.' In protesting against being 'contained' on a performance site away from the parade, representatives referred to the wider repertoires that members turned to:

> Locating Sound Systems together on sites such as Wormwood Scrubs – would this not again place larger crowds together and cause more friction between both sounds and their followers? I can only see this as banishing sound systems away from the main part of the Carnival. We play a big part over the two days and are culturally a part of the Carnival, playing music from the Caribbean and recently from all over the world.[2]

To reinforce their arguments, local community initiatives in the form of combining 'Djing skills with a stage show for up and coming young talent from our local borough' were also mentioned.[3]

Representatives of the British Association of Steelbands suggested that another part of the Trinidad Carnival be reintroduced, but only for their art form: 'Steelbands would like to see the reintroduction of J'Ouvert – the opening of Carnival – for steelband performances only.'[4] In Trinidad, J'Ouvert takes place in the early hours of Monday morning with carnivalists dancing along the streets until dawn, covered in mud, to steelbands and drumming. The British Association of Steelbands recommended that *j'ouvert* within the Notting Hill structure should take place on Sunday morning from around 4am until midday and that the steelband competitions should take place at this time.

The Associations expressed specific concerns, but a series of broader questions can be posed in considering these Notting Hill Carnival debates. How can the renewed calls to a performance authenticity based on the Trinidad Carnival model be explained? How do discussions on musical repertoires reveal attitudes within Caribbean communities towards inclusion and exclusion from Carnival and how can these be addressed? Why do some Notting Hill carnivalists wish to return to 'tradition', to a restriction of repertoires, and why do they offer critiques against other Caribbean genres – such as reggae, sound systems and zouk?

What does this tell us about home in the global city? What does it tell us about home in the diaspora?

Stuart Hall suggests that cultural identity is a 'matter of "becoming" as well as of being' and that such a sense of identity 'belongs to the future as much as to the past' (Hall 1996a [1990]: 112). Alleyne-Dettmers discusses Carnival in London as a performance with ties to the past and aspirations for the future that therefore tells us something about identity as a 'matter of becoming'. She observes that Carnival performance can 'regenerate the past', but that there is also a 'hidden agenda to re-inscribe it into new formulations' (Alleyne-Dettmers 2000: 161). One of the consequences of the Greater London Authority review was to make explicit the agendas for re-inscribing Carnival into new formulations. While immediate concerns revolved around safety issues, the broader project was to think about how Carnival, as London's major musical spectacle, could be developed as a tourist attraction (Lee Jasper, Chair of the Greater London Authority Review Group, personal communication, 2001). Notting Hill Carnival was described as Europe's largest street festival. In debates, contradictions between those aspiring towards development and those arguing for the maintenance of Carnival as a specifically Trinidadian performance space arose from not fully acknowledging the various ways in which the Trinidad Carnival itself has changed. Invoking 'authenticity' to 'regenerate the past' and assessing current performance practices by referring to past ones led some performers to argue that from an island (Trinidad and Tobago) perspective, musical genres such as reggae, salsa and zouk are not authentic or specific Carnival sounds.

The emphasis of some carnivalists on authenticity is something more than Hutnyk's perspective of 'authenticity' discourse as the marketing of exotica, a descriptor only applied to performers at the 'margins', or cultural sites for appropriation in which materials can be taken over and re-presented by more powerful artists with slicker and richer marketing agencies (Hutnyk 2000). Carnivalists raised authenticity as a medium for exploring inclusion and exclusion from Carnival performance spaces, but did so by speaking from within those performance spaces. Their ideas about authenticity revealed the importance of matters relating to performance practices, as well as of ideologically orientated questions about to whom Carnival belongs or for whom it is performed. These are aesthetic and performance-orientated debates that go beyond the view of musical practices as being only about commodities and products in commercial markets.

Moreover, conflicting ideas about what should be performed, where the performance should take place and how music should be performed show how musical performance provides a medium for exploring a wide array of social questions.[5] The Carnival Review Group meetings illuminated the tensions between Caribbean island attachment and general identification with a Black minority in Britain. What do these tensions tell us? The contributions of carnivalists to Carnival discussions provoke an analysis that overturns some assumptions about the sameness of Black performance spaces. While complaints about underfunding as a result of Carnival being viewed as a Black art form were voiced, the renewed emphasis on performance authenticity nevertheless highlighted one way in which carnivalists questioned the similarity of Black expressive cultures. Carnival, then, is not simply a 'Black' spectacle. And such an assertion gains potency in the diasporic context of Britain. For Trinbagonians (from the Republic of Trinidad and Tobago), the Notting Hill Carnival is modelled on the Trinidad spectacle with all of its specific performance traditions. Moreover, Carnival is not just a performance that we can view to gain insights into the playing out of various ideological positions. In debates, carnivalists – from performance-orientated perspectives – privileged aesthetic concerns and traditional performance practices over 'Black issues'. In doing so, they certainly demonstrated ideological positions and something of the 'richness of cultural struggle in and around "race"' (Gilroy 1987: 154). These struggles could be read in terms of internal frictions and the loss of a mobilising political opportunity to present a united 'Black' perspective. There is that dimension to the struggles around 'race'. But in privileging 'performance' issues, as the carnivalists do, the struggles can be read with more optimism too. Gilroy suggests that

> Black British cultures have been created from diverse and contradictory elements apprehended through discontinuous histories. They have been formed in a field of force between the poles of under- and over-development, periphery and centre.... The outcomes of this cultural and political interaction reconstruct and rework tradition as they pursue their particular utopia. A vision of a world in which 'race' will no longer be a meaningful device for the categorization of human beings. (Gilroy 1987: 218)

In debating creative, aesthetic issues, some of which revolved around ideas about authenticity and tradition, carnivalists complicated simple ideas about the complicities of performance and 'race' and in their concerns over creative matters, 'race' could not be reduced to simple binary oppositions: white or black, for example.

In 2005, claims to urban spaces took a new turn. The Greater London Authority offered a Caribbean music spectacle in Hyde Park in an attempt, as perceived by carnivalists, to move Notting Hill away from the streets and transform Carnival into a mere tourist enterprise. Quoting 'the road made to walk', some participants suggested that such a spectacle should be boycotted. The Greater London Authority argued that the Hyde Park concert was a way of finding new venues for a Carnival that had outgrown its traditional route through the streets of Notting Hill. By the end of the 2006 Carnival season, these discussions had been resolved with plans to collaborate. The new performance spaces of Hyde Park would contribute to making the Notting Hill Carnival even bigger in the future.

Caribana

As in Trinidad and Tobago and in London, Caribana provoked discussion about developing Carnival in Toronto as a tourist economy. Indeed, Carnival commentaries focused on the issue of Caribana's economic status in 2001. Reports such as the Whistler document (exploring consumer profiles for the Canadian Department of Communications) have noted the increasing importance of festivals in the 'creation and dissemination of artistic work' and the significant economic impact of this 'cultural industry' (Holgerson 1991). Despite acknowledgement of Caribana's market potential, the financial management of this Carnival was much criticised in press reports. The *Toronto Star* noted: 'Over the years, Caribana has been plagued by money and organizational problems and marred by violence. The Caribbean Cultural Committee still needs to get its house in order' (*Toronto Star*, 3 August 2001: A22). Internal frictions within the organising committee (the Caribbean Cultural Committee) became a matter for public contemplation. *Metro Today* reported: 'For the past few months, the 2001 committee began breaking down because of infighting. It was touch and go for a while – half of the committee resigned and the chief executive officer was suspended over a contract dispute' (*Metro Today*, 2 August 2001: 13). The City Council accused the Caribana festival board of being incapable of handling public money and had to take over Caribana's expenditure from an allotted 350 million dollar fund (*Eye News*, 2 August 2001: 12). Carnivalists, too, contributed to debates about this tourist economy, complaining about the lack of sufficient support for their activities from the finances raised during the Carnival season. Louis Saldenah, for example, a mas bandleader in Toronto, commented on Caribana economy in the following terms:

> Caribana really doesn't sell itself but everyone knows it's one of the largest festivals in North America. It brings in over $350 million into the economy. And if you try to get a hotel downtown it's almost impossible. [It is government funded] from the City and the Province, but you know when we are bringing $350 million into the economy and the provincial government is taking over $25 million in taxes, $450,000 given to the bandleaders is absolutely nothing. This is where all the negativity breaks out in the media because I agree that Caribana doesn't operate correctly especially where finances are concerned. But on the next hand, Caribana is really under funded concerning the impact it has on the economy. (Louis Saldenah, personal communication, July 2001)

Toronto carnivalists, like Saldenah, expressed a wish (as in the Notting Hill debates) to see the generated revenues redirected back into community initiatives:

> I always believe it's like protecting your investment and when you look at Caribana and you look at the overall picture, and you look at the people who are making all the money, it's not Caribana, it's not the artistes who are putting on the show. Airlines, vendors, TTC, ferry, hotels – they're making more money than anyone else. (Louis Saldenah, personal communication, July 2001)

Hunter notes that the lack of demonstrable benefit to Canadian Caribbean communities has been a general criticism made by community members (Hunter 1996: 13). Despite the wealth that Caribana seems to generate for the local economy, the organising committee itself has been operating at a deficit almost since the beginning – from 1968 (in Caribana's second year). By the mid 1990s, the Caribbean Cultural Committee recognised that it needed to move from being a community-based organisation to a streamlined, professional structure that would encourage corporate and public sector funding and therefore set up, with the Chairperson of the Municipality of Metropolitan Toronto, a Task Force that would make recommendations regarding the future development of the event. These recommendations included changing the parade route, charging for festival site events, drawing on volunteers to reduce the amount of public services needed, marketing and sponsoring events that hold the potential to generate income, and establishing better communications with interested parties (Hunter 1996, Report of the Task Force). Despite attempts to maximise infrastructural potential, the following years brought even greater debts to the organising committee.

River of Life. Against the background of organisational controversy, the main concerns of Caribana carnivalists revolved around artistic questions. In this respect they paralleled the Notting Hill carnivalists, who insisted in the Greater London Authority Review Group meetings that whatever organisational problems were faced in setting up Carnival, an appreciation of this performance as an art form should remain paramount. For the tourist, too, it is the spectacle itself that matters. While discourses about tourist economies, Carnival histories and development strategies provide a context within which Carnival politics may be understood, other kinds of discourses around authenticity, repertoires, performance legitimacy and competition reveal some of the aesthetic as well as political dynamics that shape Carnival as a musical spectacle. In discussing the Notting Hill Carnival debates, I asserted the importance of considering aesthetic as well as ideological realms, based on the concerns expressed by various carnivalists in the Carnival review exercise. I want to develop this point with further ethnographic evidence from the Canadian context. I shall turn therefore to an example of a mas band in Toronto to consider Carnival preparation processes and the extent to which Canadian Caribbeans continue to be informed by Trinidad Carnival performance aesthetics.

Louis Saldenah has been involved in Caribana as a mas bandleader for twenty years and has won the mas band competition 'band of the year' ten times in the past twelve years. Winning bands tend to attract the largest following (Foster and Schwartz 1995: 48) and Saldenah's has around 1,200 people in costume: 'We have been the biggest band in Caribana for the past ten years. We have people from the islands (Caribbean), we have people from the States, from England, we have people from Saudi Arabia who registered with us through the internet' (Louis Saldenah, personal communication, July 2001).

Saldenah comes from a family famous for its participation in the Trinidad Carnival. His father played mas in Trinidad for 35 years. Despite this background, he asserts an individual style and notes how his Canadian experiences shape his Carnival themes:

> So I really don't look to Trinidad for ideas. My ideas are instilled in me and I try to be just as good as Trinidad Carnival. Basically, I have my own ideas and my own identity where Carnival is concerned. I have to have the feeling. The feeling just comes to me when I'm ready and then I go with my instinct. So a few years ago we played, 'Ontario – Yours to Discover' [he won the band of the year with this theme]. So it's something that once it happens in my brain then I go with it. One year I was driving my car and

> there was a radio station saying 'night out' and I played 'Night Out' because of that and I just interpreted that in costumes. (Louis Saldenah, personal communication, July 2001)

The music that he chooses to play with his costumes, however, comes from Trinidad and Tobago. He turns to some of Trinidad's most popular singers. In making this musical choice he points to the reproduction in Canada of struggles for performance space by different kinds of Carnival musics: steelbands, calypso and soca singers, and DJ sound systems.

> I'm using two live bands from Trinidad – top bands, Traffik and Charlie's Roots with David Rudder. And also a DJ. There are two parts in Caribana there's the steelband parade and then there's the costume with live music bands and I'm on the side with live music bands because people who participate in these fabulous costumes like to be having a good time and the music has to be a little quick tempo. And as you know the steelband plays pretty slow and those people who play with me like to get into it and have a good time. David Rudder has played with me for the past few years and I've noticed when we get on a show he plays a lot of his old music – 'Bahia Girl', 'Dust in Yuh Face', and so on, which I like a lot. He brings in the old hits because it has a nice tempo, and upbeat, you know and I don't mind. (Louis Saldenah, personal communication, July 2001)

Musical choices as much as costume designs may determine which mas band attracts the most followers and wins the Carnival competitions. As Foster and Schwartz put it: 'the band will also be remembered the next time for the music that kept onlookers swaying, for the rhythms that caused spectators to jump spontaneously into the band and become a part of the extravaganza, for the lyrics that kept everyone singing and joining the response and call of the chorus or the song's reprise' (1995: 45). Bandleaders generally confirm what the band's music will be several months in advance and pay deposits to secure the contribution of a well-known calypso band or sound system, often choosing musicians from the Caribbean.

Similarly, planning the costumes begins months in advance of the Carnival parade. Mas bands consist of several sections which all offer various perspectives on a central theme. The themes are chosen for their potential to be expressed through costumes. Sections have their own leaders, the section captains. In choosing themes, a mas bandleader will work with the section captains to explore ideas and to decide colour schemes and costume shapes. Saldenah related how the theme for his Carnival 2001 appearance was chosen:

> [The theme is] 'River of Life'. This is the first time I didn't bring the theme of the band. Normally it's my theme. What happened is, originally I wanted to play puppetry, but the committee that work with me said it was a little difficult to bring because of the time. So Steve, my co-designer, said 'Well let's bring survival'. I told him I didn't like the name 'survival' because it's on TV so many times. You know they will think we copy, and so on. So he came with 'River of Life' and so we developed the theme and that's what we did this year. Once the theme was developed we started sourcing materials and because we have a large amount of people working with us it took us about a month to produce all the costumes.... We have about five tables at night working on costumes, so it's like mass production. (Louis Saldenah, personal communication, July 2001)

Tony Ishmael was one of the section captains with this mas band. He headed a section called 'Faith'. I asked him about his section and whether he was following Carnival trends in Trinidad and Tobago to develop his costume ideas for Caribana. In his response we can note how 'survival', that had been rejected as a broad unifying theme, endured as a way of thinking about costume designs. Like Saldenah, Ishmael emphasises his own creative processes. He is part of the circulation of carnivalists between Caribbean island and diasporic metropolitan city, but even though he travels to see the Trinidad Carnival and to collect his materials for the Caribana season, he insists on his practice as an independent designer:

> Our Band theme this year is the 'River of Life'. In the 'River of Life' we picked out twelve themes as we have twelve sections. Obviously we couldn't pick everything so between the twelve section leaders we got together and decided which section we wanted to bring. It's sort of like a survivor band.

You can't survive without water so we have the water section. You can't survive without the sunlight so we have the sun section. Same thing, I feel that if you don't have faith you could as well give up. We have the hope section. All that reflects survival. The emblem used on our sign is like an upside down heart, which is the international symbol of faith. The colours I chose: the black, yellow and gold. Each section leader chooses their own colours and they work with the designer, Steve, and I gave my ideas to him so he works with that so that each section complements each other. I wouldn't say that anything in Trinidad influences me because I am a designer in my own right. Obviously we all copy from each other, we see something we like. For instance, my headpiece here may not be very steady but if I try to make it more steady it will be heavier. And the person who is using this headpiece does not want anything heavy on her head. So I have to make it extremely light. So even though I saw a way of reinforcing it in Trinidad, to make it more rigid, she will not wear it because it becomes more heavy. So there are certain things you could see and learn and copy, other things you can't. Where going down to Trinidad assists me is because when I go down I already know the colours I want for Caribana and I already know what I'm doing for Caribana, so I'm able to go and scout around for fabrics because that's the home of fabrics, and I select all my samples. And when I come up here I show it to the designer and I say 'This is what I want...' and he works around that and then I order it from Trinidad, all my body suits are flown up from Trinidad. I deal with a company called Chaos and they do everything for me every year. If you look at my storyboard here you can see the designer's rendering and you can see how I source all the materials for my section. Everything I'm using here is on that board. (Tony Ishmael, personal communication, July 2001)

Aspects of Tony Ishmael's biographical details and Carnival practice throw light on issues about specific island attachment and on a generalised sense of Caribbeanness in Canada. He has been playing in Caribana since its first year, 1967. He used to be a bandleader, but joined Saldenah's camp because of other work commitments. He has been part of the camp as a section leader for 18 years. Although Ishmael travels to the Trinidad Carnival he migrated to Canada from St Lucia. He had been active as a carnivalist in St Lucia since childhood and had won the Band of the Year competition in St Lucia seven times before moving to Canada. When he took part in the 1967 Caribana he was involved with a section entitled 'We are the Caribbeans' and led participants from St Lucia. He reminisced that the first Caribana was just a festival that brought Caribbeans together because that was a tradition that they had in common. There were ten sections representing different Caribbean islands. Later on, Ishmael launched the Junior Carnival and then the Miss Caribbean Carnival Competition. He was motivated, like others in his community, by a wish to transmit traditional performance practices to Canadian-born children of Caribbean parentage. His daughter, then, is also a carnivalist and has won the title 'Queen of Carnival' as a junior and as an adult performer. (She was defending her crown in 2001 for the third year, and successfully retained it with a costume of a fish.) Since migrating to Canada, Ishmael has pursued Carnival practice in the Caribbean, in Trinidad and Tobago. He has been involved with Carnival education projects in Trinidad and has not missed the Trinidad Carnival season for many years. Although he displays particular enthusiasm for this art form, he is aware of the extent to which Carnival participation depends on aesthetic and performance interest, and not just on a sense of identity represented as 'Caribbean'. He noted:

> Even when I'm in Trinidad I'm surprised at the number of people who don't care about Carnival. Carnival, Sunday, Monday and Tuesday they plan to go on picnics with their friends and family and they have nothing to do with the festival in Port-of-Spain or other major cities. The same thing in the rest of the Caribbean islands. There are people who are not into Carnival and no matter what you do, if they're inside their home[s] they may not even look out to see what's passing outside. They absolutely have no interest. But for those who are Carnival people in the islands, once they migrate to Toronto they get hooked up with one of the masquerade camps. (Tony Ishmael, personal communication, July 2001)

The testimonies of a mas band leader and of a section captain point to some of the specific ways in which the Trinidad Carnival continues to provide a model for Carnival practice in Toronto. Carnival practices had been transmitted through family involvement in the Caribbean and a familial interest continues to shape ongoing participation in the Canadian context. The musical choices of mas band participants are shaped by the contemporary musical scenes of the Caribbean. Canadian carnivalists may continue to take an active role in Caribbean Carnivals and thus remain up-to-date with performance aesthetics. There are also Trinidad and Caribana Carnival economic networks. Ishmael, for example, buys his costume materials for Caribana in Trinidad. Yet, these testimonies also point to the ways in which Caribana is seen as being a Canadian spectacle. Saldenah hears something on the local radio and thinks of a mas band theme that celebrates Ontario. Mas band participants insist on their own creative contributions. They are not just reproducing a Trinidad model. In the same way that Springer noted that the Trinidad Carnival could not be a simple reproduction of a Wosirian drama, the Toronto event has taken on its own form. Launching Junior and Miss Caribbean Carnival competitions has been a way of familiarising and involving Canadians of 'Caribbean parentage' with some of the performance traditions of the Caribbean.

Concluding Thoughts

For Saldenah and Ishmael, history is an important concept that shapes their Carnival activities in Toronto. But they are conscious, too, of forging a new kind of Carnival that is specific to the Canadian context and that is partly a reminder for their Canadian children of a Caribbean island 'heritage'. In 1998, Saldenah set up an all-year-round mas camp in Toronto (Figure 7.1). His aims were pragmatic and political: to preserve the costumes that had been designed for future use, to have costumes available for other kinds of events (such as in the city's Olympic bid displays), and to make Caribana a more permanent feature of Toronto's musical landscape by providing an exhibition space that would also record this mas camp's costume history:

> I set up this permanent mas camp three years ago.... We were moving from warehouse to warehouse every year. We were just renting out for

three months. I realised all of our good costumes were being destroyed because we couldn't afford storage.... We organise a lot of different stuff all year round and actually if you come in here at any time of the year you will see the costumes displayed here so you would know that we take part in Caribana and shows outside of Toronto.... Everybody just happens to think about Caribana for the two months period and you know we make elaborate costumes. And what happens in previous years – once Caribana is over the costumes are destroyed because there's no place to store the costumes and if we do get a place it's really expensive. So I decided to get something permanent for our group so the costumes can be reused right during the season. (Louis Saldenah, personal communication, July 2001)

Figure 7.1 Louis Saldenah (right) at his mas camp

Keith Nurse notes that

> Since the 1990s, carnival has become big business, especially in terms of cultural tourism and cultural industry in each of the three key art-forms: mas, pan and calypso. The Trinidad carnival has grown to be the premier festival in the region, attracting between thirty and forty thousand visitors for the festival which generates foreign exchange earnings of over US$30 million.... The carnivalists benefit from the transnational economic flows that have been generated by the growth of the overseas Caribbean carnivals

in North America and Europe. The consolidation of the diasporic community has led to the creation of year-round work for musical artists, masquerade designers and other professionals from Trinidad. (1999: 673)

My ethnographic snapshot of Carnivals linked through transnational networks of economic and aesthetic exchange resonates with Nurse's analysis. The transnational and national interact in complex ways, on one hand embracing the tourist as a 'stranger' (a transient visitor) in Carnival as a cultural industry, and on the other exploring Carnival as a performance practice through which histories across the national and the diasporic can be recovered. I hope that what has been highlighted here are the ways in which discourses about Carnival's economic benefits interweave with questions about performance practices and histories, and the extent to which these revolve around the localised political concerns of participants.

Saldenah's ideas about the display of Carnival costume history in this mas camp were reminiscent of museums in Halifax, Nova Scotia and Ellis Island, New York, that similarly display material artefacts that give insights into the histories of migrations to the New World. Within a broad history of migration the idea of some people living at 'home' and others in a 'host land' loses its force. The testimonies of Saldenah and Ishmael do not sit well in the formula that presents Carnival as little more than a performance that plays out binary oppositional states (between 'diasporic' and 'at home' communities). For Saldenah and Ishmael, Carnival in the diaspora is more than a performance of being at and away from home. It is, or should be, more than just a 'Black festival' in Canada (Louis Saldenah, personal communication, 2001). Theorisation of 'hybridity' grapples with some of the complexities of their experiences but does not offer a ready and easy way of conceptualising them. Hutnyk critiques hybridity as being another aspect of ethnic politics at work in cultural production:

> Hybrid cultural practice is assigned to the ethnicised zones of the margin from the very outset. That the most rigid versions of the centre-and-margin model operate a hegemonic white supremacist vision has often been pointed out. That its more sympathetic renderings also carry a perniciously

homogenising 'future' vision of an integrated Western culture-in-multiplicity is the grand trick of capitalist 'difference'. (Hutnyk 2000: 123)

Ethnicised zones at the margins in centre-periphery models recur in the distinctions of homelands – host-lands. We find people living in 'host-lands' through generations as they live in 'ethnicised zones'. The descriptor 'host-land' applied to Caribbean diasporic communities in Britain is inappropriate, however, given the historical connections over centuries. The struggles over 'race' that have taken place in Carnival performances also demonstrate a response against the limits of 'ethnicised zones'.

I would like to briefly take up that idea of 'hybridity' as a 'grand trick of capitalist 'difference'. I shall juxtapose it with Harris's notion of the 'trickster gateway' (1999 [1970]) to make the point that carnivalists who engage in debates about performance authenticity, diaspora and belonging cannot merely be seen as the victims of a 'grand trick of capitalist difference' that represents a Western triumph over its 'ethnic others' and reinforces the idea of separation. In this regard, Harris's refusal to see the Caribbean as only an 'adjunct of imperialism' (1999 [1970]: 158) is instructive in warning against the simplicities of binary polarisations between the powerful and the powerless.

Hutnyk points out that hybridity-talk contains the paradox of essentialism (the idea that somewhere there is a 'pure' something that has contributed for instance to a 'new' practice in cultural mixes). In exploring the use of the term to describe the cultural practices of 'others' located at the margins he launches a critique of 'difference' that fits well with my view of musical practice in the Caribbean Diaspora as a medium for creative expression, empowerment and political visibility that pushes against the borders of non-belonging. Are people who identify themselves as part of a Caribbean Diaspora 'tricked' in Hutnyk's formulation into remaining on the margins? I think they are not and that centre–periphery models do not always reflect the real movements of people. When carnivalists struggle to create a musical spectacle that speaks as a multiply situated performance they are demonstrating the scope of the creative imagination and claiming major urban spaces as their own. How can one conceptualise these creativities? In Chapter 2, I discussed the importance of adopting historical perspectives that reveal centuries of interconnectedness such that it would be incorrect to interpret diasporic musical production only in terms of new creative and cultural mixes. In Chapter 3, I argued for an understanding of creativity as everyday process that works against the politics of 'difference'. Such are the legacies of empire and the projects of creating others that the politics of difference have to be addressed and, in fact, struggled over (as I suggested in Chapter 5). If hybridity seems to be about combinations, about encounters, Harris provides an alternative to our understanding of creativity as emerging from things taken away. Exploring limbo in the Caribbean, Harris plays on the idea of limb and dismemberment to talk about people who have been 'dislocated' and 'violated by economic fates'. In limbo, a dancer moves under a bar that is gradually lowered. Harris describes the movements as becoming spider-like, a description that enables him to tap into the Anancy (the 'trickster' spider) stories. A second thread in his analysis is his word play on limb/limbo, to draw attention to physical displacements, the locus of the imagination and creative spirit within the body, and the dancing body as a site of historical memory. The creative spirit remains powerful despite severance – the dismembered limb that is the legacy of slavery (separation from a homeland). The reassembly of those limbs occurs in the Anancy (spider-like) dance of limbo. His interpretation of the limbo dance ultimately provides a profoundly optimistic vision of the creative spirit in face of the ruptures and fragmentations that have characterised Caribbean societies. When Harris wrote this piece, his vision forced us to rethink the Caribbean as being history-less. What is remarkable, too, about this analysis is Harris's insistence that the points he makes extend beyond the particularities of African voyages across the Middle Passage. Harris writes:

> For limbo (one cannot emphasize this too much) is not the total recall of an African past since that African past in terms of tribal sovereignty or sovereignties was modified or traumatically eclipsed with the Middle

Passage and with generations of change that followed. Limbo was rather the renascence of a new corpus of sensibility that could translate and accommodate African and other legacies within a new architecture of cultures. For example, the theme of the phantom limb – the re-assembly of dismembered man or god – possesses archetypal resonances that embrace Egyptian Osiris, the resurrected Christ, and the many-armed deity of India. (1999 [1970]: 158)

The reference to ancient Egyptian and Indian deities in this description of limbo is reminiscent of recent analyses of Carnival in relation to the Wosirian drama or to Saivism. Harris sees limbo as a 'ground of accommodation' and as an 'art of creative coexistence' that points 'away from apartheid and ghetto fixations' (1999 [1970]: 158). Such an interpretation is essential to free creative expressions from the 'prison' of the past: 'the limbo dance becomes the human gateway which dislocates (and therefore begins to free itself from) a uniform chain of miles across the Atlantic' (1990 [1970]: 159).

Let me restate the central question posed at the outset of this book: where is home in the diaspora? In exploring this question, I have been considering what 'a new architecture of cultures' might be – the ways in which diasporic creativity make us rethink ideas about 'culture' as property and as attribute; the ways in which homes are made; and the ways in which claims to history and to performance spaces are asserted. While carnivalists in Trinidad and Tobago look, for example, to the homeland in Africa or India, for the Caribbean Diaspora, the homeland is the Caribbean island as much as other preceding homelands in Africa or India. This tells us something about home in the diaspora such that Trinidad and Tobago, London and Toronto also become 'homes'. Carnivals as public musical spectacles in the Caribbean and in the Caribbean Diaspora open up Harris's 'gateways', offering themselves either as sites of conflict or as performance expressions that point to visions of another kind of social order. Harris lays the onus on the artist to strive for those gateways. Writing about intellectual and legal suspicion towards the imaginative arts, he notes:

> Therefore the rise of the poet or artist incurs a gamble of the soul which is symbolised in the West Indian trickster (the spider or anancy configuration). It is this element of tricksterdom that creates an individual and personal risk absolutely foreign to the conventional sanction of an Old Tribal World: a risk which identifies him (the artist) with the submerged authority of dispossessed peoples but requires of him, in the same token, alchemic resources to conceal, as well as elaborate, a far-reaching order of the imagination which, being suspect, could draw upon him a crushing burden of censorship in economic or political terms. He stands therefore at the heart of the lie of the community and the truth of community. And it is here, I believe, in this trickster gateway – the gamble of the soul – that there emerges the hope for a profoundly compassionate society committed to freedom within a creative scale. (1999 [1970]: 166)

Striving to go beyond the limits of difference might take us through the 'trickster gateway' into Aunty Nansi's Beautiful Cosmos, which is a vision of freedom within a creative scale. If the idea of separation still appears in Harris's rhetoric of 'creative co-existence' and 'accommodation' (resting on assumptions of difference and conflict), so too does it appear in discourses on 'hybridity' and 'multiple subjectivity'. Trinidad Carnival, Notting Hill Carnival and Caribana show us that the 'reassembly' of a performance art in diasporic contexts offers the potential, one that would take us beyond the boundaries of both hybridity as creative mixes and performance as an oppositional, conflictive practice, to forge new creative expressions (Harris's 'arts of the imagination') that are themselves performances of being at home.

Agawu observes that there 'is no method for attending to sameness, only a presence of mind, an attitude, a way of seeing the world' (Agawu 2003: 169). Through ethnographic attention to musical performances, this book has attended to similarity rather than difference. It has explored the gateways between remembering and forgetting, between solidarity and conflict, between home and diaspora. The metaphor of the 'trickster gateway' has served a dual purpose. It has been a way of highlighting alternatives, reflecting on the ways in which we might imagine and work towards different kinds of social and political possibilities, and pointing to the mediations necessary to bring these about. It accommodates disagreement and contradiction. The metaphor of the gateway has also pointed to the unknown, to the 'gamble' that must be taken in moving through it. Ethnography is a way of exploring contradiction, possibility and the socio-political world through a close-up view of musical performances. It is a way of writing about the ways in which people use musical expression to assert specific cultural histories and diasporic identities. It is also a way of writing about just 'how tangled music really is' (Slobin 1993: ix) so that we do not end up with uncomplicated understandings of performances as spaces of conflict or utopia. The entanglements of diasporic musical expression have been explored in relation to historical narratives (connections through imperial histories, steelband histories, the dancing body as a site of historical memory and Carnival performance histories) and political visions (the struggles for 'One Love' and thinking beyond 'difference'). Such an approach leaves us on one side of the trickster gateway. I have wrestled, however, with the ambiguities of the trickster gateway in considering the politics of human relatedness through the world of musical performances, the processes of creativity as a way of conceptualising home in the diaspora, and the disjunctures between a politics of difference and a politics of possibility that works towards global equity. In looking at musical production and innovation in diasporic politics, I have found myself considering the same issues that troubled writers over a century ago. In *The Souls of Black Folk*, Du Bois turned to musical expression to discuss the problems of the 'color-line' (1999 [1903]: 17), to present an argument about being both Black and American (thereby thinking about national exclusions and inclusions on the basis of 'race'), and to state a broad political vision concerned with the equality of people – the 'human brotherhood'. This kind of politically engaged scholarship remains relevant today. But for now, Aunty Nansi, in John Agard's transformation of Kwaku-Ananse, divinely associated with the sky god and whose musical ability in singing and playing the fiddle is celebrated, will have the last word. Stepping through the trickster gateway between diasporic 'difference' and performances 'out-of-place' (on one side) and diasporic reassembly and performances 'at home' (on the other), we might hear Aunty Nansi laughing as she asks: 'Am I Afro-Celto-Euro-Indo or just beautiful byproduct of cosmos?'

APPENDIX

British Calypsonians

Admiral Jack
Alexander D. Great
Kerwin Dubois
Kizzie Ruiz
Lord Cloak
Mighty Explorer
Mighty Tiger
Peace and Love
Rev. Sweetfoot
Sister Sandra
The Astronaut
Totally Talibah

Table A.1 Members of the Trinidad All Steel Percussion Orchestra

Player	Age at the time of the tour	Instrument	Steelband affiliation in Trinidad
Sterling Betancourt ('Sty Woa')	21	Alto pong (or 'second pan')	Crossfire Steel Orchestra (based in St James)
Belgrave Bonaparte	19	Alto pong (or 'second pan')	Southern Symphony Orchestra (La Brea)
Philmore Davidson ('Boot')	22	Bass ('booms')	City Syncopators
Andrew De La Batisde	23	1st ping pong	Chicago
Orman Haynes ('Patsy')	21	2nd ping pong	Casablanca

Table A.1 continued

Player	Age at the time of the tour	Instrument	Steelband affiliation in Trinidad
Neville Jules (He did not attend rehearsals regularly and de-selected himself from the tour.)			Trinidad All Stars
Ellie Mannette	22 or 25	1st ping pong	Invaders (Woodbrook)
Sonny Roach (He was taken ill and returned to Trinidad once the orchestra had reached Martinique.)	24	Ping pong	Sun Valley Orchestra (St James)
Winston Simon ('Spree')	24	1st ping pong	Tropical Harmony (changed its name later on to 'Fascinators')
Dudley Smith	24	Tenor boom	Rising Sun Orchestra (Belmont)
Theodore Stephens	17 or 18	2nd ping pong	Free French Steelband (San Fernando)
Anthony Williams ('Muffman')	20	Tenor boom	North Stars (St James)

Note: The orchestra was directed by Nathaniel Joseph Griffiths (from Barbados where he had been the director of a police band).

Table A.2 Steelbands in Britain listed by the British Association of Steelbands, 2001

Steelband	Area
Dayspring Steelband	Coventry
Ebony (1969)	West London
Eclipse Steel Orchestra (1987)	North London
Forest Gate Steel Orchestra	East London

Steelband	Area
Glissando Steel Orchestra (1975)	West London
Hammered Steel	Penzance
London All Stars	South West London
Maestros	Birmingham
Man Tab Next Generation	West London
Mangrove Steelband (1980)	West London
Metronomes Steel (1971)	West London
New World Steelband	Leeds
North Stars Steelband	Huddersfield
Nostalgia Steelband	East London
Pan Nectar	North West London
Pan Vibes Steel Orchestra	North London
Pantasia	North London
Pantonic Steel Orchestra (1988)	North London
Phase 1 Steel Orchestra	Coventry
Rainbow Steel Orchestra	Bath
Real Steel	Plymouth
Southside Harmonics (originally Lambeth Youth Steel Orchestra, 1976)	South West London
Stardust Steel Orchestra	West London
Steelasophical	Middlesex

Note: The date when the steelband was established is given, where known.

NOTES

Memories

1. I am grateful to participants at the Remembered Rhythms seminar for raising these points in discussions about the importance of music in the diaspora, especially those about representation (Ashok da Ranade) and portability (Anthony Seeger).
2. One reason for this emphasis is that the former British Caribbean territories of Trinidad and Jamaica have produced some of the most well-known musical styles including calypso, soca, chutney, rapso, steelbands, ska, reggae and dancehall. The practice of these musical genres in the former colonial centre provides an apt space for reflecting on some of the dynamics of diaspora identities in the postcolonial moment and for engaging with postcolonial studies. The poignant realisation of postwar Caribbean migrants to Britain that they were not returning to a place that they had been taught to regard as a homeland and to which they had been invited to provide a labour force for transport and health systems, for example, has brought to the forefront issues of inclusion and exclusion that continue to be played out over five decades later. Another reason is that the dissemination of Caribbean popular music, even in North America, has often been mediated via Europe, particularly in the early twentieth century. The Caribbean music recordings of the British gramophone company HMV were distributed widely: to the Caribbean, Latin America, the United States and West Africa. Similarly, other European centres (France and Spain) have been important in the spread of Caribbean music. Musicians from the French-speaking Caribbean islands and from Cuba were recording at the French Odeon from the late 1920s, and performers undertook concert tours of the United States from their Paris base (Cowley 2001). A third reason is that the Caribbean Diaspora in Britain highlights multiple perspectives across the Atlantic, the centuries of interconnectedness, the historical legacies that might propel us towards rethinking the paradoxes of diasporic sensibilities and that strike against the core of ideological fictions centred on 'identity' and 'difference'. In fact, an appreciation of these colonial and postcolonial histories, of the entanglement of European imperial powers (mainly Britain, the Netherlands, France and Spain) with territories in the New World, of global commerce and

traffic of people since the sixteenth century, is crucial to reassessing the polarities of diaspora and home.
3. Avtar Brah raises a series of questions that turn our attention to the inscription and articulation of difference: 'How does difference designate the 'other'? Who defines difference? What are the presumed norms from which a group is marked as being different? What is the nature of attributions that are claimed as characterising a group as different? How are boundaries of difference constituted, maintained or dissipated?' (1996: 115). A shift away from difference does not evade such questions, but highlights the point that the inscription of difference does not have to be accepted uncritically or taken for granted.

Chapter 1

1. In a study of multi-ethnic discourses in London, Baumann compares different strategies for establishing community in the West London suburb of Southall and highlights the importance that musical spaces have had in bringing African-Caribbeans together. In terms of the Caribbean community's infrastructure, Baumann notes that there are few formal political or religious institutions that unite this community in the same ways as other Southall communities: 'Unlike Sikhs and Hindus, but like Muslims, Afro-Caribbeans are not represented among the elected councillors and are few and far between in the other civic power structures. Unlike the Muslim community, however, there is no one place of worship around which community leadership, collective resources, and joint initiatives could crystallize. The settlement pattern in West London, spread widely and thus thinly, helps to render Southall marginal to many Afro-Caribbeans, and Afro-Caribbeans are often regarded as marginal to Southall' (1996: 91). The opening of musical venues has changed this social mapping. The opening of a nightclub in 1988 (Tudor Rose) was the 'biggest thing to happen for the black community in Southall' and with the opening of a second music venue (Mona Lisa) that put on soul, reggae and calypso nights, African-Caribbeans from across West London were drawn to Southall. The night–life landscape, then, was visibly African-Caribbean in contrast to the predominantly public daytime Asian presence (1996: 91). The glimpse into musical spaces given in Baumann's analysis of multi-ethnicity and visibility in Southall is relevant to my focus on performance in the Caribbean Diaspora since many of these spaces have figured prominently in the debates on, and politics of, belonging, identity and 'race'.

2. Cited in Berrian (2000: 26) and translated by Berrian from the French ('Une vielle chanson dit: "Nous ne somme pas gens d'ailleurs. Nous sommes gens d'ici".').

Chapter 2

1. Fifty years later, a BBC documentary, *The Windrush Years*, celebrated the 'arrival' of Caribbean populations in Britain. The programme inspired some debate. Comments like 'There's not a lot to celebrate. Those years were difficult. My parents struggled to even find a place to live' drew nods of understanding from an audience of 'second generation British Caribbeans'. I noted these comments and the responses they drew at a meeting exploring Caribbean Musics in the Institute of Commonwealth Studies, University of London 1998.
2. Listings of recordings and newspaper reports are the source materials that contribute to a portrait of early twentieth century Caribbean music in Britain. Cowley's 1990 study has provided a main reference for the history outlined here.
3. In works like *In The Castle of My Skin* (George Lamming 1998 [1953]), *The Lonely Londoners* (Sam Selvon 1956), *Moses Ascending* (Selvon 1975), *Moses Migrating* (Selvon 1983), *An Area of Darkness* (V. S. Naipaul 1964), *The Mimic Men* (Naipaul 1967), writers explored the experience of migration to Britain, describing a (usually) male world marked by a sense of transience and loneliness.
4. Through educational projects aimed at London's schools, British calypsonians exert a much wider influence and bring into play questions about which musics should receive attention in the national forum even if they are associated with minority interest groups. Another forum in which British calypsonians exercise some influence is the Notting Hill Carnival, one of Europe's largest street events (see Chapter 7).
5. The role of folk music in the construction of national identities has been studied in various European contexts (for example, Bohlman 1988, Goertzen 1997, Ramnarine 2003, Rice 1994, Slobin 1996).
6. For Gordon Rohlehr, post-Independence Trinidadian calypsos are essentially 'texts of survivalism' that often portray the small or weak in the 'grip of dominant forces that work resolutely towards his extinction' (2000: 29). Rohlehr does not see 'active rebellion' in the post-Independence calypso text, but a hope for 'divine justice; desperate faith in the power of the Cosmos to correct social imbalance and firm resolve to "hold on" until divine purpose works itself out'. In this 'universe of inequity', calypsonians take on the role of prophets, commenting on social, political and moral processes, defending

freedoms, predicting disaster and singing the praises of the virtuous, righteous and outstanding (2000: 29). There are differences between the post-Independence Trinidad and Caribbean diasporic calypso scenes. In contrast to Rohlehr's assessment of the post-Independence calypso in Trinidad as texts of resignation to divine justice rather than political will, the urge to 'active rebellion' is evident in British calypso practice. This may be because while Trinidadian calypsonians deal with national concerns from a position of some power as 'voices of the people', British ones are marginal voices in the national chorus. If the British calypsonian can be described as a 'prophet', the prophecy is above all a political one. And the prophecy turns out to be about the place of the calypso genre in British musical life, though one can note the irony in aligning calypso practice to the expressive domain of folk music in England that has itself been recently perceived to be marginalised by its practitioners.
7. Greater London Authority Notting Hill Carnival Review. Recommendations Form (RF1) and Issues Form (IF1) submitted by the Association of British Calypsonians, 9 May 2001.
8. Alexander D. Great became a member of the Association of British Calypsonians in 1995 and he promotes calypso performance through educational and media work. Since 1999, he has appeared on the radio with a weekly topical calypso (on *Choice* and then *London Live*) and he has released some CDs through his own recording venture (personal communication, October 2000). He has also run workshops as part of 'world music' programmes at higher education level at Trinity College of Music, Brunel University and Queen's University Belfast.

Chapter 3

1. At that time, I was only vaguely aware that the Inner London Education Authority ran a steel orchestra alongside the symphony orchestra, of which I was a keen member, in its central London Music Centre. It was some years later that I began to visit panyards in Trinidad, to attend performances in various parts of the world and to look up information about steelbands on the Internet – different locations which offer a way of engaging with steelband projects in and beyond Trinidad and Tobago.
2. Live performance is important in experiencing steelband: 'people desire to be enveloped by the pan sound – not only actually to feel the rhythms and hear the range of voices in the orchestras but to immediately connect with the music's creators' (Steumpfle 1995: 233). While the live performance aesthetic of the principal steelband

competition, Panorama, includes fast tempos that result in some blurring of pitch, recorded performances of Panorama arrangements, largely produced by Simeon Sandiford since the 1980s, present a more controlled sound. His recordings have been made at the panyards during the weeks preceding Panorama, rather than at the event itself, since background noises (crowds and traffic) are easier to control. The relaxed mood of the performers reduces mistakes and their slower tempos result in greater clarity in the pan sound. Ingram suggests that Sandiford's personal preferences determine the kind of Panorama recordings that feature in international spaces and that he therefore presents an example of local actors shaping global media processes (see Ingram 2001). If recorded aesthetics depart from the aesthetics of live performance, opportunities to hear steelbands in the Caribbean are manifold, from large competitions such as Panorama in Trinidad to hotels throughout the region.
3. Early makers also experimented with making the steelpan mobile – from pans around the neck to pans on wheels. They experimented with tuning layout, hammering pitches in cycles of fourths or fifths. Changes in tuning, from tuning by ear to using a strobe-tuning machine, indicate further developments in steelpan technology.
4. Tamboo bamboo consists of tuned bamboo tubes beaten rhythmically against the ground.
5. The assimilation perspective was criticised as it: 'fails to challenge negative views and is itself racist; requires people to ignore their own cultural backgrounds if they are to succeed in the education system; miseducates everyone in reflecting an inadequate view of Britain in relation to world society; does not learn from other people's experiences'. The cultural diversity perspective informed by beliefs that teaching about culture would promote positive self-images and that issues of racism should maintain a low profile was similarly rejected because it 'emphasises culture while ignoring issues such as economic disparity between communities; reflects a white view of black cultures as homogenous, static, conflict-free, exotic; and does not promote racial equality'. The Inner London Education Authority chose the perspective emphasising equality as one that should inform pedagogic practices. The aims were to 'recognise that racism in wider society is reflected in education systems; draw on Black perspectives to dismantle discriminatory practices; provide social, political and moral education; remove discrimination in educational establishments including courses and textbooks that ignored the validity of black experience; and train staff on principles for combating racism' (Inner London Education Authority, 1983).
6. Some of the details of teaching sessions are provided in this description: 'The bass line is normally taught by listing the notes arhythmically and

then the player is expected to interpret the pitches in an appropriate style. For pieces with very straightforward harmonisation, no help is given by the director; the player works out the key and chord changes unaided and plays them in a suitable rhythm. Gerry [Gerald Forsythe] may glance at the section if he is unhappy with the interpretation but it is very rare for him to speak to them once a tune has been played through satisfactorily by the whole band.... The parts for double seconds, guitars and cellos serve as both chordal harmonies and melodic decoration. Players are expected to know what notes are in major, minor, diminished, seventh chords, although these are usually spelt out for them eventually, if they appear confused' (Spencer 1986: 37–8).
7. For further discussion on the sitar in Trinidad, see Ramnarine (2001).
8. See Ramnarine (1998/99) for a more extensive discussion of the speech given by Daphne Philips.
9. Kronman (1991) speculates that its harmonic spectrum is generated by intricate interaction between the non-linearity of the fundamental and the octave mode.

Chapter 4

1. The musicologist Richard Taruskin follows an anthropological lead in his essay 'Tradition and Authority', looking at how musical authority has been constructed. He considers the context of so-called 'historically authentic performance', which could be understood as conforming to a modern aesthetic. Authority is constructed through a scholarship that operates as an 'inventing agent'. The sources in which musical authority has been invested identified by Taruskin are oral tradition, the composer, the text, the performer, the musicologist and the 'personal' – those who claim to speak on behalf of others such as the conductor who asserts an alliance with the composer (Taruskin 1995).

Chapter 5

1. Nowhere is this privilege more apparent than in the disregard for the voices of those 'natives' who might be able to challenge ethnographic authority. Trouillot notes anthropology's 'flagrant contempt for the most obvious and recognized forms of metasocial commentary emanating from local voices: the discourses of local politicians, local media, and especially local scholars' (2003: 132). Challenging the discursive privileges of ethnographic production, the voices of those

once easily dismissed as 'local' are refusing to be ignored. In the introduction to her study of Jamaican dancehall, for example, Cooper (whose institutional base is in the University of the West Indies) takes issue with the ways in which other scholars have misinterpreted, ignored and appropriated her own arguments (Cooper 2004).

2. Commissioning people to write texts for him as part of his fieldwork, Blacking later presented the texts of one of these writers in a study of the childhood of a Venda girl in what is effectively her autobiography (1964). The girl, however, was given a pseudonym (at her request) and the autobiographical account, prefaced by Blacking's introduction to the Venda, was published as his study of them. In co-authorship in a study of dhrupad (Sanyal and Widdess 2004) it is difficult to distinguish the individual voices of the writers due to their 'reluctance to indulge in a reflexive narrative' (2004: xv). But the text is produced on the basis of an equal partnership, to integrate performer-orientated and musicological perspectives, written by a practitioner from within the tradition and by an analyst of that tradition. In an oral history project, Bharucha composes a contrapuntal text, in which his own voice interweaves with that of his subject, Komal Kothari – captured on recordings that have been transcribed, edited and recontextualised until the written text begins to reveal some of the immediacies of the spoken word (Bharucha 2003).

3. A paradox is that while oral histories are about letting people be 'heard', what they say will be shaped by the questions they are asked so that research agendas and their resulting written narratives raise familiar problems of representation. Oral histories are no more inclusive than other historical sources as they involve processes of selection (who has been heard?), issues of trust (do people want to make sure that you do not find out what is really important to them?) and may reveal conflicting opinions or memories related to people's divergent agendas. Oral histories are performances – edited, altered in repeated telling, improvised in the moment, directed at an audience. But from 'just talking about something' to formal interviews or narrative analysis of song texts, oral histories can be used to generate ethnographic data, to compare a range of discourses on musical practice that can be used in conjunction with questionnaires, archive and written sources, and that perhaps enable a more complex view of the musical context under study to be gained.

Chapter 6

1. A report in the *Sentinel* gave the following details: 'we saw posted up in the corner of our streets a bill forbidding all persons to wear

masks.... The people resented, murmured a little and obeyed the cruel enjoinment: the masks were dropped. But, by way of compensation, they betook themselves to fancy dresses, and in droll accoutrements led many processions through the streets. The Police was immediately set on movement, and some of the gay fellows were arrested, prosecuted and fined.... The people, excited by these last provocations, would not submit; they assembled in different bands, set the Police at defiance, paraded with or without masks, hissed or hooted the Policemen, attacked them in their stronghold, beat and knocked them down, wounded some of them and presented such boisterous scenes as we had never witnessed before' (*Sentinel*, 4 March 1858, cited in Cowley 1996: 54).
2. TIDCO ceased operations on 31 October 2005.
3. Shadow's text is also a parody on those soca songs with repetitive directions to 'jump up' and 'wine'. These texts have inspired critiques on their banality in, for example, the pages of the local press.
4. Jihaji refers to a shipmate or ship family, to the relations that were established amongst the migrants travelling on the same ship from India to the Caribbean.
5. The criticisms levelled against pichakaaree are similar to those that were voiced against the Indian-Caribbean popular genre chutney, as it first began to emerge onto public performance stages in the 1980s. Like pichakaaree, chutney was viewed by its critics as being an Indian response to Carnival. In terms of instrumentation and song texts there was a corresponding emphasis on particular timbres. In the case of chutney, the *dholak*, *dhantal* (iron rod) and harmonium are essential accompaniment to the voice. Other types of chutney, such as chutney soca, may use trumpets, synthesisers and other electronic resources. Chutney song texts are often in English too with a few Bhojpuri or Hindi phrases added. See Ramnarine (2001) for further discussion on chutney.
6. Referring to primary source materials including newspaper reports, Cowley notes that as early as the 1850s African-Trinidadians were participating in the Indian Hosay celebrations (1996: 84). (Indian indentureship to Trinidad began in 1845.) There is evidence of Indian participation in Carnival stick fights during the 1870s (1996: 66) and while it was colonial policy to marginalise Indians in these arenas, reports from 1879 and 1880 indicate that these policies were not entirely successful (1996: 83).
7. Van Koningsbruggen's language reveals an all too easy dismissal of 'incorrect' historical facts. He writes, for example, of an African orientation which idolises 'an African heritage put together from a mixture of mythical and historical elements' and of the task of

'Africanizing the entire history of the world' against the misleading claims of the white world (1997: 201). Such an assessment is not entirely misleading, but Van Koningsbruggen does not explore the contemporary, postcolonial politics that give rise to such a stance.
8. 'Goodbye Columbus' in Trinidad World Music, track 12. CD. CO 295. Rituals. 1995.

Chapter 7

1. Greater London Authority Notting Hill Carnival Review. Recommendations Form (RF1) and Issues Form (IF1) submitted by the Association of British Calypsonians, 9 May 2001, and Recommendations Form (RF1) and Issues Form (IF1) submitted by the British Association of Steelbands, 16 May 2001.
2. Greater London Authority Notting Hill Carnival Review. Recommendations Form (RF1) and Issues Form (IF1) submitted by the British Association of Sound Systems, 6 June 2001 (p. 3).
3. Greater London Authority Notting Hill Carnival Review. Recommendations Form (RF1) and Issues Form (IF1) submitted by the British Association of Sound Systems, 6 June 2001 (p. 6).
4. Recommendations Form (RF1) and Issues Form (IF1) submitted by the British Association of Steelbands, 16 May 2001.
5. Several studies have shown how Caribbean performance traditions provide a unique vantage point for scrutinising political and national practices and the playing out of competing ideological positions within specific island spaces. These include dancehall performance in the articulation of class in Jamaica (Stolzoff 2000); the musical codings which provoke political memories of various African social, spiritual and ancestral systems in Carriacou (McDaniel 1998); the role of zouk in adding impetus to Creole movements in the French-speaking Caribbean (Guilbault 1993) and in bringing about a changing relationship to France with a new emphasis on Caribbean identities (Berrian 2000), and the musical signification of power in Haiti (Averill 1997).

BIBLIOGRAPHY AND DISCOGRAPHY

Bibliography

Adeyinka, Olaogun Narmer. 2000. 'A Carnival of Resistance, Emancipation, Commemoration, Reconstruction, and Creativity' in *Ah Come Back Home: Perspectives on the Trinidad and Tobago Carnival*, eds Ian Isidore Smart and Kimani Nehusi. Washington DC and Port-of-Spain: Original World Press, pp. 105–29.

Agard, John. 1985. *Mangoes and Bullets: Selected and New Poems 1972–1984*. London: Pluto Press.

———. 2000. *Weblines*. Newcastle Upon Tyne: Bloodaxe Books Ltd.

Agawu, Kofi. 2003. *Representing African Music: Postcolonial Notes, Queries, Positions*. New York and London: Routledge.

Allen, Ray and Wilcken, Lois. 1998. 'Introduction: Island Sounds in the Global City' in *Island Sounds in the Global City: Caribbean Popular Music and Identity in New York*, eds Ray Allen and Lois Wilcken. New York: The New York Folklore Society and the Institute for Studies in American Music, Brooklyn College, pp. 1–6.

Allen, Ray and Slater, Les. 1998. 'Steel Pan Grows in Brooklyn: Trinidadian Music and Cultural Identity' in *Island Sounds in the Global City: Caribbean Popular Music and Identity in New York*, eds Ray Allen and Lois Wilcken. New York: The New York Folklore Society and the Institute for Studies in American Music, Brooklyn College, pp. 114–37.

Alleyne-Dettmers, Patricia. 2000. 'Beyond Borders, Carnival as Global Phenomena: "Going Bananas, Food for the Devil"', in *Ah Come Back Home: Perspectives on the Trinidad and Tobago Carnival*, eds Ian Isidore Smart and Kimani Nehusi. Washington DC and Port-of-Spain: Original World Press, pp. 131–62.

Altink, Henrice. 2000. 'More than Producers and Reproducers: Jamaican Slave Women's Dance and Song in the 1770s–1830s' in *The Society for Caribbean Studies Annual Conference Papers*, ed. Sandra Courtman. Accessed online at <www.scsonline.freeserve.co.uk/olvol1.html>.

Appiah, Kwame Anthony. 1996. 'Is the Post- in Postmodernism the Post-in Postcolonial?' in *Contemporary Postcolonial Theory: A Reader*, ed. Padmini Mongia. London, New York, Sydney and Auckland: Arnold, pp. 55–71.

Ashcroft, B., Griffiths, G. and Tiffin, H. 1989. *The Empire Writes Back: Theory and Practice in Post-colonial Literatures*. London: Routledge.

Association of British Calypsonians. 1999. *Annual Report.* London: Association of British Calypsonians.
—— 2001. Recommendations Form (RF1) and Issues Form (IF1) submitted to the Grater London Authority Notting Hill Carnival Review, pp. 1–7.
Averill, Gage. 1997. *A Day for the Hunter, A Day for the Prey: Popular Music and Power in Haiti.* Chicago and London: University of Chicago Press.
Back, Les. 2000. 'Voices of Hate, Sounds of Hybridity: Black Music and the Complexities of Racism', *Black Music Research Journal,* vol. 20 (2): 127–49.
Bakhtin, M. M. 1981. *The Dialogic Imagination: Four Essays,* trans. Caryl Emerson and Michael Holquist. Austin: University of Texas Press.
Battaglia, Debbora. 1999. 'Toward an Ethics of the Open Subject: Writing Culture in Good Conscience', in *Anthropological Theory Today,* ed. Henrietta L. Moore. Cambridge: Polity Press, pp. 114–50.
Baumann, Gerd. 1996. *Contesting Culture: Discourses of Identity in Multi-ethnic London.* Cambridge: Cambridge University Press.
Belgrave, Joseph. 1978 [1932]. 'Reflections on Carnival' in *From Trinidad: An Anthology of Early West Indian Writing,* ed. Reinhard W. Sander. New York: Africana Publishing Company.
Berrian, Brenda F. 2000. *Awakening Spaces: French Caribbean Popular Songs, Music, and Culture.* Chicago and London: University of Chicago Press.
Bhabha, Homi K. 1994. *The Location of Culture.* London and New York: Routledge.
Bharucha, Rustom. 2001. *The Politics of Cultural Practice: Thinking Through Theatre in an Age of Globalization.* New Delhi: Oxford University Press.
——. 2003. *Rajasthan, An Oral History: Conversations with Komal Kothari.* New Delhi: Penguin Books India.
——. 2005. 'Towards the Real of Time: Rethinking the Risks of Cultural Practice Today'. Keynote lecture delivered at the *Towards Tomorrow* conference, Centre for Performance Research, Aberystwyth, Wales, April.
Blacking, John. 1964. *Black Background: The Childhood of a South African Girl.* New York, London and Toronto: Abelard-Schuman.
——. 1976. *How Musical is Man?* London: Faber and Faber.
Bohlman, Philip V. 1988. *The Study of Folk Music in the Modern World.* Bloomington: Indiana University Press.
——. 1993. 'Musicology as a Political Act', *Journal of Musicology,* (4): 411–36.

Brah, Avtar. 1996. *Cartographies of Diaspora: Contesting Identities*. London and New York: Routledge.
Braziel, Jane Evans and Mannur, Anita. 2003. 'Nation, Migration, Globalization: Points of Contention in Diaspora Studies' in *Theorizing Diaspora: A Reader*, eds Jane Evans Braziel and Anita Mannur. Oxford: Blackwell, pp. 1–22.
British Association of Sound Systems. 2001. Recommendations Form (RF1) and Issues Form (IF1) submitted to the Greater London Authority Notting Hill Carnival Review, pp. 1–10. British Association of Steelbands. 2001. Recommendations Form (RF1) and Issues Form (IF1) submitted to the Greater London Authority Notting Hill Carnival Review, pp. 1–7.
Brubaker, Rogers. 2005. 'The "Diaspora" Diaspora', *Ethnic and Racial Studies*, Vol. 28 (1): 1–19.
Budge, Wallis E. A. 1973 [1911] *Osiris and the Egyptian Resurrection*. New York: Dover.
Chamberlain, Mary. 2001. 'Migration, the Caribbean and the Family' in *Caribbean Families in Britain and the Trans-Atlantic World*, eds Harry Goulbourne and Mary Chamberlain. London and Oxford: Macmillan Education Ltd, pp. 32–47.
Chen, Kuan-Hsing. 1996. 'The Formation of a Diasporic Intellectual: an Interview with Stuart Hall' in *Stuart Hall: Critical Dialogues in Cultural Studies*, eds David Morley and Kuan-Hsing Chen. London and New York: Routledge, pp. 484–503.
Cohen, Robin. 1997. *Global Diasporas: An Introduction*. London: University College Press.
Concepción, Alma. 2002. 'Dance in Puerto Rico: Embodied Meanings' in *Caribbean Dance from Abakuá to Zouk: How Movement Shapes Identity*, ed. Susanna Sloat. Gainesville: University Press of Florida, pp. 165–75.
Cook, Nicholas and Everist Mark, eds. 1999. *Rethinking Music*. Oxford and New York: Oxford University Press.
Cooper, Carolyn. 2004. *Soundclash: Jamaican Dancehall Culture at Large*. New York and Basingstoke: Palgrave Macmillan.
———. 2006. 'Torrid Zones: Sexual Politics in Jamaican Dancehall Culture', Keynote lecture delivered at the British Forum for Ethnomusicology annual conference on Sexuality and Gender in Performance, Fieldwork and Representation, University of Winchester, April.
Cowley, John. 1990. 'London is the Place: Caribbean Music in the Context of Empire 1900–1960' in Black Music in Britain: Essays on the Afro-Asian Contribution to Popular Music, ed. Paul Oliver. Basingstoke: Open University Press. pp. 58–76.

——. 1996. *Carnival, Canboulay and Calypso: Traditions in the Making.* Cambridge: Cambridge University Press.
——. 2001. 'West Indian Recordings in France and Britain, 1929–1951', Paper presented at the Latin American Music Seminar, Institute for the Study of the Americas, October 2001.
Crowell, Nathaniel Hamilton Jr. 2002. 'What is Congolese in Caribbean Dance' in *Caribbean Dance from Abakuá to Zouk: How Movement Shapes Identity*, ed. Susanna Sloat. Gainesville: University Press of Florida, pp. 11–20.
Csordas, Thomas J. 1999. 'The Body's Career in Anthropology' in *Anthropological Theory Today*, ed. Henrietta L. Moore. Cambridge: Polity Press, pp. 172–205.
Dabydeen, David and Samaroo, Brinsley. 1987. *India in the Caribbean.* London: Hansib Publishing Ltd.
Daniel, Yvonne. 2002. 'Cuban Dance: An Orchard of Caribbean Creativity' in *Caribbean Dance from Abakuá to Zouk: How Movement Shapes Identity*, ed. Susanna Sloat. Gainesville: University Press of Florida, pp. 23–55.
Delgado, Fraser and Muñoz, José Esteban, eds. 1997. *Everynight Life: Culture and Dance in Latin/o America.* Durham and London: Duke University Press.
Desmond, Jane C. 1997. 'Embodying Difference: Issues in Dance and Cultural Studies' in *Everynight Life: Culture and Dance in Latin/o America*, eds Celeste Fraser Delgado and José Esteban Muñoz. Durham and London: Duke University Press, pp. 33–64.
De Verteuil, Anthony. 1989. *Eight East Indian Immigrants.* Port-of-Spain: Paria Publishing Co. Ltd.
Doodhai, Michelle. 2001. 'Chowtal vs Pichakaree', *Sunday Guardian* (Trinidad), 11 March p. 5.
Du Bois, W. E. B. 1999 [1903]. *The Souls of Black Folk*, ed. Henry Louis Gates Jr and Terri Hume Oliver (a Norton critical edition). New York and London: W. W. Norton and Company.
Dudley, Shannon. 2001. 'Ray Holman and the Changing Role of the Steelband, 1957–72', *Latin American Music Review*, vol. 22 (2): 183–98.
Elder, J. D. 1994. *Folksongs from Tobago.* London: Kamak House.
Elliot, David J. 1984. 'The Role of Music and Musical Expression in Modern Society: Toward a Global Philosophy of Music Education', *International Journal of Music Education*, vol. 6 (4): 3–8.
——. 1989. 'Key Concepts in Multicultural Music Education', *International Journal of Music Education*, vol. 13: 11–18.
Erlmann, Veit. 2004. 'Communities of Style: Musical Figures of Black Diasporic Identity' in *Identity and the Arts in Diaspora Communities*,

eds Thomas Turino and James Lea. Michigan: Harmonie Park Press, pp. 81–91.
Foehr, Stephen. 2000. *Jamaican Warriors: Reggae, Roots and Culture*. London: MPG Books.
Foster, Cecil and Schwartz, Chris. 1995. *Caribana: The Greatest Celebration*. Toronto: Ballantine Books.
Francis, Pepe. 2001. 'Fifty Years of Steelpan in the UK', *Pan Podium: The Official Magazine of the British Association of Steelbands*, issue 2: 6–7; continuing at 20.
George, Rosemary Marangoly. 1996. *The Politics of Home: Postcolonial Relocations and Twentieth-Century Fiction*. Cambridge: Cambridge University Press.
Gilbert, Helen and Tompkins, Joanne 1996. *Post-colonial Drama: Theory, Practice, Politics*. London and New York: Routledge.
Gilroy, Paul. 1987. *There Ain't No Black in the Union Jack: The Cultural Politics of Race and Nation*. London and New York: Routledge.
——. 1993a. *Small Acts: Thoughts on the Politics of Black Cultures*. London: Serpent's Tail.
——. 1993b. *The Black Atlantic: Modernity and Double Consciousness*. Cambridge, Mass.: Harvard University Press.
——. 2000. *Between Camps: Nations, Cultures and the Allure of Race*. London: Penguin Books.
——. 2005. *Postcolonial Melancholia*. New York: Columbia University Press.
Glasser, Ruth. 1998. 'Buscando Ambiente: Puerto Rican Musicians in New York City, 1917–1940' in *Island Sounds in the Global City: Caribbean Popular Music and Identity in New York*, eds Ray Allen and Lois Wilcken. New York: New York Folklore Society and Institute for Studies in American Music, Brooklyn College, pp.7–22.
Goertzen, Chris. 1997. *Fiddling for Norway: Revival and Identity*. Chicago and London: University of Chicago Press.
Goldman, Vivien. 1997 [1979] 'Uptown Ghetto Living: Bob Marley in his own Backyard' in *Reggae, Rasta, Revolution: Jamaican Music from Ska to Dub*, ed. Chris Potash. New York: Schirmer Books, pp. 39–47.
Goulbourne, Harry. 2001. 'The Socio-political Context of Caribbean Families in the Atlantic World' in *Caribbean Families in Britain and the Trans-Atlantic World*, eds Harry Goulbourne and Mary Chamberlain. London and Oxford: Macmillan Education Ltd, pp. 12–31.
Goulbourne, Harry and Chamberlain, Mary, eds. 2001. *Caribbean Families in Britain and the Trans-Atlantic World*. London and Oxford: Macmillan Education Ltd.

Grant, Cy. 1999. *Ring of Steel: Pan Sound and Symbol*. London and Basingstoke: Macmillan Education Ltd.

Greater London Authority. 2001. *Notting Hill Carnival Review: Interim Report and Public Safety Profile Recommendations for 2001*. London: Greater London Authority.

Guilbault, Jocelyne. 1993. *Zouk: World Music in the West Indies*. Chicago and London: University of Chicago Press.

Hall, Catherine. 2000. 'Introduction: Thinking the Postcolonial, Thinking the Empire' in *Cultures of Empire: Colonizers in Britain and the Empire in the Nineteenth and Twentieth Centuries. A Reader*, ed. Catherine Hall. Manchester: Manchester University Press, pp. 1–33.

Hall, Perry A. 1997. 'African-American Music: Dynamics of Appropriation and Innovation' in *Borrowed Power: Essays on Cultural Appropriation*, eds Bruce Ziff and Pratima V. Rao. New Brunswick, NJ: Rutgers University Press, pp. 31–51.

Hall, Stuart. 1996a [1990] 'Cultural Identity and Diaspora' in *Contemporary Postcolonial Theory: A Reader*, ed. Padmini Mongia. London, New York, Sydney and Auckland: Arnold, pp. 110–21.

——. 1996b. 'When was "the Post-Colonial"? Thinking at the Limit' in *The Post-Colonial Question: Common Skies, Divided Horizons*, eds Iain Chambers and Lidia Curti. London and New York: Routledge, pp. 242–60.

——. 2000. 'Conclusion: The Multi-Cultural Question' in *Un/settled Multiculturalisms: Diasporas, Entanglements, Transruptions*, ed. Barnor Hesse. London and New York: Zed Books, pp. 209–41.

——. 2001. Public lecture presented at the South Bank Centre, 18 October.

——. 2002. 'Calypso Kings', *Guardian Unlimited*, <www.Guardian.co.uk/friday_review/story/0,3605,744905,00.html>, accessed 31 December.

Harris, Wilson. 1999 [1970]. 'History, Fable and Myth in the Caribbean and Guianas' in *Selected Essays of Wilson Harris: The Unfinished Genesis of the Imagination*, ed. Andrew Bundy. London and New York: Routledge, pp. 152–66.

Hebdige, Dick. 1987. *Cut 'n' Mix: Culture, Identity and Caribbean Music*. London and New York: Routledge.

Henry, Frances. 2003. *Reclaiming African Religions in Trinidad: The Socio-political Legitimation of the Orisha and Spiritual Baptist Faiths*. Barbados, Jamaica, Trinidad and Tobago: University of West Indies Press.

Henry, W. A. 2002. 'Reggae/Dancehall Music: The "Hidden Voice" of Blak British Urban Expression', PhD thesis, University of London.

———. 2006. *What the Deejay Said: A Critique from the Street!* London: Learning By Choice Publications.
Herbst, Edward. 1997. *Voices in Bali: Energies and Perceptions in Vocal Music and Dance Theater.* Hanover: Wesleyan University Press.
Herskovitz, M. J., and Herskovitz, F. S. 1947. *Trinidad Village.* New York: Octagon Books.
Hesse, Barnor. 2000. 'Introduction: Un/settled Multiculturalisms' in *Un/settled Multiculturalisms: Diasporas, Entanglements, Transruptions*, ed. Barnor Hesse. London and New York: Zed Books, pp. 1–30.
Hill, Donald. 1998a. 'West African and Haitian Influences on the Ritual and Popular Music of Cariacou, Trinidad, and Cuba', *Black Music Research Journal*, vol. 18 (1/2): 183–201.
———. 1998b. '"I am Happy Just to be in this Sweet Land of Liberty": The New York City Calypso Craze of the 1930s and 1940s' in *Island Sounds in the Global City: Caribbean Popular Music and Identity in New York*, eds Ray Allen and Lois Wilcken. New York: The New York Folklore Society and the Institute for Studies in American Music, Brooklyn College, pp. 74–92.
Hobsbawm, Eric. 1987. *The Age of Empire 1875–1914.* London: Abacus.
Holgerson, Ronald. 1991. *Festivals: A Market with Potential.* Whistler Report. Canadian Arts Consumer Profile, Department of Communications, Canada.
Hunter, Patrick. 1996. *A Jewel Worth Polishing: The Report of the Caribbean Cultural Committee/Metropolitan Toronto Chairman's Task Force on Caribana.* Toronto: Metropolitan Toronto Task Force on Caribana.
Hutnyk, John. 1997. 'Adorno at Womad: South Asian Crossovers and the Limits of Hybridity-Talk' in *Debating Cultural Hybridity*, eds Pnina Werbner and Tariq Modood. London: Zed Books Ltd.
———. 2000. *Critique of Exotica: Music, Politics, and the Culture Industry.* London: Pluto Press.
———. 2005. 'Hybridity', *Ethnic and Racial Studies*, vol. 28 (1): 79–102.
Ingram, Amelia. 2001. 'Reinventing Steel Pan on Records: Local and Global Dialectics', *Center for Black Music Research Digest*, vol. 14 (1): 16–18.
Inner London Education Authority. 1983. *Race, Sex and Class. Multiethnic Education in Schools.* London: Inner London Education Authority.
———. Inner London Education Authority Music Centre. 1982. *Germany Tour Press Reports.* London: Inner London Education Authority Music Centre.

Innes, C. L. 1995. 'Wintering: Making a Home in Britain' in *Other Britain, Other British: Contemporary Multicultural Fiction*, ed. A. Robert Lee. London and East Haven, Conn.: Pluto Press, pp. 21–34.

James, C. L. R. 2003 [1932]. *Letters from London*. Oxford: Signal Books.

James, Louis. 1995. 'The Disturbing Vision of George Lamming' in *Other Britain, Other British: Contemporary Multicultural Fiction*, ed. A. Robert Lee. London and East Haven, Conn.: Pluto Press, pp. 35–47.

Jones, Anthony Mark. 1973. *Steelband, A History: The Winston 'Spree' Simon Story*. Port-of-Spain: Educo Press.

Kasinitz, Phillip. 1998. 'Community Dramatized, Community Contested: The Politics of Celebration in the Brooklyn Carnival' in *Island Sounds in the Global City: Caribbean Popular Music and Identity in New York*, eds Ray Allen and Lois Wilcken. New York: New York Folklore Society and Institute for Studies in American Music, Brooklyn College, pp. 93–113.

——. 2004. '"New York Equalise You?" Change and Continuity in Brooklyn's Labor Day Carnival' in *Carnival: Culture in Action – The Trinidad Experience*, ed. Milla Cozart Riggio. New York and London: Routledge, pp. 270–82.

Kershaw, Baz. 1992. *The Politics of Performance: Radical Theatre as Cultural Intervention*. London and New York: Routledge.

Klass, Morton. 1961. *East Indians in Trinidad: A Study of Cultural Persistence*. Prospect Heights, Ill.: Waveland Press Inc.

Kronman, Ulf. 1991. *Steel Pan Tuning: A Handbook for Steel Pan Making and Tuning*. Accessed via <http://hotpans.se/pan/tuning/>.

Kuper, Adam. 1999. *Culture: The Anthropologist's Account*. Cambridge, Mass., and London: Harvard University Press.

Lamming, George. 1992 [1960]. *The Pleasures of Exile*. Ann Arbor: University of Michigan Press [London: Michael Joseph].

——. 1998 [1953] *In the Castle of My Skin*. Essex, Kingston, San Juan, New York and Ontario: Longman Ltd.

Levine, Lawrence W. 1977. *Black Culture and Black Consciousness: Afro-American Folk Thought From Slavery to Freedom*. Oxford, London and New York: Oxford University Press.

Liverpool, Hollis. 2001. 'Reexportation and Musical Traditions Surrounding the African Masquerade' in *Culture and Mass Communication in the Caribbean*, ed. Humphrey A. Regis. Gainesville and Tallahassee: University Press of Florida.

Lo, Jacqueline. 2000. 'Beyond Happy Hybridity: Performing Asian-Australian Identities' in *Alter/Asian*, eds Ien Ang, Sharon Chalmers,

Lisa Law and Mandy Thomas. London: Pluto Press. Accessed via <http://dlibrary.acu.edu.au/research/adsa/lo.htm>.
Lundberg, Dan, Malm, Krister and Ronström, Owe. 2003. *Music, Media Multiculture: Changing Musicscapes*. Stockholm: Svenskt Visarkiv.
Maharaj, Parsuram 2001. 'Pichakaree polluting Phagwa', *Newsday*, 6 March, p. 10. Trinidad: Daily News Ltd.
Maharaj, Satnarayn 2001. 'Maha Sabha, Kendra in Battle over traditions of Phagwa', *Sunday Guardian*, News Desk feature, 11 March, p. 1.
Malm, Krister and Sarstad, Monika. 1997. 'Rap, Ragga Reggae in East Africa'. <www.musikmuseet.se/mmm/africa/mission.html>, accessed 17 May 2001.
Manuel, Peter. 2000. *East Indian Music in the West Indies: Tān-singing, Chutney, and the Making of Indo-Caribbean Culture*. Philadelphia: Temple University Press.
Marcus, George. E. 1992. 'A Broad(er) Side to the Canon, Being a Partial Account of a Year of Travel Among Textual Communities in the Realm of Humanities Centers, and Including a Collection of Artificial Curiosities' in *Rereading Cultural Anthropology*, ed. George E. Marcus. Durham, NC, and London: Duke University Press, pp. 103–23.
McAlister, Elizabeth. 2002. *Rara! Vodou, Power, and Performance in Haiti and its Diaspora*. Berkeley, Los Angeles and London: University of California Press.
McDaniel, Lorna. 1998. *The Big Drum Ritual of Carriacou: Praisesongs in Rememory of Flight*. Gainesville, Tallahassee, Tampa, Boca Raton, Pensacola, Orlando, Miami and Jacksonville: University of Florida Press.
Minh-ha, Trinh T. 1994. 'Other than Myself/My Other Self' in *Travellers' Tales: Narratives of Home and Displacement*, eds George Robertson, Melinda Mash, Lisa Tickner, Jon Bird, Barry Curtis and Tim Putnam. London and New York: Routledge, pp. 9–26.
Monson, Ingrid, ed. 2003. *The African Diaspora: A Musical Perspective*. New York and London: Routledge.
Murray, Stuart, ed. 1997. '(Un)belonging Citizens, Unmapped Territory: Black Immigration and British Identity in the Post-1945 Period' in *Not on Any Map: Essays on Postcoloniality and Cultural Nationalism*. Exeter: Exeter University Press, pp. 43–66.
Myers, Helen. 1998. *Hindu Trinidad: Songs from the India Diaspora*. Chicago and London: University of Chicago Press.
Naipaul, V. S. 1964. *An Area of Darkness*. London: Andre Deutsch.
——. 1967. *The Mimic Men*. London: Andre Deutsch.
——. 1984. *Finding the Centre*. London: Penguin Books.

NCC (National Carnival Commission, Trinidad and Tobago). 2001. 'Carnival History... Who Gets the Credit?' in *Before and Beyond Mas*, ed. Avion Taylor-Roach. Trinidad: NCC.

Nehusi, Kimani. 2000. 'The Origins of Carnival: Notes from a Preliminary Investigation' in *Ah Come Back Home: Perspectives on the Trinidad and Tobago Carnival*, eds Ian Isidore Smart and Kimani Nehusi. Washington DC and Port-of-Spain: Original World Press, pp. 77–103.

Nettl, Bruno. 1995. *Heartland Excursions: Ethnomusicological Reflections on Schools of Music*. Urbana and Chicago: University of Illinois Press.

Noel, Terry. 1978. 'Ethnic Minorities: Steel Bands', *Music in Education*, vol. 42: 118–19.

——. n.d. *The Steelband: From Bamboo to Pan*. London: Commonwealth Institute.

Nurse, Edmund 'Prince', ed. 2001. *Downtown Mas 2001: Souvenir*. Trinidad: Edmund Prince Nurse.

Nurse, Keith. 1999. 'Globalization and Trinidad Carnival: Diaspora, Hybridity and Identity in Global Culture', *Cultural Studies*, vol. 13 (4): 661–90.

Olwig, Karen Fog. 1993. *Global Culture, Island Identity: Continuity and Change in the Afro-Caribbean Community of Nevis*. London: Harwood Academic Publishers.

Owen, David. 2001. 'A Profile of Caribbean Households and Families in Great Britain' in *Caribbean Families in Britain and the Trans-Atlantic World*, eds Harry Goulbourne and Mary Chamberlain. London and Oxford: Macmillan Education Ltd, pp. 64–91.

Persad, Kamal. 2001. 'Carnival and Shivratri', *Sunday Express* (Trinidad), 25 February, p. 16. Trinidad.

Phillips, Caryl. 2001. 'The High Anxiety of Belonging', *Brick: A Literary Journal*, issue 67: 8–12.

Pieterse, Jan Nederveen. 1995. 'Globalization as Hybridization' in *Global Modernities*, eds Mike Featherstone, Scott Lash and Roland Robertson. London, Thousand Oaks and New Delhi: Sage Publications, pp. 45–68.

Radano, Ronald and Bohlman, Philip, eds. 2000. *Music in the Racial Imagination*. Chicago and London: University of Chicago Press.

Ramnarine, Tina K. 1996. '"Indian" Music in the Diaspora: Case Studies of Chutney in Trinidad and in London' *British Journal of Ethnomusicology*, vol. 5: 133–53.

——. 1998. 'Brotherhood of the Boat: Musical Dialogues in a Caribbean Context', *British Journal of Ethnomusicology*, vol. 7: 1–22.

——. 1998/99. 'Historical Representations, Performance Spaces and Kinship Themes in Indian-Caribbean Popular Song Texts', *Asian Music*, vol. 30 (1): 1–33.

——. 2001. *Creating Their Own Space: The Development of an Indian-Caribbean Musical Tradition*. Jamaica: University of West Indies Press.

——. 2003. *Ilmatar's Inspirations: Nationalism, Globalization, and the Changing Soundscapes of Finnish Folk Music*. Chicago and London: University of Chicago Press.

——. 2004. 'Music in the Diasporic Imagination: The Performance of Cultural (Dis)placement in Trinidad' in *Island Musics*, ed. Kevin Dawe. Oxford: Berg, pp. 153–70.

——. 2007. 'Beyond Borders: Memory and Creativity in the Diaspora' in *Remembered Rhythms: Issues of Diaspora and Music in India*, eds Shubha Chaudhuri and Anthony Seeger. Oxford: Berg.

——. Forthcoming. 'Beyond the Academy' in *The New (Ethno)Musicologies*, ed. Henry Stobart. Lanham, Md: Scarecrow Press.

Ravi Ji. 2001. 'Empowerment through Culture' in *Trinidad Guardian*, 5 March, p. 21.

Rawlins, Trevor, ed. 1983. *ILEA at the Barbican Centre*. Surrey: ILEA Information Service.

Reddock, Rhoda. 1995. 'Contestations Over National Culture in Trinidad and Tobago: Considerations of Ethnicity, Class and Gender' in *Contemporary Issues in Social Science: A Caribbean Perspective*, eds Ramesh Deosaran and Nasser Mustapha. University of West Indies: Ansa McAl Psychological Research Centre, pp. 106–45.

Rice, Timothy. 1994. *May it Fill Your Soul: Experiencing Bulgarian Music*. Chicago and London: University of Chicago Press.

Riggio, Milla Cozart, ed. 2004. *Carnival. Culture in Action – The Trinidad Experience*. New York and London: Routledge.

Rohlehr, Gordon. 2000. 'Change and Prophecy in Calypso', *Trinidad and Tobago Review*, Vol. 22 (11–12): 29–33. Trinidad: Trinidad Express Newspapers.

Román-Velazquez, Patria. 1999. 'The Embodiment of Salsa: Musicians, Instruments, and the Performance of a Latin Style and Identity', *Popular Music*, vol. 18 (1): 115–31.

Said, Edward. 1993. *Culture and Imperialism*. London: Chatto & Windus.

——. 1999. *Out of Place: A Memoir*. London: Granta Books.

Samson, Jim. 1999. 'Analysis in Context' in *Rethinking Music*, eds Nicholas Cook and Mark Everist. Oxford and New York: Oxford University Press, pp. 35–54.

Sanyal, Ritwik and Widdess, Richard. 2004. *Dhrupad: Tradition and Performance in Indian Music*. Aldershot: Ashgate.
Schechner, Richard. 2002. *Performance Studies: An Introduction*. London and New York: Routledge.
Selvon, Sam. 1956. *The Lonely Londoners*. London: Alan Wingate.
———. 1975. *Moses Ascending*. London: Davis-Poynter.
———. 1983. *Moses Migrating*. Essex, Kingston, San Juan, New York and Ontario: Longman Ltd.
Sharma, Sanjay, Hutnyk, John and Sharma, Ashwani, eds. 1996. *Dis-Orienting Rhythms*. London: Zed Books Ltd.
Sharp, Cecil. 1907. *English Folk-Song: Some Conclusions*. London: Simpkin and Novello.
Shepherd, Verene A. 2000. 'Image, Representation and the Project of Emancipation: History and Identity in the Commonwealth Caribbean' in *Contending with Destiny: The Caribbean in the 21st Century*, eds Kenneth Hall and Denis Benn. Kingston: Ian Randle Publishers, pp. 53–79.
Shukra, Kalbir. 1998. *The Changing Pattern of Black Politics in Britain*. London and Sterling, Va: Pluto Press.
Sloat, Susanna, ed. 2002. *Caribbean Dance from Abakuá to Zouk: How Movement Shapes Identity*. Gainesville: University Press of Florida.
Slobin, Mark, 1993. *Subcultural Sounds: Micromusics of the West*. Hanover and London: Wesleyan University Press.
———. ed. 1994. 'Music in Diaspora: The View from Euro-America', special issue of *Diaspora: A Journal of Transnational Studies*, vol. 3 (3).
———. ed. 1996. *Retuning Culture: Musical Changes in Central and Eastern Europe*. Durham, NC, and London: Duke University Press.
———. 2000. *Fiddler on the Move: Exploring the Klezmer World*. New York: Oxford University Press.
———. 2003. 'The Destiny of "Diaspora" in Ethnomusicology' in *The Cultural Study of Music: A Critical Introduction*, eds Martin Clayton, Trevor Herbert and Richard Middleton. New York and London: Routledge, pp. 284–96.
Smart, Ian Isidore. 2000. 'Carnival: The Ultimate Pan-African Festival' in *Ah Come Back Home: Perspectives on the Trinidad and Tobago Carnival*, eds Ian Isidore Smart and Kimani Nehusi. Washington DC and Port-of-Spain: Original World Press, pp. 29–76.
Smart, Ian Isidore and Nehusi, Kimani, eds. 2000. *Ah Come Back Home: Perspectives on the Trinidad and Tobago Carnival*. Washington DC and Port-of-Spain: Original World Press.

Solís, Ted. 2005. '"You Shake Your Hips Too Much": Diasporic Values and Hawai'i Puerto Rican Dance Culture', *Ethnomusicology*, vol. 49 (1): 75–119.
Spencer, Sally-Anne. 1986. 'A Study of a Steel Band: The ILEA Schools Steel Orchestra', MA thesis, University of London.
Springer, Pearl Eintou. 2000. 'Carnival: Identity, Ethnicity, and Spirituality' in *Ah Come Back Home: Perspectives on the Trinidad and Tobago Carnival*, eds Ian Isidore Smart and Kimani Nehusi. Washington DC and Port-of-Spain: Original World Press, pp. 17–27.
Steumpfle, Stephen. 1995. *The Steelband Movement: The Forging of a National Art in Trinidad and Tobago*. Philadelphia: University of Pennsylvania Press.
Stolzoff, Norman C. 2000. *Wake the Town and Tell the People: Dancehall Culture in Jamaica*. Durham, NC, and London: Duke University Press.
Sugarman, Jane C. 2004. 'Diasporic Dialogues: Mediated Musics and the Albanian Transnation' in *Identity and the Arts in Diaspora Communities*, eds Thomas Turino and James Lea. Michigan: Harmonie Park Press, pp. 21–38.
Taruskin, Richard. 1995. *Text and Act: Essays on Music and Performance*. New York: Oxford University Press.
Thompson, Robert Farris. 2002. 'Teaching the People to Triumph over Time: Notes from the World of Mambo' in *Caribbean Dance from Abakuá to Zouk: How Movement Shapes Identity*, ed. Susanna Sloat. Gainesville: University Press of Florida, pp. 336–44.
Tölölyan, Khachig. 1996. 'Rethinking Diaspora(s): Stateless Power in the Transnational Moment', *Diaspora*, vol. 5 (1): 3–7.
Trouillot, Michel-Rolph. 2003. *Global Transformations: Anthropology and the Modern World*. New York and Basingstoke: Palgrave Macmillan.
Turino, Thomas. 2004. 'Introduction: Identity and the Arts in Diaspora Communities' in *Identity and the Arts in Diaspora Communities*, eds Thomas Turino and James Lea. Michigan: Harmonie Park Press, pp. 3–19.
Van Koningsbruggen, Peter. 1997. *Trinidad Carnival: A Quest for National Identity*. London and Basingstoke: Macmillan Education Ltd.
Vaughan Williams, Ralph. 1963 [1934]. *National Music and Other Essays*. London: Oxford University Press.
Volk, Terese M. 1998. *Music, Education, and Multiculturalism: Foundations and Principles*. New York and Oxford: Oxford University Press.
Walcott, Derek. 1992. *The Antilles*. New York: Farrar Straus Giroux.
Walker, Robert. 1986. 'Music and Multiculturalism', *International Journal of Music Education*, vol. 8 (2): 43–52.

Waterman, Christopher A. 1990. *Jùjú: A Social History and Ethnography of an African Popular Music*. Chicago: University of Chicago Press.

——. 1991. 'The Uneven Development of Africanist Ethnomusicology: Three Issues and a Critique' in *Comparative Musicology and Anthropology of Music: Essays on the History of Ethnomusicology*, eds Bruno Nettl and Philip V. Bohlman. Chicago and London: University of Chicago Press.

Welsh, Sarah Lawson. 1997. '(Un)belonging Citizens, Unmapped Territory: Black Immigration and British Identity in the Post-1945 Period' in *Not on Any Map: Essays on Postcoloniality and Cultural Nationalism*, ed. Stuart Murray. Exeter: University of Exeter Press, pp. 43–66.

Werbner, Pnina. 1997. 'Introduction: The Dialectics of Cultural Hybridity' in *Debating Cultural Identity*, eds Pnina Werbner and Tariq Modood. London: Zed Books.

——. 2002. *Imagined Diasporas among Manchester Muslims: The Public Performance of Pakistani Transnational Identity Politics*. Oxford: James Currey.

Wilson, Salah A. 1999. *Steelpan Playing with Theory*. Quebec: Salahpan.

Witmer, Robert. 1987. '"Local" and "Foreign": The Popular Music Culture of Kingston, Jamaica, before Ska, Rock Steady, and Reggae', *Latin American Music Review*, vol. 8 (1): 1–25.

Yelvington, Kevin A., ed. 1993. *Trinidad Ethnicity*. London and Basingstoke: Macmillan Press.

Discography (main recordings referred to in the text)

Alexander D. Great. 1994. *Lash dem Lara!* CD. London: Lion Valley Records. LVR001.

——. 1997. *Panorama Attack*. CD. London: Lion Valley Productions. SAR004.

——. 1998. *Rum Shop Kaiso Chronicles, volume 2: The Windrush Collection*. London: Lion Valley Records. SAR005.

Association of British Calypsonians. 1999. CD. *The Very Best of Born in Britain*. London: Association of British Calypsonians. ABCD2.

Bob Marley. Island Records and various compilations/ re-releases.

Burning Flames. 1994. *Klatye*. Cassette. New York: Burning Flames Music BMI. 012CA.

Cachao. 1995. *Cachao Master Sessions volume 2*. CD. New York: Sony, A CineSon Production for Crescent Moon Records. EK 67319.

Calypso Awakening. 2000. *Calypso Awakening: from the Emory Cook Collection, 1956–1962*. CD. Washington: Smithsonian Folkways Recordings. SFW CD 40453.

Celia Cruz. 1995. *Celia Cruz Queen of Cuban Rhythm: The Legendary Seeco Recordings, 1959–1965.* CD. EU: Music Collection International Ltd. MCCD 220.
D Rapso Nation. 1998. *D Rapso Nation: Anthology of the Best of Rapso.* CD. Trinidad: Rituals. CO5598.
Dark Latin Groove. 1996. *Dark Latin Groove.* CD. Sony Discos CDZ 81694/2–469807.
David Rudder. *David Rudder International Chantuelle.* CD. New York: JW Productions. CR 029.
Eyesburn. 2001. *Eyesburn Gabu.* CD. Beograd: Metropolis Music Company. MCD 040.
Linton Kwesi Johnson. 1997. *Reggae Greats.* CD. Germany: Spectrum Music. 552 881–2.
Lomax 1962 field recordings. 1999. *Caribbean Voyage: The Alan Lomax Collection.* A series produced by Rounder Records, Massachusetts, USA.
'London is the Place for Me'. 2002. *London is the Place for Me: Trinidadian Calypso in London, 1950–1956.* CD. EU: Honest Jon's Records compilation. HJRCD2.
Lord Invader. 2000. *Calypso in New York.* CD. Washington: Smithsonian Folkways Recordings. SFW CD 40454. (From the Asch Recordings, 1946–1961.)
Mungal. 2000. *Dreadlocks.* CD. Rituals/Virgin France. 72438 505612 3.
Phase One. 1999. *Phase One Steel Orchestra.* Coventry: Butts College Theatre, live recording.
Ras Shorty I and the Love Circle. 1999. *Jamoo Victory.* CD. Trinidad: Jamoo Good News Ltd. J007.
Reggae around the World. 1998. *Reggae around the World.* CD. EEC: Putumayo Records. PUTU 142–2.
Salah & Family Steelpan Workshop. 1995. *Good Feelings.* CD. Canada: Salahpan. 8000–2.
Shadow. 2001. *Just for You.* CD. Mount Hope: McGarland Music. CRCD008.
Sheldon Blackman. 2004. *One Big Fat Love Bomb.* CD. Trinidad: Jamoo Good News Ltd.
Skiffle Bunch. 2003. *Skiffle Bunch and Stalin Live at the Naparima Bowl.* CD. Trinidad, San Fernando.
Tambu. n.d. *Once Upon a Time.* CD. Petit Bourg: Bangaseed Limited. BSCD104.
Yothu Yindi. 1992. *Tribal Voice.* CD. Australia: Mushroom Records. MUSH32463.2.

INDEX

acoustic research, 80
aesthetic
  judgement, 69
  movement, 109
  practice, 23
African-American spirituals, 5, 13
Afroblocos, 12
Agard, John, 2, 50, 108, 158, 205
agency, 179
agent
  body as intentional, 117
  musical, 32, 156
  scholarship as, 112, 115
Allen, Kurt, 164
alterity, 34
analysis, musical, 21, 22, 33, 115
  social relevance of, 22
analytical models, 10, 30, 88, 108
  mapped onto experiences, 32
Anancy, 202
  see also Aunty Nansi
ancestors, 10, 28, 65
anthropologists, 64, 106, 110
anthropology, 14, 100, 122, 133
appropriation, 23, 24, 32
arrangement, musical, 70, 79, 85, 93, 94, 148, 149, 169
arrival
  in-between states of, 7
  postponed, 8
articulation, 5, 24, 133
Association of British Calypsonians, 52, 56, 68, 185
  see also calypso

Atlantic, 2, 4, 11
  performance traditions in the Black, 38
audience, 25, 44, 45, 51, 54, 69, 74, 120, 129
Aunty Nansi (Kwaku-Ananse), 106–8, 112, 204–6
  see also Anancy
authenticity, 185, 188–90
authority, 154
  ethnographic, 132, 133
  exercise of, 32
  in canon formation, 42
authorship, ethnographic, 132

Babylon, 5, 134, 135, 153
Barbados, 11, 14, 15
Beacon, The, 162
Belafonte, Harry, 12, 51
Belgrave, Joseph, 162
belonging, 2, 6, 10, 17, 25, 179
  asserted, 12
  borders of, 8
  multi-local, 9, 15, 19, 20
  national, 24, 35
  sense of, 38, 39
  within racist structures, 35
benga, 136
Berlin school of comparative musicology, 115
Betancourt, Sterling, 84–5
bhangramuffin, 159
Big Drum Ritual of Carriacou, 27–8
'Big Party for your Golden Jubilee', 73–4
biguine, 11, 44
Black History Month, 71

Black Lyrics, 159
Black Power, 53, 70
Blackman, Sheldon, 129, 159, figure 5.1
Blekbala Mujik, 137
body, 109, 110, 111, 117
　female, 125
　stereotypes of, 114
borders, 3, 8
　sonic crossings of, 13, 160
Born in Britain (CD), 50, 69
borrowing, 23
boundaries, 5, 20, 35, 64
　musical, 69
　permeability of, 9
　questions about, 12
　setting, 125
　tropes of cultural, 29, 77
British Association of Steelbands, 85
British Association of Sound Systems, 186
British Caribbean fiction, 50
British folk music, 42, 55–62
British Museum, 164, 166
British Parlophone, 43
Brother Resistance, 129, 159, 179
Burning Flames, 104
busker, 77

3Canal, 157, 159
Cachao, 109
call and response, 159
calypso, 42–75
　tents, 37, 42
　verbal mastery in, 43
calypsonians, 42, 43
　Andall, Ella, 180, 181
　Attila the Hun, 51
　Baptiste, Mona, 48
　Belasco, Lionel, 49

calypsonians *continued*
　Chalkdust, 149, *see also* Liverpool, Hollis
　Duke of Iron, 50
　Herbert, Chris Tambu 18
　Invader, 52
　Lady Spencer
　Liverpool, Hollis 56, *see also* Chalkdust
　Lord Beginner, 48, 52
　Lord Cloak, 52
　Lord Kitchener, 11, 48, 52, 69, 70, 145, 149, 168
　Lord Melody, 43
　Lord Shorty, 129, *see also* Ras Shorty I
　Lovey, 51
　Manning, Sam, 49
　Mighty Explorer, 54
　Mighty Sparrow, 43, 69, 145
　Mighty Tiger, 52
　Plummer, Denyse, 164
　Roaring Lion, 51, 52, 145, 149
　Shadow, 94, 168, 173
　Short Shirt, 168
　Sister Ava, 159
　Sister Sandra, 149
　The Mighty Terror, 52
　Totally Talibah, 54
　Young Tiger, 44, 45
canon, 42, 47, 53, 57, 70
　mixing of, 31
　questioning of, 64
　'race' as, 126
Carnival Development Committee, 167
Carnival, 36, figures 2.5 and 6.2
　contested histories of, 164–7, 181
　London (Notting Hill), 183–90
　New York (Brooklyn), 37
　Trinidad, 161–73
　Toronto (Caribana), 190–200

Caribbean Diaspora, 7, 9, 10, 201
   as a term, 24
   spread of, 11
censorship, 39, 43
centre-periphery models, 201
Césaire, Aimé, 38
Césaire, Ina, 39, 41, 48
Césaire, Mano, 39, 41
cha cha cha, 126
choice, 118, 127
chord symbols, 148
choreography, musical, 123
chowtal, 176, 178
chutney, 12, 99
   'conscious', 130
   soca, 159
citizenship, 6, 55, 62
civil rights, 5, 183
Classics and Carols Festival, 93
classification, 112
   of repertoire, 65
Cliff, Jimmy, 12
colonial
   accounts, 111
   authorities, 163
   desires, 111
   documents, 3
   education, 8
   experiences, 2
   politics, 48
colonialism, 33, 38, 160, 179
   political spaces of, 15
   see also postcolonialism
comedy, 2, 45
commodity, 23
Commonwealth Institute, 86, 92
Commonwealth, 63
competition
   European Steelband, 83
   Notting Hill Panorama, 92
   Panorama, 79
   pichakaaree, 176

salsa dance, 117
Toronto Panorama, 94
compositional process, 27, 62
Connor, Edric, 84
consciousness, 5, 6, 7, 54, 149
consumer, 36
contradiction, 156, 188, 205
   ideological, 14
   of 'fusions', 95
Cook, Emory, 6, 43
copyright, 52, 105
'Coronation Calypso', 44–5
corporate marketing, 127
cosmos, 107, 108, 204
counter-hegemonic practice, 133, 160
creative
   expressions, 2
   interactions, 13
   processes, 31, 77, 94
creativity, 10, 23, 30–1, 101, 103
   as process and as choice, 124
   cultural, 6
   everyday processes of, 17, 102
   intercultural, 29
creolisation, 95, 99, 102
Cruz, Celia, 109
Cuba, 11
Cugat, Xavier, 126
cultural heritage, 4
cultural theorists, 13, 16, 33
culture, moral dimensions of, 102–8
culture theory, 106, 107

D'Bhuyaa Saaj, 99
Damas, Léon, 39
dance
   as celebration of 'community', 109
   as embodied practice, 118
   as ritual and spiritual practice, 128

scholars, 110
styles, 110, 115
troupes, 37
dancehall, 34–5, 37, 125, 152–4
Dark Latin Groove, 109
Dekker, Desmond, 12
dhantal, 99, 129, 176
dholak, 129, 176
diaspora(s), 2–10, 14, 18, 160,
   figure 1.1
  and nation, 44–6, 55–7, 64–7
  as contested terrain, 27
  convergence of, 26
  defining, 19
  ethnographic literature on, 6
  experiences of, 24, 27
  overlapping, 29
  secondary, 19, 24
  struggles over, 3
  universalisation of, 19
  see also home
diasporic
  consciousness, 130
  creativity, 30, 203
  experiences, 5
  histories, 130
  memories, 2
Dickson, Dudley, 81
didgeridu, 23, 137
difference, 10, 23, 102, 103, 180
  challenge to, 46
  colonial preoccupations with, 116
  embodiment of, 110–12
  interruptions to, 32
  multicultural assumptions of, 87
  within communities, 25
digital technologies, 83
displacement, 4, 19
  ambiguity of, 26
  diaspora as, 7
  dilemmas of, 27

DJ Lezlee Lyrix, *see* Henry, W. A
DJ Mike Tabor, 137
double bass, 105
double entendre, 63
Dreadlocks (CD), 95
drum kit, 100, 129
Du Bois, 5, 13, 205
dub, 130, 159
Dunbar, Rudolph, 49
Dynamic Tassa Group, 97–9, figure 3.3

Elder, J. D, 64
embodiment, 110, 112
  across culture, 122
empire, 1, 4, 11, 44, 48, 63, 64
  fallouts of, 19
empowerment, 90, 166, 173
encounter, musical, 31
entanglements, of musical expression, 205
equality, 90, 91
essentialism, 14, 31, 95, 110, 125
  paradox of, 201
Estefan, Gloria, 12
Ethiopianism, 135
ethnic absolutes, challenge to, 45
ethnicity, 46, 88, 179
ethnographic
  analysis, 33
  approaches, 16
  attention, 204
  descriptions, 21
  experiment in 'chatting', 130–4
  literature, 6
  modes of thinking, 10
  production of cultural difference, 29
ethnography, 131–4, 156
  decentring strategies of, 157
ethnomusicologists, 30, 33, 47

ethnomusicology, 14, 29, 100, 116
  intersections with cultural studies, 23
  of engagement, 22
  on diaspora, 6
  phenomenological approaches within, 45–6
  recent trends in, 30
  salvage, 116
  theories in, 101
European Pan Festival, 86
everyday, 108
  process, 105
  volatility of, 102
evolutionary thinking, 106
exclusion, 5, 8, 25, 34, 46, 87
'Exil', 39, 41
exile, 3, 4, 8, 19, 24, 38, 104
Exodus, 5
experience, 3
  diasporic, 5, 7, 8
  of migration, 7
  particularities of, 123
  postmodern, 24
exploitation, 160
Eyesburn, 12

Festival of Britain (1951), 1, 84
festivals, 32, 82, 92, 98
  ancient Egyptian, 164
  Classics and Carols, 93
  Diaspora Music Village, 97
  Europe's largest street, 188
  Indian religious, 80
  Kendra Phagwa, 175–8
  Pan Jamboree, 93
  Shivratri, 165
fiddle, 137, 205
fieldwork, 14–15, 82
film songs
  American, 78
  Indian, 176, 180
film, 78
folk music, 56
  of Tobago, 64–7, figures 2.3 and 2.4
Forsythe, Gerald, 91
freedom, vision of, 204
fusions, 94–6, 99–100, 107

Garvey, Marcus, 134, 155
gateway, trickster, 203–6
gender, 115
generation, 2, 3, 6, 8, 9, 13, 17
genocide, 160
genre, 67, 68
geopolitical shifts, 3
gesture
  dance, 114
  musical, 124
  narrative, 16
Ghana, 48
gharana (Visnupur), 95
Gilroy, Paul, 13, 20, 21, 46–7
global political action, 20, 23–4, 39, 40, 160
global politics of equity, 128
globalisation, 6, 14, 20, 31, 40
  as interruptive paradigm, 101
  via diaspora, 56
gospelypso, 159
Grant, Eddy, 12
Great, Alexander D., 2, 57–63, 132, 145–51, figures 2.2 and 5.1, *see also* calypsonians
Greater London Authority, 1, 184, 185, 188, 190
guitar (acoustic and electric), 129, 147
Guyana, 11

Haiti, 11, 38
Hajj, 165
Hall, Stuart, 7–8, 25, 63
harmonic partials, 80

harmonium, 99, 176–8
Harris, Wilson, 109, 181, 201–4
Heidegger, phenomenological tradition of, 124
Henry, W.A., 34–6, 132, 152–8
Herder, 13
heritage, 71, 94, 185, 198
  African, 104, 130
  cultural, 165
  Indian, 19
  musical, 95
heterophony, 133
highlife, 48
hip-hop, 34
history, 3, 18, 39, 63, 156
  divergent notions of, 27
  ideas of, 26
  imperial, 67
  knowledge of, 178–9
  social, 65
  stories of, 181
home, 2, 6, 9, 19, 22, 25, figure 1.1
  as a mode of dwelling, 5
  in the diaspora, 3-4, 8, 9, 10, 16, 203
  musical spaces of, 15
  play of, 161
  see also diaspora
homeland(s), 2, 4, 5, 8, 19, 24, 27, 28
  ancestral, 6
  classical concern with, 19
  displacement from, 7
Hornbostel, Erich von, 115–17
humanoecotourism, 167
hybridity, 29–33, 100–2, 112, 119–22, 124, 127, 200–2
  'happy', 120
  'intentional', 120
hyperpolitics, 40

identity, 7, 28–9, 102, 107
  ancestral, 28
  boundaries of, 13
  conceptions of, 14
  ethnic, 53, 54
  formation, 6
  sense of, 38
ideologies, 87, 102, 107, 110
imagination, 110, 202
  creative, 20, 201
  diasporic, 12, 19, 185
  musical, 23
  national, 48, 56, 57
Immigration Act (1965), 51
imperial, legacy, 55, 67
improvisation, jazz, 93
inclusion, 25 46, 87, 172
indentureship, 4, 25
independence movements, 5, 52
industry, 126
  Carnival as, 168
  cultural, 162, 191
  music, 54, 67, 68, 128
  salsa as, 118
Inner London Education Authority, 90, 91, 92
innovation, 16, 68
  cultural, 166
  musical, 69
inscription, 118, 126
instrumentation, 99
insurgency, 156, 157
intentionality, 118
intercultural, 14
Ishmael, Tony, 195–8, 200

Jah Kimbute, 136
Jah-Mbo Rebels Band, 136
JAHngle, 135
Jai, Rikki, 180, 181, figure 6.4
Jamaica, 2, 11, 44, 52, 111, 153
James, C. L. R, 119–20, 122
Jami Moja, 135
jamoo, 129, 130
  chutney, 159

jazz, 93, 95, 147
'Jean and Dinah', 43
Jennings, Gerald 'Al', 49
Jewish dispersion, 5
jhaal, 176
jigs, 65
Johnson, Ken, 49
Johnson, Linton Kwesi, 50
jonkonnu, 38
J'Ouvert, 37, 187
jùjú, 48
jumbies, 65

kaherwa taal, 130
Kassav, 11
Kendra Phagwa Festival, 174, 178, figure 6.5, *see also* pichakaaree
Kenya, 136
kinaesthetic semiotics, 110, 124
King, Martin Luther, 183
kinship, 4, 6
Kronman, Ulf, 83
Kwaku-Ananse *see* Aunty Nansi

label
  of culture and identity, 108
  marketing, 94
labour, 3, 4, 19, 25
  control over, 111
  in postwar shortages, 25
  of identity formation, 29
  of plantation production, 182
Lamming, George, 25
language, interpretation of, 158
Lara, Brian, 148
'Lash Dem Lara', 148
Le Mar, Angie, 2–3
learning, 108, 118
liberal-democracies, 91
limbo, 109, 202
listening, 132, 137, 138, 145, 152

location, 180
Lomax, Alan, 6, 43
'London is the Place for Me', 48
London, 14, 49, 97
  education in, 90–3
loss, 8, 17
Love Circle, 129–30
lyricism, 34, 135, 153–7, 160

Malavoi, 39
mambo, 84, 127
Mannette, Ellie, 81
marches, 65, 84
marginalisation, 38
marginality, 40, 77
marketing strategy, 70, 126
Marley, Bob, 5, 12, 134–7, 139, 142, 144, 149, 154–5, 158, 160
Marshall, Wayne, 132, 138–45
Martin, Ricky, 12
Martinique, 39, 44
mass media, 14
meaning, 127, 157
  embodied, 126
  social, 27, 33
mediation, 25, 127, 205
memory, 2, 10, 27, 39, 63
  collective, 18
  in the body, 109–11
  kinetic, 126
  sacred, 165
mento, 147
Miami, 14
micromusics, 52–3
migration, 2–5, 9, 14, 18, 24, 51
  as interruptive paradigm, 101
  patterns of, 11
  to New World, 18, 200
military wind bands, 138
mimicry, 31
minority, 9, 22, 55, 161, 189
missionary work, 65

modernity, 24
Motown, 70, 147
multiculturalism, 87–91, 107–8
multi-sited field research, 14
music, 12–13, 23, 32
   'a society with a', 30, 39
   as commodity, 105
   ontologies of, 36
   portability of, 13
   study of, 19, 22, 33
   therapy, 86
musical
   mappings, 29
   spaces, 34, 39, 42, 46, 50, 55
   see also analysis
musicology, 22
'My Kinda Music', 54, 55
myth of flight, 28

Naipaul, V.S., 26–7
narrative, 18
   gesture, 16
   historical, 26, 27, 179
   musical, 25
   personal, 8
   strategies, 88
nation, 3, 15, 20, 32, 45, 46, 56
   interplay with diaspora and generation, 6
   treasures of, 57
national, 3, 15
   development, 97, 161
   form of musical expression, 43
   identities, 34, 44
   politics, 161
National Carnival Commission (in Trinidad and Tobago), 167
National Carnival Institute (in Trinidad and Tobago), 167
nationalism, 6, 15, 57
nationalist, 44
   enterprises, 56
   projects, 13

neo-African unity, 38
'New British Calypso', 69–70
'new ethnicities', 53
New World, 18
New York, 11, 36–8, 43, 51, 55
Nigeria, 48
Noel, Terry, 86
non-belonging, 3, 9, 201
nostalgia, 10
notation, musical, 5, 13, 93, figure 2.1
nursery rhymes, 65, 157

'Oh Gosh Man', 54
'One Love', 135, 155, 156, 160
'One World', 20
oral
   history, 16, 71, 152, 156
   testimonies, 3
origin, 3, 9, 24, 162
   assessment of, 65–7
   myths of, 56
   thesis, 165
Orisha, 164
otherness
   construction of, 40, 91
   dilemma of 48
ownership, 161, 164, 172

Pan European, 86
Pan Jamboree Festival, 93
Pan Québec, 91, 93
Pan Teachers' Association, 92
pan-Africanism, 37, 134, 136
pan-Caribbeanness, 37, 130
   in music scenes, 49
Pantar, 95
Paris, 11, 14, 39
Patasar, Mungal, 95–6, 101
patois, 136, 140, *see also* Patwah
Patwah, 158, *see also* patois
Pearse, Andrew, 43, 64

pedagogy
  alternative, 34
  musical, 87–94
percussion, 148
performance, 5, 10, 16, 20, 22, 25
  as empowerment, 28
  as history, 27
  in a theory of global political action, 39, 40
  poetry, 50
  transnational, 162
  visibility and audability of, 13
Phagwa, 173–8
Philip, Clive, 86
Phillip Stephon, 85
Phillips, Caryl, 8, 9
Phillips, Daphne, 96, 97
Phillips, Victor, 85
pichakaaree, 175–7, see also Kendra Phagwa Festival
pizzicato (plucked string technique), 137
place, 9, 124
  and generation, 10
  connections to, 6
  juxtaposition of, 27
  politics of, 4
  Said on, 7
planetary humanism, 20, 31, 160
policing, 161
policy-making, 96, 97, 178
political activism, 2, 13, 22, 130, 166
politics, 3, 10, 15, 18, 134
  diaspora as, 9
  of creativity, 102
  of ethnicity, 107, 176
  of exclusion, 34, 67
  of hybridity, 31
  of nationhood, 13
  of possibility, 16
  of 'race', 46

of rethinking difference, 17
of scholarship, 22
spiritual, 160
polkas, 65
'Pong and Chant', 104, 105
popular music, 11, 37, 53, 65, 135
  charts, 12
population figures, 11
possession, 28
postcolonial, 3, 29
  discourses, 130, 156
  experiences, 2
  Jamaican society, 7
  movements, 25
  musical experiments, 23
  politics, 53, 57
  polyvocality, 157
  projects, 26, 62–4
  studies, 31
postcolonialism
  and diaspora, 178–82
  and multiculturalism, 91
  political spaces of, 15
  see also colonialism
post-Emancipation song, 65
power, 23, 31–3, 62, 64, 105, 111
  imbalanced relations of, 3
practice, 5, 6, 23, 117–18, 127
  subjective, 9
  theory and, 155
preservation
  of cultural knowledge, 6
  musical, 13
prestige, 55
production, 32
  diasporic cultural, 7, 16, 20, 200
  of identities, 110
protest song, 145
Puente, Tito, 127
Puerto Rico, 11

pyramid pans, 81

quadrilles, 65

'race', 6, 32, 46–8, 50, 57, 89
racism, 36, 40, 46, 47, 63, 90
radio, 49, 138
ragga, 135
rajamuffin, 159
rap, 130, 135, 159
rapso, 129, 157, 159
'Rapso Nation', 159–60
rara, 38
Ras Inno, 136
Ras Pompidou, 136
Ras Shorty I, 129–30
Ras T, 136
Rastafarianism, 96, 134
RCA Victor, 55
reclamation
  historical, 126
  of the past, 166
recording technology, 36
recordings, 6, 11, 13, 43, 48, 55
reels, 65
reggae, 34, 52, 130, 134–8
reggae on benga, 136
Regrello, Junia, 97, 98, 101
rehearsal, 93, 169
repertoire, 12, 37, 54, 65, 78, 92, 96, 178, 185
representation, 32, 64, 79, 90, 162
  of the body, 125
resistance, politics of, 23, 134
retention, cultural, 6
revelation, 129
rhyming lines, 150, 151, 159
Rhythm Section, 99
rhythm, 22, 28, 35, 80, 109, 112–18
ritual, 6, 13, 28, 38, 126
Road March, 42

rocksteady, 138
Rollock, Frank, 92
Royal Festival Hall, 1, 77, 92
Royal Opera House, 70
Rudder, David, 180–1, 194
rumba, 44

Said, Edward, 7, 104, 105, 106
Saivism, 165, 203
Salah and Family Steelband Academy, 93, figure 3.2
Saldenah, Louis, 191–200, figure 7.1
salsa, 11, 109–10, 113, 117
  aficionado, 111, 123, 126–7
  footwork, 114
Salsa y Aché, 118
Samaroo, Jit, 82
samba, 84
sameness, social, 40
Sanatan Dharma Maha Sabha, 174, 176–8
Sawhney, Nitin, 96
sax, 148
scholarship
  engaged, 133, 160, 205
  musical, 112, 116
Schools' Steelband Music Festival, 92
scottisches, 65
sea-shanties, 65
Senator Asher, 152
Senegal, 39
Senghor, Léopold, 39
sensibility, 12, 28
  diasporic, 3, 9, 13, 16
  multilocal, 20
  national, 16
  postcolonial, 16, 48
sexuality, 125
Shaggy, 12
Sharp, Boogsie, 169
Sharp, Cecil, 57

significance, 78
  historical and political, 157
  musical, 28
similarity, 20, 204
  human, 40
sitar, 95
ska, 52, 138, 159
skill, 118, 123, 127
  choreography of musical, 123
slavery, 4, 25, 179
Slobin, Mark, 6
Smith, Rudy, 83
soca, 15, 37, 69, 129
social theory, 12
sokah, 129, see also soca
Solomon, Titi, 135
song, texts, 5, 42, 130, 136, 181
  as politics, 130
  circulation of, 38
  folk, 44, 65
  'jump and wave', 69
sonic environment, 24, 100, 102, 181
spaces, 39
SS *Empire Windrush*, 1, 11, 48, 49, 63
St Kitts-Nevis, 4
St Lucia, 1, 196, 197
Stax Soul, 147
Steelband Association of Great Britain, 86
steelbands, 77–9
  College Boys' Band Dixieland, 85
  Cosmo Pans, 81
  Desperadoes, 76, 78
  Ebony, 86, 87, figure 3.1
  Exodus, 76, 93, 95
  Flamingoes, 94
  Harpsi Drum, 81
  Hot Pans, 83
  Invaders, 76, 78
  Leicester Melodians, 86
  London All Stars, 92
  London Schools' Steel Orchestra, 91
  Mangrove, 86
  Paddington Youth, 92
  PANch, 87
  Pantastic, 103
  Phase II Pan Groove, 76, 169–72, figures 6.1 and 6.3
  Phase One, 85
  Red Army, 78
  Renegades, 76, 177
  Skiffle Bunch, 96–9, figure 3.3
  Starlift, 169
  Steel Harps, 82
  Steel Pan Lovers, 83, 87
  Trinidad All Steel Percussion Orchestra, 83, 84
Steelband Association of Great Britain, 86
steelpan, 76, 78–9
  technology, 80–3
'Stranger', 94
struggle, 2, 3, 10, 17, 160
subjectivity, 6, 13, 20, 47, 108
  multiple, 5
suite, baroque dance, 149
Suriname, 11
sustainability, 181
symbol, 78
synthesiser, 148

tamboo bamboo, 84
'Tamborilero', 109
Tanzania, 136
tassa, 80, 97, 98, figure 3.3
tempo, 129, 130
Tervala, Esa, 82–3
text, 32, 43, 124
  body as, 117, 125, 126
textuality, 124
texture, 23, 70, 96
  heterophonic, 133
  instrumental, 129
theatre orchestras, 138

Them Mushrooms, 136
'They Came Upon the Windrush', 57, figure 2.1
timbre, 19, 22, 23, 95, 100, 104
Tobago, 64–7
tonal quality, 80
Toronto, 14, 183
tourism, 68, 168, 185
tourist economies, 161
  Carnival in, 167–73, 190, figure 6.2
trade, 1, 3, 4
tradition, 187
  bearers, 13, 107
Traffik, 194
transmission
  cultural, 6, 10, 95, 103
  media, 135
  oral, 83
transnational, 6, 13, 15, 33, 38, 42
  communities of relatedness, 4
  music market, 12
transformation
  of identity, 68
  of place, 4, 21, figure 1.1
  social, 74
transposition, 148
transruption, 100–1, 104
Trinidad and Tobago, 4, 11, 14
trombone, 148, 149
trumpet, 148, 149
tuning techniques (steelpan), 83

universality, 39, 54

urban spaces, 74
utopia, 17, 25, 35, 40

Vaughan Williams, Ralph, 55, 57
Victor Talking Machine Company, 43
Victoria and Albert Museum, 71, 74
village life, Caribbean, 6
violence, 160, 191
virtuosity, 42, 114
Vishnu Purana, 173
vocal backing, 129
voice, 132, 156
  in heterophonic debates, 133
  of the tourist, 168
  'rebel', 135

Wailing Souls, 158
waltz, 84
Windrush Years, 1, 43, 48
World Music, 32, 56
World Steelband Festival, 82
Wosirian drama, 164, 198, 203

X, Malcolm, 183

Yaa Asentawaa Arts and Community Centre, 52
yard-tapes, 34, 35, 36, 154
Yothu Yindi, 12, 135

Zambia, 137
Zephaniah, Benjamin, 50
zouk, 11, 159, 188

www.ingramcontent.com/pod-product-compliance
Lightning Source LLC
Chambersburg PA
CBHW022048290426
44109CB00014B/1027